What others are saying …

"Whether you're an owner hoping to prevent your pet from becoming lost or stolen, an owner struggling to improve the chances of recovering your missing pet, or a good Samaritan trying to reunite a lost pet with his owner—you'll feel the authors' strong commitment to helping keep people and pets together. This book is a must-read for everyone who is concerned about the ultimate safety of pet animals."

— *Martha Armstrong, Vice President for Companion Animals and Equine Protection,*
The Humane Society of the United States

"A great resource for owners of pets large and small. It covers all the techniques for avoiding losing a pet, and has a concise, easy to follow plan if, despite everything, prevention fails. As a reference, it consolidates all the time-consuming research needed following the loss of a pet, with names, phone numbers, and web addresses immediately at hand. We look forward to displaying *The Complete Guide to Lost Pet Prevention & Recovery* in our hospital waiting room soon."

— *Rodney and Elizabeth Boden, VMD*

"*The Complete Guide to Lost Pet Prevention & Recovery* is a truly comprehensive resource that will assist anyone who owns a pet. More importantly, the authors have discovered what every doctor has always known; prevention is the best medicine. Every veterinarian and pet owner should have this book in his or her library."

— *Marko Sima, VMD*

"This comprehensive guide is unique in its scope and mission. Not only does it serve as a how-to manual on keeping pets of all sorts from getting lost or stolen, it also presents a clear and sound philosophy on responsible pet ownership. All concerned pet owners should read this book, and all libraries that serve pet owners should have at least one copy."

— *John J. Trause, Director, Wood-Ridge Memorial Library*

"As the editor of *The Pet Gazette*, and a dog owner myself, I find *The Complete Guide to Lost Pet Prevention & Recovery* to be an 'essential must-have' for any pet owner, an invaluable tool that brings all the important instructions and facts together in one place…like no other! So many times I have had questions, or our readers have sent in questions that can now be answered through this book. I can't imagine any pet owner not having a copy on their book shelf, especially those who travel with their pets."

— *Stephanie Smith, Editor, The TIMES at the Jersey Shore/The Pet Gazette*

"Few things are as devastating to an animal lover as not knowing where his or her pet is. Preventing your animal companion from becoming lost and finding your lost pet as quickly as possible are critical for every pet owner to know. If you have a pet, reading this book will make a difference for you."

— *Lani Kian, Communications Manager, Dumb Friends League*

"An invaluable resource. The information in this book could, quite possibly, save your pets life. The research is painstakingly accurate and thorough, and the authors' commitment to the welfare of animals is evident on every page."

— *Elisa Schmidt, Kennel Manager, Monmouth County Society for the Prevention of Cruelty to Animals*

The Complete Guide to

LOST PET

Prevention & Recovery

The Complete Guide to

LOST PET

Prevention & Recovery

- How to *prevent* your pet from becoming lost or stolen
- How to *recover* your lost pet
- What to do if you find a stray pet

by

Joseph Andrew Sapia

and

Patricia Sapia

El Jebel
PRESS

Atlantic Highlands, NJ

First Edition
Printed in the United States of America

Publisher's Cataloging-in-Publication
(Provided by Quality Books, Inc.)

    Sapia, Joseph Andrew.
       The complete guide to lost pet prevention & recovery
    : how to prevent your pet from becoming lost or solen,
    how to recover your lost pet, what to do if you find a
    stray pet / by Joseph Andrew Sapia and Patricia Sapia.
    -- 1st ed.
      p. cm.
      Includes index.
      ISBN 0-9718336-0-5

      1. Pets--Safety measures. 2. Pet loss. 3. Pet
    theft. I. Sapia, Patricia. II. Title.

    SF411.5.S37 2002   636.088'7
                    QBI02-200326

Published by: El Jebel Press
                P.O. Box 288
                Atlantic Highlands, NJ 07716
                Phone: (732) 872-2414
                Email: ElJebelPress@lostpetfoundpet.com
                Web: www.lostpetfoundpet.com

Editor: Paul M. Howey
Cover and Interior Design: Sherry Stinson, The Printed Image
Cover Photo Credit (Dog/Gunner): Bonnie Nance, Rural Images Photography
Proofreader: Megan Nodwell, Red Letter Editing
Indexer: Dorothy Hoffman, Lilbun Productions

How to order:
Single copies may be ordered from El Jebel Press, P.O. Box 288, Atlantic Highlands, NJ 07716, (732) 872-2414.

Quantity discounts are available on bulk purchases of this book for resale, educational purposes, gifts, corporate premium sales, or fundraising. Special books or excerpts can be created to fit specific needs. For information, please contact El Jebel Press.

For Midnight

and for
Marama, Tra, and Kitty

and for
all the lost, missing, and stolen pets—

it is for them this book is dedicated,
with love

We can judge the heart of a man
by his treatment of animals.
—*Immanuel Kant*

Acknowledgments

We first want to thank our Mom, Eileen Sapia, for without her *inexhaustible* support and patience this book might very well not have been a reality. Thanks Mom!

Next in line are the many friends and family members who supported our efforts. Each and every one of you contributed something different on our behalf and we sincerely wish to acknowledge and thank you for your part in our success.

Joel Allegretti	Serge Kostin	Maureen Sapia
Adele Fister	Joseph Noonan	Joseph Sapia
Eugenia Gould	Robert F. O'Grady	Joni Young Sayers
Lawrence Gould	Barbara Rampino	MaryAnne Smith
Elizabeth B. Havard	Pat Rampino	Sandra Tom
Kent Jarratt	John Sapia	Father Charles Weiser

We are deeply indebted to Nancy Peterson for her consistent support, her availability, her optimism, and her encouragement. Thanks for the time you took from your busy life to help ensure this book was the very best it could be. And an extra special thanks on behalf of all the animals you help on a daily basis—you are a very special lady!

Also, we wish to extend a sincere thanks to the other professionals who took the time from their busy schedules to review our book. Thanks to: Rodney Boden, VMD; Elizabeth Boden, VMD; Lani Kian; Marko Sima, VMD; Elisa Schmidt; Stephanie Smith; and John J. Trause.

A special thanks goes to Linda Radke and the Five Star Support Team, and to our editor, Paul M. Howey.

Additionally, we would like to acknowledge the many fine individuals, organizations, and companies who offered their services and/or resources, and the written materials many have provided for inclusion in this book. These certainly helped in making this book the complete resource we intended it to be.

A special mention goes to our local animal shelter, the SPCA of Monmouth County. We find them to be a model example of just what an animal shelter is supposed to be.

And finally, the true inspiration for this book goes to our ever-faithful companions—past and present—thanks guys! Hugs to: Midnight, Marama, El Jebel, TS Eliot, Blue, Sable, Winnie, Tra and La La, Kitty, Tripper, Gumba, Kimba, Lassie, Bonnie, Smokey, Tom Tom, Maddie, Rush, Beast, Tisa, Pastel, Peter Peck, Jessie, Mazie, Kiska, Boo Boo, Betty, Sky, Speck, Tippy, Dot, Earheart, Satch, Moe, Cooper, Inky, Cat, Jonnie Cat, Fluffy, and Edgar.

Contents

Section I: PREVENTION
Keeping Your Pet Safe

Section II: RECOVERY
How to Find Your Lost Pet

Section III: ADDITIONAL TOPICS

Foreword

LOST!

Large orange male cat with white paws, striped tail, and green eyes.
Last seen wearing a blue collar the first Wednesday in August,
near the Audubon Society. Call (999) 999-9999.

If you think it only happens to other people's pets, think again. I could not have foreseen what occurred one pleasant evening as I relaxed in our living room, watching TV in the semidarkness. It was one of those rare summer evenings in Charleston, South Carolina, when you could have the windows open. And what windows they were—stretching from floor to ceiling to catch any breezes to cool the warm night air.

The stillness of the evening was broken only by the sounds of the TV and the cicadas, until suddenly, a crashing sound pierced the calm. In an instant, my sister's cat, Obe, flew across the room, charged the window, tore through the screen, and disappeared.

Obe was adopted from the John Ancrum SPCA in Charleston, South Carolina. He had been named Romeo, and his previous owners had given him up because he was constantly underfoot. He was a love. My sister knew the dangers faced by cats allowed outdoors and chose to keep Obe safe as an indoor-only cat. She provided all the fun of the great outdoors without the risks. Instead of chasing leaves, he chased ping-pong balls; instead of lying in the outdoor sun, he perched on a window shelf; and instead of clawing a tree, he had his floor-to-ceiling cat condominium. He was spoiled.

The next sounds I heard were high-pitched screams. I ran out the front door to the backyard where I could barely make out Obe and an unknown cat in a face off. "Oh, please, don't let them chase each other into the street," I thought. My heart was pounding as I approached Obe. I picked him up very carefully, quickly turned away from his howling opponent, and walked around to the front of the house and back inside.

I put Obe in a bedroom to survey the damage to the window. Thank goodness, it was only the screen—Obe was safe, not hurt or lost.

Just walk through any animal shelter, and you'll see countless wonderful pets waiting for homes. Many of them were lost and never found by their heart-broken families; others were abandoned by irresponsible people; and some were relinquished by owners who could not keep them. Of stray cats and dogs, an estimated 14% of dogs and 4% of cats are reunited with their families nationwide. Weren't the others wearing identification? Didn't their owners try to find them?

If it can happen to an indoor-only cat like Obe, it can happen to anyone's pet. You may have an indoor-outdoor cat who "always comes home," until one day he doesn't appear at dinner time. And countless numbers of cats and dogs have crashed through screens, windows, and sliding glass doors, or escaped out the door and over the fence to quickly become disoriented in the "great outdoors."

No one wants to think of the possibility of a pet becoming lost, but it can happen despite your best efforts to prevent it. I hope your beloved pet is never lost. This book can help you minimize that risk. If your pet becomes lost, I hope you've had the foresight to read this book and develop a plan of action. Don't get caught in the dark. Your pet is counting on you.

Nancy Peterson
Issues Specialist for Companion Animals
The Humane Society of the United States

Preface

Losing a beloved pet is one of the worst feelings in the world. Your emotions will no doubt race from panic and fear to guilt, anger, and helplessness. These are compounded by the worry for your pet's safety and the uncertainty as to its fate. Is your pet dead or alive? Is it sad or frightened? Is it suffering? Did it run away or was it perhaps stolen?

The sad fact is our cherished pets are lost or go missing on a daily basis and statistics for lost pets in the United States are positively sobering. If you own or have owned pets, chances are you have already experienced a missing pet or at the very least know of someone who has. And if you have been thus far fortunate enough to not have experienced the frightful ordeal of a pet gone missing, chances are very real that over the course of a lifetime of pet ownership, you may one day have to deal with a missing or even a stolen pet.

We've lost a number of cherished pets. Some were recovered immediately (in unusual places around the house and not really "lost" at all) and others were recovered after much effort and heartache. Unfortunately, some pets were never found and are still missing (and missed!) to this very day.

Sadly, some pets we've lost could probably have been recovered had we not been given well-intentioned but wrong information, or if we had been better prepared and more knowledgeable about how to recover a missing pet. And we could have increased our chances for the safe return of our pets if we had had on hand a decisive plan of action to follow immediately. There are many things we wish we'd known then which we know now that could have made our pet recovery efforts fruitful. We want to share with other pet owners what we've learned the hard way—so if you ever have a pet go missing, you can significantly increase your chances of recovery.

While much has been written on the subject of lost pets, until now there has been no single resource available to help pet owners locate a lost pet, and just as importantly, how to prevent a pet from becoming lost in the first place. A knowledgeable pet owner can do a lot to prevent his or her pets from becoming lost.

Being prepared is your first line of defense and the best advice we can give to assist you in finding your lost pet. **Section One** ("Prevention") was written with the hope that you, the pet owner, will become knowledgeable and therefore better prepared to prevent pet loss from occurring in the first place. In the event your pet is lost, however, the knowledge you've gained, along with the preparedness steps we've outlined, if implemented, will help you to *prevent your pet from staying lost.*

Section Two ("Recovery") gives pet owners a decisive plan of action to follow. When a pet is discovered missing, not only do you need to act quickly, you need to know exactly what to do, and more importantly, what to do first. Trying to find your pet while you're in a state of panic and distress only makes a chaotic situation all the more difficult. Our recovery plan is clear and systematic, thus eliminating much of the panic and confusion that often accompanies the loss of a beloved pet, and will afford you the best opportunity to bring your missing pet home safely.

Our ultimate goal is for every pet owner to have this book in hand *before* disaster strikes, so you are prepared in case your pet ever goes missing.

But there is no need to feel disheartened. There are many ways to successfully recover your lost pet. In fact, many lost pets are recovered. We have included wonderful stories of pet owners reunited with their pets in what seemed like the most unlikely of circumstances for recovery. Some pet owners have been reunited with a lost pet after many years, or with hundreds of miles separating them from each other. Yes, lost pets are recovered!

Introduction

Many of us have seen *The Incredible Journey* and *Lassie Come Home*, both classic films about heroic animals finding their way home across great distances, as if guided by some unseen hand. Alas, as with most Hollywood movies, they are simply the creations of screenwriters. Yes, there have been true stories of pets making astounding treks in search of their owners. Unfortunately, however, too often Lassie doesn't come home and the journey for many lost pets is less than incredible. Instead, the journey often leads such pets to the animal shelter where, if their owners don't claim them and responsible homes can't be found, they are destroyed. The journey can also lead to being hit by a car or worst of all, to being nabbed by a pet thief and sold to a research laboratory.

Most missing pets are not brought home by some magic force, but by specific steps taken by their owners prior to and immediately following their pet's disappearance. These steps include preventive maintenance and in the event of pet loss, having a decisive plan of action for recovery.

The subject of lost pet prevention and recovery is complex and covers a wide range of topics and situations, from proper pet identification to how to create an effective flyer. There are so many different ways that pets are lost, and under so many different circumstances, from being stolen to being left behind or lost during a disaster such as a hurricane or earthquake. You might lose your pet while on vacation or during a major holiday. All of these situations require different types of preparation as well as different responses.

There is much in the way of helpful information already available in the form of books, informational pamphlets, magazine articles, and now Internet web sites. However, much of the information is scattered and incomplete or specialized.

This book is a comprehensive, user-friendly reference guide intended to educate pet owners about preventing pet loss and, in the event of pet loss, to aid them in the recovery of their missing pets. We believe strongly in promoting responsible pet ownership through humane education. We also believe that having a good general knowledge as to the proper care and maintenance of whatever a person's chosen pet may be is one of the most effective means of preventing pets from becoming lost. Throughout this book we point pet owners in that direction.

We also believe that the Internet, while not indispensable, is an incredibly helpful tool and that having a pet is reason enough to have access to the Internet. If your pet is ever lost, the Internet will prove its worth a thousand times over. Our book contains many helpful Internet resources. We created our web site (**www.lostpetfoundpet.com**) to assist our readers in quickly accessing the various web sites found throughout our book. (See "How to Use This Book.")

We've divided this book into three sections. **Section One** addresses prevention, where education is the key. The "Prevention" section is intended to be read, assimilated, and the preventive steps implemented *before* pet loss occurs. In this section, we cover all the basics of lost pet prevention and preparedness.

What do we mean when we say lost pet prevention and preparedness? Think of it as preventive medicine—you exercise, eat right, and take the steps necessary to remain healthy. While taking these preventive steps towards a healthy lifestyle does not guarantee you will never become sick, chances are good that you will probably not get sick as often, and recover more quickly if you do. The same is true of lost pet prevention and preparedness. Not all of the steps we outline, if implemented, will physically prevent your pet from becoming lost, but they will significantly improve your chances of recovering a lost pet.

Take permanent identification: a tattoo or a microchip for example. Having your pet tattooed or microchipped is something you do before your pet is missing. While these will not prevent your pet from becoming lost, they will dramatically improve your chances of getting your pet back should it ever go missing.

Section Two of this book addresses recovery. The "Recovery" section is intended to be a quick reference that will help you act decisively in the event that your pet is lost or stolen. According to National Pet Detectives, 89% of missing pets actively pursued in the first twelve hours are recovered. Because time is such a critical factor in missing pet recovery, we have kept the commentary to a minimum and simply laid out the steps you need to take, beginning with the first most important things to do if your pet goes missing, where and how to conduct an effective search, how to organize searches, who to call, who to talk to, and where and how to tell others about your missing pet. Special topics include how to make an effective flyer, how to place an eye-catching classified ad—everything you need to aid in the recovery of your lost pet.

You will note that some of the topics in the "Prevention" section of the book are repeated in the "Recovery" section. We did this because there are special situations (disasters, for example) that require further treatment. What we've done is to come up with a recovery plan that can be modified to fit almost any situation, and then we've addressed the concerns unique to these special situations. We found this to be the most efficient way to cover almost every situation in which a pet might become lost.

Section Three of this book addresses four additional helpful and hopeful topics pertaining to pet loss. "You've Found Your Pet—Now What?" gives pet owners a few simple guidelines to follow when their missing pet is recovered, from assessing their pet's condition (is a veterinary visit in order?) to most importantly, how to prevent it from happening again.

"Found Strays" addresses exactly what to do when you find a stray (which could very well be someone else's lost pet).

"Knowing When to Give Up"—here we offer some guidance in the form of a heartfelt letter to help pet owners with this difficult and deeply personal decision.

Despite one's best recovery efforts, the fact remains that not all lost pets will be recovered. Closure is a big part of losing a pet that is never recovered. The "not knowing" can be as hurtful as the loss itself. The last section advises you on how to overcome your grief and help bring closure to your loss. When writing this topic, we did not set out to reinvent the wheel. Instead, we chose to briefly cover the basics of grieving as it relates to the loss of a beloved pet, referring our readers to the many valuable resources already available to them: from books and pet-loss grieving hotlines to memorial web sites where pet owners can share their stories, post poetry, and share photographs of their beloved animals.

Of course, preventing your pet from becoming lost is always best. Preparing ahead of time for the possibility of pet loss is also one of the most effective means of recovering a lost pet. It is our hope that you purchased this book as a preventive measure. Read it carefully and become thoroughly familiar with every aspect of prevention and preparedness, assimilating the information and implementing the preventive steps we've outlined. And if your pet should ever go missing, we hope this book is the motivational force in helping bring your "Lassie" home safely.

How to Use This Book

This book is a user-friendly reference guide intended to assist pet owners in all aspects of lost pet prevention and recovery. Its two primary audiences are those who have lost a pet (for whom time is critical) and those who have purchased this book as a preventive measure (for whom time is less of a concern). Following a few simple guidelines will help you get the most out of this book.

Recovery

Time is critical! 89% of pets actively searched for in the first twelve hours are recovered, according to National Pet Detectives. If your pet is lost, waste no time reading further. Skip the "Prevention" section altogether and proceed immediately to **Section Two**, "Recovery," and begin the search for your missing pet. Everything you need to know to aid you in the recovery process can be found there. Once you've recovered your pet, go back and read "Prevention," and begin implementing the various prevention and preparedness strategies we've outlined there.

Special Recovery Situations

If your pet was lost under unusual circumstances (while vacationing, during a move, or in a disaster situation, for example), be sure to read the "Special Recovery Situations" section and incorporate it into your overall recovery plan.

Prevention

If you bought this book as a preventive measure, read through the "Prevention" section carefully, and begin to put into practice the steps and other suggestions we've outlined there. Part of any effective prevention strategy must include preparing ahead of time by arming yourself with a thorough knowledge of exactly how to recover a lost pet, before that pet is ever lost. The fact is that most pet owners are unprepared and rarely give pet loss a thought until it happens. Our recovery plan is designed to aid anyone, even the most unprepared pet owner, in recovering a lost pet.

Having purchased this book ahead of time, there is absolutely no reason now for you to be caught unprepared. Once you've finished reading "Prevention," continue on to "Recovery." Then take what you learn about recovery and incorporate it into your overall prevention and preparedness strategy. Put together a "Recovery Kit," and gather the other items listed in "Preparing for Recovery" (especially your list of "Critical Contacts"). Now is the time to prepare for recovery.

Critical Contacts

Your list of "Critical Contacts" will be referred to throughout this book. Earmark this page. Compiling a list of "Critical Contacts" is one of the most important things a pet owner can do to aid in the recovery of a lost pet.

While it is best to compile this information ahead of time as a preventive measure, we've arranged the list so that it is useful to anyone in an emergency, even if they've done little to prepare. Think of it as a sort of "cheat sheet" you can use to quickly locate animal shelters, veterinarians, recovery services, etc.—the very people you would need to contact if your pet were ever lost.

Resources

Although the "Resources" section roughly corresponds to the topic titles used throughout the "Prevention" section of this book, it has been arranged alphabetically for ease of use. The contact information for the various products (videos, books, software, etc.), services (registries and recovery services, training and behavior assistance, disaster preparation help, etc.), and government and humane organizations mentioned throughout this book, can be located there. All references to resources will appear as "Resources/Topic Title." Here is an example: (See "Resources/ Humane Organizations.")

Our Web Site

We created our web site (**www.lostpetfoundpet.com**) as a companion to this book. It helps our readers easily and quickly access the important on-line prevention and recovery resources found throughout our book without having to type in each web address from the text. Just log on and click the "For Our Readers" link. In addition, pet owners can download free lost pet flyers and log sheets that are indispensable for keeping track of and organizing the leads generated during the recovery process.

Section I

PREVENTION

Keeping Your Pet Safe

Importance of Prevention

The Humane Society of the United States estimates that between 8 and 10 million animals are taken in by shelters annually. These include animals from a variety of sources, such as owner relinquishments, abandoned animals, abuse cases, and strays. It is widely known that the prospects for reuniting stray pets with no identification with their owners are bleak. According to the American Humane Association, only 14% of the stray dogs and 4% of the stray cats that enter animal shelters are reclaimed by their owners. It is true that many of these animals are adopted out to loving homes. Still, far too many are euthanized once the holding period has passed, which can be as brief as 72 hours depending on where you live. Why? The sad fact is that otherwise healthy animals are humanely destroyed because they arrive at the shelter with no identification, and their owners, for whatever reason, fail to reclaim them in a timely manner. The harsh reality is that there are too many strays, and homes cannot be found for all of them. The shelter often has no choice; space must be made for the other animals they know will be arriving the next day, and the next, and the next. This is why prevention and preparedness are so important, and why, if your pet does go missing, you must visit your local animal shelters immediately to search for and reclaim your lost pet.

As alarming as the above statistics may be, they do not tell the whole story. They are only averages gleaned from shelter statistics. Millions of pets go missing each year and never make it to an animal shelter, and therefore are never counted in official statistics. Some people estimate that the number of pets lost each year exceeds 10 million. Consider the following:

It is important to note that getting your pet back once it has been adopted by someone else can be difficult, if not impossible.

• *Pets that are stolen.* Some people estimate that as many as 1.5 million dogs and cats are stolen each year; most are never recovered.

• *Pets that are killed.* The greatest danger is of course being killed in traffic; unaltered males are at greatest risk. Lost pets face many other dangers, from ingesting toxic substances to being killed by wild animals.

• *Pets that are taken in by another family.* This is a common occurrence and, although no statistics are available, it's likely that each year tens of thousands of lost pets are kept by those who find them.

• *Roaming cats.* Many people falsely believe that cats can survive on their own. The sad truth is that many thousands of stray cats starve to death every year.

• *Pets that are caught in a hunter's trap.* Untold numbers of pets are caught in hunters' traps every year. Steel-jaw leg-hold traps do not discriminate between wild animals and pets.

Lost pets face many life-threatening dangers. Not the least among these are pet thieves ("bunchers") who routinely cruise neighborhoods rounding up stray cats and dogs and selling them to research laboratories. Another serious threat is exposure to various communicable diseases such as feline leukemia, feline immunodeficiency virus, rabies, and others.

Many people's idea of preventing pet loss is limited to pet containment (e.g., fencing, kennels, enclosures, or keeping animals exclusively as house pets). While containment can be very effective in preventing pets from

Shelters Employ Creative Strategies

In an effort to minimize the need to euthanize otherwise healthy animals, shelters employ a host of creative strategies, from temporarily placing animals in volunteer foster care homes until they are adopted, to calling on breed rescue groups to rescue purebred animals. Purebred dogs make up approximately 25% of the animal shelter dog population.

escaping, it ignores the real issue of *why* the pet escaped. Not only do we address this issue, but we also offer readers concrete solutions for curbing escaping behavior—things like spaying/neutering, obedience training, and environmental enrichment—which can dramatically reduce escaping behavior in even the most persistent and talented pet Houdini.

Because even the most carefully-designed prevention strategy cannot guarantee that an animal will never turn up missing, pet owners must be prepared. The truth is that most pet owners are not. They seldom give a thought to pet loss until it happens. Fortunately, there are many things pet owners can do ahead of time to maximize their chances of a speedy recovery in the event that containment fails and their pet is lost. These measures include proper means of identification, including some type of permanent identification, knowing how to create effective flyers and classified ads, how to keep accurate and up-to-date pet records, and having a detailed recovery plan in place before a pet is lost.

Pet loss is a devastating experience, and if the pet is never recovered, the emotional pain can linger for years. By implementing the various preparedness strategies outlined in this book, you will not only reduce the risk of pet loss, but also dramatically increase your chances of recovering your pet if it ever goes missing.

Pet Record Keeping

Keeping accurate, complete, and up-to-date pet records is an integral part of lost pet prevention and recovery. These records will be useful in a variety of situations, including when you attempt to retrieve your pet from a shelter. If your pet is ever lost, having complete records will save you valuable time. We will refer you to your pet records throughout this book.

Make at least two copies of everything, and keep them in watertight containers, one at home and one at a location away from your home (with a friend, a family member, or in a safe deposit box) in the event of a disaster or other unforeseen emergency.

Pet record-keeping involves more than simply keeping vaccination records and medical history. As soon as possible, you should create a folder for your pet's records. Be sure to include the following items:

- *Vaccination Information*—Any and all vaccination records for rabies, distemper, bordetella (kennel cough), parvo (a gastrointestinal virus that can be deadly), etc.

- *Medical History*—A complete record of your pet's veterinary visits, checkups, and emergencies, as well as any special dietary needs. X-rays can be used to positively establish ownership.

Take the Memory Test

Do you think you can accurately describe the pet with whom you share your home and life? You'd be surprised.

As a family project, have everyone get a sheet of paper and a pencil. Put your pet in another room. Then have each person write a description of your pet from memory. Try to recall every detail, unique markings, eye color, hair length and texture, tail length and type, etc. You'll be amazed at how much each person's description differs from the others, and what details each person has left out. This fun family project will clearly demonstrate the need for accurate written and photographic records of your pet.

FIGURE 1

- *Purchase Receipts*—If you purchased your pet from a breeder or adoption agency; documentation if you adopted it from a shelter.

- *Photographs*—Several photographs, preferably in color, taken from various angles and continually updated as your pet grows. (See "Photographing Your Pet.")

- *Written Description of Your Pet*—A description that includes as many physical details about your pet as possible. Human memory is faulty and should not be expected to be accurate, especially when someone is under stress. (See figure 1.)
  - Hair length (long or short)
  - Coat texture (rough, silky, smooth)
  - Patches, spots, tattoos, color patterns
  - Tail (long, short, cut, bushy, corkscrew, etc.)
  - Ear set (e.g., erect, cropped, tipped, etc.)
  - Eye color
  - Breed (Husky, Shepherd, mixed breed, etc.)
  - For birds, feather colors and patterns

- *Tags*—Keep a duplicate set of identification tags with your pet's records.

- *Registry Information*—Contact numbers and other paperwork for organizations with whom you've registered your pet's identification information.

- *Club Membership Information*—Contact numbers, membership cards, etc., for any animal clubs you belong to.

People move and addresses change, pets grow or are groomed. Many vaccinations require booster shots and must be kept current. In other words, your pet records are not static. They need to be updated *each and every time* there is a change of any kind. The advantage of keeping accurate and up-to-date pet records is that you will have immediate access to information that will be useful in a variety of situations:

- *Moving/Transporting/Vacationing*—All states have regulations regarding the transportation of animals across their borders and vaccination requirements that may vary depending on the type of animal. (See "Traveling With Pets.")

- *Making Flyers and Ads*—Many of the items in your records will enable you to quickly and accurately prepare notices about your missing pet. (See "Flyers and Classified Ads.")

- *Retrieving Your Pet from a Shelter*—Without proof of ownership and current vaccination records, you may be unable to retrieve your pet from a shelter.

- *Boarding or Kenneling Your Pet*—Reputable kennels require that you provide proof of rabies and distemper vaccination for all dogs, cats, and ferrets. (Ferrets are susceptible to canine distemper, which is often fatal.) Many kennels also require additional vaccinations for such things as bordetella and parvo, and many require that these vaccinations be administered well in advance of kenneling your pet. This is very important if you travel with your pet, since a situation could arise while traveling (e.g., if you had to be hospitalized) in which you must board your pet. (See "Pet Sitters, Boarding Kennels, and Caretakers.")

- *Finding Sitters and Caretakers*—Most professional pet sitters will require that you provide them with up-to-date health records and proof of vaccinations. It is also prudent to provide these records to any friends or family members who might be caring for your pet.

- *Licensing Your Pet*—You cannot obtain a municipal dog license without proof of rabies vaccination. In many communities the law requires that cats be licensed as well.

- *Recovering a Stolen Pet*—If your pet is ever stolen, having complete records will assist you in recovering your pet.

Like almost everything else in this world, pet record-keeping has entered the computer age. You can download a trial version of record-keeping software right from the Internet. (See figure 2.) Since computer failure is not an uncommon occurrence, you should always have a hard copy of your pet's records. Keep your records organized by creating a record-keeping folder. (See figure 3.)

Health-Minder Software

"Health-Minder software knows your pet is an important member of the family and that keeping your pet healthy is a top priority. It helps you keep detailed pet health records of vaccines, illnesses, medications, feeding requirements, license number, names and phone numbers of veterinarians and hospitals, special care needs, even track pet health insurance claims. You can print out the pet health record for travel or for leaving your dog with a caretaker."

You can download a free 60-day trial version of Health-Minder from their web site at **www.health-minder.com.**

FIGURE 2

Create Your Own Pet Record-Keeping Folder

At your local office supply store purchase a multi-pocket file folder. Use tabs to organize your pet records for quick and easy access. Staples carries a 13-Pocket Poly File made from textured polypropylene, which is 20 times stronger than paper-based material and practically indestructible.

FIGURE 3

Photographing Your Pet

Taking photographs of your pet is one of the most important things you can do to prepare for pet loss. Most people who have pets consider them part of the family and therefore have photographs of them in their family album. While these may be helpful, too often they aren't very clear, or were taken from a distance, or are outdated. Whether you do it yourself or have them done professionally, you need to have quality pictures taken. They will be crucial in a variety of recovery situations and are an important part of your pet records. (See figure 4.)

If you have children or grandchildren or nephews or nieces, include them in some of the photos. This can speed up the recovery process since a picture of a missing pet and the child who adores it has strong emotional appeal. Someone who may have considered keeping your pet may have second thoughts.

Hire a professional pet photographer. There are advantages to hiring a professional. They will have all the right equipment, know how to choose the best background, etc. If you do use a professional, be sure that he or she understands you want photos for identification purposes, and you are not looking for a portrait.

A Picture Says a Thousand Words

When it comes to recovering a lost pet, a picture truly does say a thousand words. Photographs will be useful, even critical, in a variety of situations.

• Current photographs are indispensable for making flyers. An ideal flyer should include two photographs, one face shot and one full-body profile shot. (See "Flyer Sample.")

• Photos can be scanned and then uploaded and posted online at any of the numerous missing pet web sites.

• Photos can be critical to rescue workers in the aftermath of a disaster.

• If you ever have to go to court (people do steal pets), photographs are one more way of proving ownership.

• Photos can be shown to shelter personnel to prove ownership and reclaim your pet. Shelter workers see dozens, even hundreds of pets a week; a photograph can make a real difference here.

• Photos will be indispensable if you lose your pet while traveling or vacationing.

• Photographs help you to recall important details about your pet that, in its absence, you may not be able to recall as clearly as you think.

FIGURE 4

Pet Photo Tips

- If you decide to do it yourself, set up your photo area some days in advance in order to allow your pet to explore the area. This will make your pet more comfortable and relaxed when the photo session begins. Above all, be patient. Having its picture taken is not an everyday occurrence for your pet.

- Set up in an area where there is strong natural light and use high-speed film. This will allow you to take photos without using a flash. You may want to consider a safe outside area.

- Shoot against a clean background, free of clutter. Use a sheet or blanket as a backdrop, and use a color that will contrast with the color of your pet.

- Prior to your photo session, be aware of your pet's mental state since this may determine your pet's willingness to sit still and be photographed. If your pet is anxious, hungry, tired, needs a walk, or is not feeling well, it may be best to put it off until another day.

- Take shots of the face, from several angles, whole body shots, and underbelly shots. Pay particular attention to markings, recording on film special patterns and colors unique to your pet. This can aid someone immeasurably in identifying your pet. To the average person, all Dalmatians look alike. Of course, this isn't so, as each has its own unique series of spots.

- Shoot two or more rolls of film (professionals frequently shoot several rolls of film in order to get just a few quality photos). Once developed, choose the clearest and best photos for your pet records.

- If appropriate, include children in some of the photos, but do not substitute cute shots for quality photos that give an accurate representation of your pet.

- Regularly update photos as your pet grows.

- Many people groom their pets and even shave their coats in the summer. This can make your pet look quite different. If you alter your pet's appearance in any radical way, be sure to update its photos.

Pet Identification

Proper ID—Your Pet's Ticket Home

Proper pet identification provides a vital link between you and anyone who may find your lost pet. Although most people's idea of pet identification is the standard identification tag, there are many other options available today and new pet identification methods and products are continually being developed. (See figure 5.) While tags are indispensable and indeed remain the most popular form of pet identification, they can become lost, leaving your pet vulnerable. That so few animals are reunited with their owners is mostly due to the lack of identification.

With no positive means of identification, it is impossible for animal control, shelter workers, or anyone else finding your lost pet to contact you. For this reason, many national pet organizations now encourage pet owners to supplement visible forms of identification like ID tags with permanent identification such as tattoos and microchip implants. (See figure 6.) By using multiple forms of identification, including some form of permanent identification, you greatly increase the chances of recovering a lost pet. Although the reasons for proper pet identification are obvious, please consider these other facts:

The Future of Pet Identification

Global Positioning Satellite (GPS) technology, the ability to track and pinpoint via satellite one's precise location anywhere on the planet, has been in use for some time now. While originally developed for various government, scientific, and military purposes, every day it seems to find another commercial application, the most recent being tracking lost pets.

According to the March 2001 issue of *Pet Product News,* "A recent agreement between Paradigm Advanced Technologies Inc. of Toronto and iTrackPets Inc. of Point Roberts, Washington, will soon result in location-based applications that can track the location of domestic pets."

The device will mount to the pet's collar. The owner then programs it to alert them via phone, cell phone, or pager if their pet strays beyond the predetermined boundary set by the pet owner.

FIGURE 5

• Shelters will generally hold pets with some form of identification longer than pets without identification. This is actually the law in many places. In Pennsylvania, for example, shelters are only required to hold unidentifiable strays for two days. If a stray is brought in with some form of identification, however, the shelter is required to hold the animal for ten days, even if they are unable to locate its owner right away.

• If your pet is injured while it is missing, and taken to an animal hospital, it is more likely to be given medical care if it is wearing identification tags or is in some other way identifiable.

• Pets without identification are often taken in and kept by the people who find them. As your pet may have been missing for days, it may look malnourished and neglected to the people finding it. Believing the animal to be unwanted or abandoned, they understandably feel justified in keeping your pet.

- Tattoos may prevent pet theft since research laboratories will not, as a rule, purchase tattooed animals. In addition, new funding and grant requirements are beginning to force research facilities to scan for microchips.

- Microchip implants have proven very successful in reuniting owners with their missing pets. Millions of pets are now implanted with microchips, and many shelters now have universal scanners. (See "Microchips.")

- While DNA won't help someone finding your pet to contact you, it can win you a victory in court if your pet is stolen or taken in and claimed by someone who refuses to return the animal.

Permanent Identification

Your pet should never be without visible identification, whether it's inside or outside the house. The major drawback of identification tags, however, is that they can be lost or intentionally removed. Therefore, standard identification tags should be supplemented with at least one form of permanent identification. Many humane organizations now recommend the use of tattoos and microchips. The American Kennel Club not only encourages but also actively promotes the use of permanent identification.

The multiple identification approach maximizes your chance of recovering your pet. For little more than a hundred dollars, a pet owner can purchase identification tags from a registry and have their pet tattooed and implanted with a microchip.

Some Sound Advice from the American Humane Association

"It's impossible to overemphasize the importance of an ID tag, a license tag, microchip, or any other device that can better help local animal welfare professionals identify and reunite lost pets with their families again. The great tragedy is that so many animals arrive at shelters with no ID tags. That means it's up to the owner to track down the lost pet—often a very difficult thing to do. If your pet happens to become lost, yet has any form of identification with your phone number on it, then chances are it won't be lost for very long."

Jack Sparks, Associate Vice-President, Communications
*American Humane Association, **www.americanhumane.org***

FIGURE 6

Registries and Recovery Services

A pet identification registry is a company that serves as a liaison between you and the person who finds your missing pet. In our opinion, using an identification registry is one of the most important things you can do to prepare for the possibility of pet loss. If you use a pet registry, your pet's identification will have the phone number of the registry company instead of your own number. The key things here are that the registry's phone number never changes, and there's always someone to answer the phone around the clock. Also, some registries provide additional services that not only safeguard your pet, but can also be of great assistance to you in your recovery efforts. (See figure 7.)

There are several types of registries: identification tag registries, tattoo registries, and microchip registries. They all operate on the same principle; your pet wears (or is implanted or tattooed with) a unique identification number. The finder of your pet reads (or in the case of microchips, scans) the identification number and contacts the registry, where all of your information is kept in a database. The registry then contacts you or someone else whom you have designated. The system works wonderfully as long as pet owners remember to update their contact information if there is a change. Here are some additional benefits to using a registry:

- Your personal contact details and other information can be easily updated.
- The registry links you to the person who finds your missing pet.
- A registry allows you to keep personal information private.
- A registry allows you to use multiple contact numbers without multiple tags.
- Many registries provide extended services such as guaranteed payment for emergency medical care, transportation, and boarding.
- A registry can keep vital medical or dietary information in their database and can inform whoever finds your pet as to its special needs.

The Pet Club of America's Petfinders

Petfinders is the lost pet service for the Pet Club of America. They are a non-profit organization that has been involved in protecting and finding missing pets since 1976. They operate a tag registry with a 24-hour hotline. In addition to providing members with a tag and a unique identification number, Petfinders will also fax and mail your pet's description in a "Lost Pet Report" to every facility that takes in strays in a 60-mile radius of where it was lost. They maintain an extensive database of lost and found pet reports and can compare your pet's description with hundreds of pets reported found each day. Visit their web site at **www.petclub.org**.

FIGURE 7

- No matter where you go with your pet, there will be someone to answer the phone who can in turn contact you.
- Statistically, prevention-conscious pet owners who take the time to register their pets with a registry are less likely to lose them.

Although identification registries have been around for years, many are now expanding the services they provide. These services can benefit everyone and are especially beneficial to those who may be unable to conduct an extensive search effort themselves (the elderly or the housebound, for example). The services they provide vary from actual hands-on help to consulting, assistance, and long-distance support for pet owners who lose their pet away from home. Different registries offer different levels of support, so it is best to contact them to determine which best suits your needs. The benefits and services they provide may or may not require your having registered with them prior to your pet's being lost, although it is always best to register in advance since it saves you valuable time.

We strongly urge you to purchase the tags through a national registry. Using a tag registry greatly increases the effectiveness of your pet's tags. Some examples of national registries include the American Pet Association's Guardian Collar Tag system, Doctors Foster and Smith's Lost Pet Service Kit, and the Pet Club of America's Petfinders. For a list of other tag registries, see "Resources/Registries and Recovery Services." Many registries provide additional recovery services, which may include one or more of the following:

- *Professionally Designed Posters and Flyers*—Created for you and shipped to you by overnight mail.
- *Postcard Mailers*—Similar to posters and flyers only in postcard form, these are mailed to homes and businesses in the specific target area where your pet was lost. This can be very effective since a good percentage of missing pets are taken in by people right in the area where the animals were lost.
- *Contacting Facilities*—Mailing and/or faxing flyers and other important information about your lost pet to all the facilities that take in stray animals within a certain distance of where your pet was lost. This is especially helpful if you lose your pet while traveling.
- *Hands-on Help*—There are even services that do the actual legwork; not simply creating professional flyers and posters, but also distributing them for you. National Pet Recovery is one example of a company that offers such a comprehensive service. They boast an impressive 87% recovery rate. (See "Resources/Registries and Recovery Services.")
- *Database Matching and Lost Pet Reports*—Gathering and maintaining information about lost pets and then comparing and matching the descriptions of the hundreds of pets reported missing and found each day.

- **Guaranteed Payments**—Guaranteeing payment for emergency transportation, boarding, emergency medical care, etc. This must be paid back once the pet is recovered.

- **Rewards**—Offering substantial rewards for information on lost and stolen pets.

ID Tags

A secure collar and a legible tag combine to make the first line of defense in lost pet prevention and recovery. Your pet should never be without them, both inside and outside of the house. Animal shelter workers across the country attest to the fact that when a pet is brought in wearing an ID tag with current contact information, reunions can be made quickly and easily, and the possibility of the pet being euthanized is virtually eliminated. When pet owners reclaim their pets quickly, it allows shelters to provide more space for other lost and homeless pets.

A tag, which is the first thing that an animal control officer or anyone else will look for when finding a stray, should have your phone number, including your area code. If possible, use more than one contact number (e.g., day, evening, and cell phone numbers).

Tag Day

On the first Saturday of each April, the American Humane Association celebrates Tag Day. The purpose of this annual event is to raise public awareness about the alarming number of strays entering our nation's animal shelters each year, and to encourage pet owners to use proper pet identification such as ID tags, license tags, microchips, and tattoos.

For more information on Tag Day, contact the American Humane Association at (800) 227-4645, or visit their web site at **www.americanhumane.org**.

Remember that you're not always going to be available, so be sure to have an answering machine or a voice mail service. If you are uncomfortable with including your own phone number on a tag, consider using a national tag registry (they will keep all your personal information private). (See figure 8.)

Keep Information Current

One common problem with tags is that people move and change their phone numbers and fail to update the information on their pets' tags. Make sure you update the information immediately when something changes. Don't wait! Most tag registries will update your information free or for a nominal fee. A tag without accurate, up-to-date contact information is as good as having no tag at all. If your pet's tags are lost or if your contact information changes, use a temporary tag until they're replaced. Temporary tags can be purchased in

---

1-800-HELP-4-PETS

This comprehensive service works like 9-1-1 for your pet in any emergency, anywhere in the U.S. Membership includes a highly visible tag inscribed with your pet's unique ID number, which is recorded in a database along with your contact information, alternative contacts, and a complete medical history of your pet. The finder of your lost pet is linked to you via the 24-hour 1-800-HELP-4-PETS hotline where all emergency calls are handled by their own staff of highly trained professionals, not an answering service. If your pet is found injured and you can't be reached, 1-800-HELP-4-PETS can even arrange for emergency medical treatment. Other benefits include emergency veterinarian referral, travel protection, and natural disaster assistance.

To find out more call 1-800-HELP-4-PETS or visit them online at **www.help-4-pets.com**

FIGURE 8

---

most pet supply stores, through pet magazines and product catalogs, online at **http://salamander.bc.ca**, or you can make them yourself. (See figure 9.)

Types of Tags

Standard Tags—The standard tag remains the most popular. It comes in a variety of shapes, from a simple square to the shape of a bone or fire hydrant. They are made of aluminum, brass, stainless steel, or plastic. They are inexpensive and are easily engraved or written on with relevant information.

Municipal Licenses and Rabies Tags—Many cities require that all dogs within their municipality are licensed and vaccinated against rabies, and more and more towns are requiring this for cats as well. When you license your pet or get a rabies vaccination, you get a tag. A rabies tag is proof that your pet has been vaccinated. This is important because if your pet is brought into a shelter, isn't wearing its rabies tags, there is evidence of its having had an altercation with a wild animal, and the offending animal is not available for testing, your pet is at serious risk of being destroyed. (See "Rabies.") Licensing and vaccinating your pet are a

---

A Quick Tag Idea

In the absence of standard temporary tags, try wrapping a piece of paper around your pet's collar and writing the information on it with a permanent marking pen, then covering it with clear tape to prevent smudging. It may not look pretty, but the important thing is that your pet is always wearing its tag and that the tag has accurate information!

FIGURE 9

fundamental part of responsible pet ownership, and while many pets have been reunited with their owners through both license and rabies tags, they are not ideal for identification purposes. Municipal licenses and rabies tags are a must, but should be seen as a supplement to, rather than a substitute for, more reliable methods of pet identification, as they do not contain your phone number and can only be used as a form of identification during regular business hours.

Alternative Tag Ideas

- *Shrinkable Tags*—Sold under the brand name GoTags, these are a great way of teaching children the importance of pet identification. Just use a permanent marking pen to write your name, address, and phone number on one of these plastic tags, pop it in the oven for five minutes, and watch it shrink down to a tag ready to be hung on the pet's collar. Visit **www.gotags.com**, and check out their whole assortment of standard ID tags, "tiny tags" (for pups and kittens), slide-on tags, and embroidered collars.

- *Slide-on Tags*—These tags have slits at both ends and slide onto your pet's collar (it must be an open-ended collar). They are less likely than hanging tags to fall off.

- *Nameplate Tags*—Permanently attached with rivets to your pet's collar, these tags are not likely to come loose.

- *Pet Wallets, Cylinders, and Kaleidoscope Tags*—These all work on the principle of allowing you to include a lot more information than standard tags can hold (the information is miniaturized and is read through a magnifying glass on the end of the tag). A friend of ours has a little Beagle that has a life-threatening disease and requires twice-a-day medication. His owners use a kaleidoscope tag that contains all the medical and emergency prescription information necessary to keep their pup alive until they're reunited with him.

- *Small Pet Necklace Tags*—TagXpress (**www.tagxpress.com**) makes a tiny necklace ID tag that is perfect for cats and tiny dogs such as Chihuahuas.

- *Talking Pet Tags*—Sold under the brand name IDeclare, the tag contains a tiny computer chip that allows you to record a message of up to 20 seconds. It can be purchased online at **www.interplanetarypets.com**. Click on the "ID Tags" link.

- *Temporary Tags*—These can be filled out and customized when you are traveling or moving with your pet, or when you need to update information while waiting for new permanent tags. (See "Resources/ID Tags.")

- *Embroidered Collars*—Although not actually a tag, they serve the same function. You can have your pet's name and a contact number custom-embroidered right on the collar.

- ***Fluorescent Collars***—Again, while not an ID tag, using a collar that stands out significantly increases the chance of recovering your pet. People are much more likely to remember spotting a stray with a brightly-colored collar. A bright fluorescent collar works well.

Tattoos

Tattooing doesn't mean your pet will join the ranks of sailors and motorcycle gangs. No skulls and crossbones or spitting cobras here, simply a unique identification number tattooed on your pet, a number that is issued by a pet registry. Tattooing is an excellent supplementary means of identification. A pet tattoo is a permanent form of identification, a numbered mark that is unique to your animal and one that cannot be lost. The American Kennel Club and many other national pet and humane organizations support the use of tattoos and other permanent methods of identification.

Tattooing is also an effective deterrent against pet thieves who make their living stealing dogs and picking up strays and selling them to research facilities and laboratories. Since laboratories will not, as a rule, accept tattooed animals, tattooing is a major deterrent. (See "Stolen Pets.") Also, a tattoo, along with the tattoo registration papers you receive from the registry, establishes proof of ownership that will stand up in a court of law, according to Tattoo-A-Pet.

Does tattooing work? Tattoos have been responsible for reuniting many lost pets with their worried owners. Some recovery stories can only be described as miraculous. (See figure 10.) An animal control officer we spoke to told us that in the course of his 25 years of dealing with stray animals, he has only come across a handful of tattooed pets. However, he said every one of them was returned to its owner. Tattooing works, as long as the tattoo number is registered. The problem is that not enough people use them, mainly because they just don't know how to go about having their pet tattooed.

Shelter workers, veterinarians, and animal control officials are trained to search for tattoos on stray animals that come into their custody. If a tattoo is discovered, they will immediately contact the tattoo registry. Tattoo companies use a unique number assigned to your pet and prefixed with a code identifying which registry the tattoo is affiliated with: for example "NDR" for the National Dog Registry or "T" for Tattoo-A-Pet. These professionals, whose job involves regular contact with stray animals, are familiar with these markings and know who to call.

Tattoo Registries

According to the National Dog Registry, approximately 200 registries have come and gone since NDR was established in 1966. That's why it's so important to go with a national registry. The National Dog Registry and Tattoo-A-Pet (which has been around since 1972) both have long track records of successfully reuniting owners with their lost pets.

Although these two companies are competitors, they work together as their main concern is for the animals. Even if they're contacted about an animal that's not registered with them, they will contact the other registries in an effort to locate the owners. "Commercial concerns always take a backseat when it comes to locating the owner of a missing pet," says Bette Rapoport of the National Dog Registry. Julie Moscove of Tattoo-A-Pet assures us that they have the same policy.

Miracles Can Happen

"It could never happen to me. That's what I have always thought… I have always been so conservative, especially where safety and security are concerned, almost to the point of fanaticism, or so I thought.

"Well, the worst happened to me. Star, my nine-year-old Sheltie, slipped through a gate a service man had left open. She was in a new neighborhood and frightened. At some point, she must have panicked and just started running.

"I had delivered over 2,000 flyers… I was getting so upset that I usually started weeping when I was talking to people.

"Star was lost a few days before Halloween. On Monday, February 13 (nearly four months later), I got a call from the National Dog Registry. That evening, the rescuers drove to my house and brought Star home to me.

"Star was rescued by some young men who were four-wheeling in the desert 40 miles southwest of where she had been lost, and had found her in a leghold trap almost dead. Star was with the mother of the rescuer for two weeks and nursed back to health. At two weeks she was given a bath and the tattoo was found.

"There are no words to describe my emotions at this point… But the bottom line is, without the (National Dog Registry registered) tattoo, I would never have gotten her back. The whole ordeal has made a believer out of me. Dog-people friends of mine from all over the country are now making sure their dogs are tattooed (and registered with NDR). THE SYSTEM WORKS!!! And MIRACLES CAN HAPPEN, BECAUSE ONE HAPPENED TO ME!!!"

–Brenda Mileski
Henderson, Nevada

FIGURE 10

If your animal is already tattooed, many registries will list the existing tattoo with their registry. It is actually pretty routine, as many smaller registries have gone out of business over the years, and the larger registries have picked up their clients. Agents will also tattoo other numbers of a client's choice, such as a Social Security number. It is advisable, however, that pet owners use the tattoo registry's assigned number system, since these markings are easy to trace and are well known among shelter workers.

Tattoo Agents

Another good reason for using one of these two companies is the tattoo agent—an independent tattooer affiliated with a registry. Both the National Dog Registry and Tattoo-A-Pet have thousands of tattoo agents. Most tattoo agents are already involved in some aspect of pet care (e.g., pet grooming, pet store owners, breeders, veterinarians, etc.) and so are experienced in handling animals.

You can locate a qualified tattoo agent by contacting either the National Dog Registry or Tattoo-A-Pet (See "Resources/Registries and Recovery Services.") Simply tell them your zip code or area code, and they will put you in touch with an experienced tattoo agent near you. Both of these national registries carry a blanket liability insurance policy that covers all of their agents.

The Tattooing Procedure

The tattooing process is safe, humane, virtually painless and bloodless, and no anesthetic is necessary. (See figure 11.) The entire procedure takes about three minutes to complete. You will also receive an ID tag with a toll-free number when you sign up.

For dogs, the tattoo is inscribed in an inconspicuous spot, usually on the belly or sometimes under the thigh of the hind leg. Cats are generally tattooed on the inner ear. Wherever it is, the fur around the tattoo should be trimmed regularly so the tattoo is always visible.

A cat or dog can be tattooed from the age of six weeks, but pet owners are urged to have it done at no later than eight weeks. The longer your pet is not tattooed, the longer it has no permanent link to you. One of the problems with tattooing that is often raised is that tattoos can fade and become unreadable as a pet grows. The folks at Tattoo-A-Pet say that if the tattoo is done properly, there should be no fading. This is one more reason to go to a professional tattoo agent who is experienced in tattooing animals. If a letter or number does fade or blur, many agents will touch it up free of charge. In any event, it is better to have a tattoo that is a little faded than to have no form of permanent identification at all, as faded tattoos are difficult but not impossible to trace.

You can view a video clip demonstration of the tattoo procedure at www.tattoo-a-pet.com.

Tattooing Other Pets

Tattooing is not just for cats and dogs. Almost any type of animal can and has been tattooed. Ferrets, hamsters, goats, rabbits, and even horses can be and have been tattooed.

Cost of Tattooing

Depending on the agent, the cost to tattoo your pet will run about $20. In addition, there is the cost of registering the number, which is currently $10 to $15 and has remained so for years (quite inexpensive when compared to the peace of mind you will gain). All registrations with the National Dog Registry and Tattoo-A-Pet are for the lifetime of the pet, and both organizations have a rate for single pets and a breeder rate. The breeder rate is also available to people who own multiple pets, allowing you to register as many pets as you own or ever will own.

Pros and Cons of Tattooing

There are some people who complain that tattoos can fade, that many shelter workers are reluctant to get close enough to look for a tattoo for fear of being bitten, or that a tattoo can be deliberately altered by someone. While these criticisms have some validity, the positive aspects of tattooing far outweigh the potential negatives. As already stated, fading should not happen if the tattoo is done properly, and it can always be touched up. As for fear of being bitten, shelter workers are justifiably cautious because they know that while a pet may be docile and happy-go-lucky at home, it may, out of fear in a strange environment, attempt to bite. Most shelter employees, however, are very good at handling frightened stray animals, and it is part of their standard procedure to check stray animals for tattoos. It's certainly possible that someone would go as far as deliberately altering a tattoo, but we believe that would be a rare exception. In any event, this is just another good reason to use multiple forms of identification!

Why Pet Tattooing is Painless

According to the National Dog Registry, which has been tattooing pets for more than 30 years, "Pet tattoos are not like human tattoos, because there are distinct dimensional differences between the structures of human and animal skin. On humans, the tattoo must go much deeper into the skin, because of the thickness and uneven shape of the epidermis. Canine and feline epidermis is much thinner… Because the tattoo needle does not reach the nerve endings of a cat or dog's skin, it is not possible for your pet to feel pain. The only sensation your pet will feel is the vibration of the marker."

To find out more, visit the National Dog Registry's web site at **www.natldogregistry.com.**

FIGURE 11

Microchips

A microchip implant is a tiny micro-electronic device consisting of a silicon chip and a passive coil all inside a bio-compatible glass pellet about the size of a grain of rice. It's actually a tiny radio transponder. The chip is encoded with a unique, unalterable identification number. Once the chip is implanted under the skin, you simply register the chip with the registry company, who will keep all of your contact information in its database in much the same way other registries keep track of tattoo numbers and tag identification numbers.

If your pet is taken into a shelter or to a veterinarian, scanned, and a chip is discovered, they will contact the registry who in turn will contact you. Chips can even be traced to the veterinarian who did the implant. This is important because if you have a chip implanted and your pet escapes before you've had a chance to register it (or if you move and forget to update your contact information with the chip registry), the chip can be traced to the veterinarian who implanted it. She or he will likely know how to get in touch with you. A microchip could also save your pet from becoming a research experiment, as new grant and funding requirements are forcing research laboratories to scan animals that have been slated for experimentation or research for microchips.

In August of 2001, the one-millionth pet was enrolled with Companion Animal Recovery (CAR), the lost pet registry run by the American Kennel Club. CAR has been responsible for over 60,000 lost pet recoveries since 1995. CAR is also the official registry for the Home Again microchip, one of the two leading microchip implants on the market today. AVID (American Veterinary Identification Devices), another leader in microchip implants and the maker of the FriendChip, reports equally impressive results. AVID's PETtrack system has helped recover 132,000 pets since 1991.

Although microchipping pets has been done for several years, it is only since the invention of the universal scanner that it has become widely accepted. In the earlier days of microchipping, there were several different chip manufacturers, each requiring a different scanning device. The situation was so bad that it was not unusual for shelter workers to have to use four different scanning devices on a single animal. Fortunately for us and our animals, the industry has standardized, with the development and subsequent proliferation of the universal scanner. More than 100,000 universal scanners have been sold to veterinarians and animal shelters, or given away through free scanner placement programs. (See figure 12.)

Also, the newer chips employ anti-migration technology which allows the chip to adhere to the tissue almost immediately, thus preventing it from moving around under the skin, which was a major drawback of earlier chips.

With the incompatibility and migration problems solved, with organizations like the American Kennel Club endorsing the technology, and with major corporations like Schering-Plough (Home Again microchip) involved, consumer as well as professional confidence is growing. More and more veterinarians are doing implants and promoting the use of chips.

Implanting the Microchip

The microchip is injected into the animal with a large-gauge needle, and is normally implanted between the shoulder blades. The whole procedure only takes a few seconds and is painless, so no anesthetic is necessary. Because the chip is bio-compatible, there is virtually no chance of an allergic reaction or rejection.

As soon as an animal is weaned—six to eight weeks—it can have a microchip implanted. A good time to do it is at the time of initial vaccinations. In fact, many veterinarians will offer a discount if it is done at the same time as another procedure. And your pet is never too old to be implanted with a microchip. Many animal shelters microchip the animals they adopt out to new homes. The fee for microchipping is included in the adoption cost.

Cost of Microchipping

The price is set by the veterinarian and is separate from the cost of registration, so it is best to call for an exact price. However, it is very affordable and well within the means of most people. The registration is for the lifetime of your pet, and enrollment is free for dogs that assist the disabled. Also, many shelters offer discounts to people who adopt animals if they microchip them.

AVID's Free Reader Placement Program

"The purpose of the program is to improve the probability of recovering a pet who has been permanently identified with the AVID FriendChip. Since many animals who are lost will end up at a shelter, AVID will provide an Identity Tag Reader free of charge to any qualifying shelter. In order for a shelter to qualify, only two criteria must be met:

1. A veterinarian who purchases an AVID system can designate a shelter to receive a free reader.

2. The designated shelter must promise to scan all animals upon admission and prior to euthanasia, placement, or sale."

To find out more about AVID's Free Reader Placement program or how an AVID microchip implant can protect your pet, call AVID at (800) 336-AVID (2843), or visit their web site at **www.avidid.com**.

Reprinted with permission from Avid Identification Systems Inc. Copyright 1996-2000. All rights reserved.

FIGURE 12

Where to Get a Microchip

This is a medical procedure and must be done by a veterinarian or under a veterinarian's supervision. Your veterinary clinic or animal shelter should be able to give you a referral in the event that they don't do implants themselves. Or you can simply call AVID at (800) 336-AVID (2843) or log onto the Schering-Plough web site at **http://usa.spah.com** to locate a participating Home Again veterinarian in your area. Shelters may offer inexpensive microchipping services or special microchipping clinics.

Microchipping Birds, Ferrets, and Other Animals

Other animals that are commonly microchipped are ferrets, pygmy goats, horses, and birds. AVID makes a smaller chip that can be implanted in birds as small as five ounces (about the size of a Cockatiel), while standard chips are used for larger exotic birds such as Macaws.

Pros and Cons of Microchipping

The most common objection to microchips is that not every scanner can read every type of chip. This is still a problem in some places, but is rapidly being resolved through projects such as AVID's "Free Reader Placement Program" and Home Again's free shelter placement. Home Again placed their scanners free for three years and now offer them at cost.

Another objection has been that the microchips tended to move after being implanted, sometimes far from the implant site. As mentioned above, this may have been true in the early days of this technology; new chips employ anti-migration technology and begin to bond with the animal's tissue within hours of implantation.

A third criticism is that shelter workers simply don't scan for chips. Again, this was more widely true when the technology was first being introduced. Microchip implants are endorsed by so many organizations now that professional animal handlers routinely scan for chips when they pick up a stray. Part of AVID's agreement for placing a free scanner in a shelter is that the shelter agrees in writing to scan all animals for microchips upon entry and just before euthanizing them.

The simple fact is that microchips work and are responsible for tens of thousands of lost pet recoveries. (See figure 13.) You need to be aware, however, that no identification method is 100% effective. Therefore, none of the methods described in this book should be relied on alone, but rather used in conjunction with other identification methods.

DNA

Having your pet's DNA profile done is yet one more way of identifying your pet. Your pet's DNA "fingerprint" is a permanent, tamperproof record of your pet's identity that is every bit as conclusive as the DNA evidence that can positively link a suspect to a crime or exonerate him. Similarly, a DNA profile of your pet can win you a victory in court if your pet is ever lost and claimed by someone else refusing to return the animal. (See figure 14.)

The leader in DNA profiling for pets is Celera AgGen, a subdivision of PE Applied Biosystems. This company works closely with several animal-related organizations including the American Kennel Club. In 1996, the AKC began an ambitious DNA pilot program and now has the largest collection of DNA profiles involving purebred dogs ever

---

"Tails" with Happy Endings from Companion Animal Recovery (CAR)

Tashatu, Female Rottweiler Dog

"Tashatu was stolen over a month before turning up at the dog pound. Before Tashatu was euthanized, they scanned a Home Again microchip and we called the owner. The owner was thrilled and said without the chip she would have never gotten her dog back!"

Bucc, Male Labrador Retriever Dog

"We received another call on a lost Labrador Retriever. This is our most recovered dog breed by far with over 5,000 successfully recovered Labs and counting. In this recovery, Bucc wandered approximately 40 miles until he was found in Valrico, Florida. The owner was in St. Petersburg, and she was amazed! So were we!"

Bob, Male Domestic Long-Hair Cat

"Bob had been lost for two weeks when the owner called us. We told her not to give up hope because she had had Bob implanted with the Home Again microchip from her vet. Two months later, we received a call at midnight that Bob had been found. The owner cried for several minutes when we gave her the wonderful news. We cried too!"

For more exciting recovery stories visit the
AKC web site at **www.akccar.org.**

FIGURE 13

assembled. In addition, there are other, smaller companies that also offer DNA services direct to consumers.

DNA and Pets

There are companies that provide a variety of services related to the DNA profiling of dogs (e.g., parentage verification, various breeding applications, as well as a method of permanent identification). Celera AgGen provides these services directly to dog owners via their direct-to-client program. Your pet's DNA profile will be done and the record kept in their database.

Due to a lack of sufficient public interest, AgGen no longer offers DNA profiling for cats and only provides limited, although very effective, services for birds. The company maintains a gene match registry for birds where your bird's blood specimen will be preserved indefinitely. If you do end up needing it to prove ownership, they will then do the DNA testing after the fact. Avian Biotech International of Tallahassee, Florida, has a blood sample storage service for birds similar to AgGen's gene match registry. Charles River Therion, Inc., located in Troy, New York, will do a DNA profile on just about any animal. According to Ann Seman, Senior Product Coordinator with Therion, "To date, we have worked with over 400 species of animals ranging from shrimp to emus to elephants to mice to dogs, horses, cats, cougars, and cell lines for biotechnology. You name it, we have probably worked or could work with it." Therion uses a more sophisticated, more labor intensive, and therefore more expensive technique that requires a blood sample be drawn by a veterinarian. The advantage to pet owners is that they will work with any animal. (See "Resources/DNA.")

While DNA services are not required for registering your dog, two of the largest kennel clubs—the American Kennel Club and the United Kennel Club—do offer DNA services to their members as well as to the general public. However, the services are limited to owners of purebred dogs. Both clubs provide DNA test kits upon request.

DNA Sample Kits

Celera AgGen will send dog owners a DNA sample kit upon request. DNA sampling is safe, easy, non-invasive, and you can take

DNA Analysis and the Legal System

"DNA-based evidence is admissible in court. DNA analysis has been used in criminal cases to link a suspect to the crime scene; it has been used in civil trials to provide evidence for paternity disputes; and it has been used for evidence in lawsuits against suspected animal smugglers.

"Can DNA-based identification satisfy the burden of proof? In civil cases, the burden of proof is less exacting than in criminal trials. Once DNA-based evidence has been admitted into a civil case, it is essentially a matter of satisfying a jury. This will undoubtedly vary from case to case and, naturally, other lines of evidence play a role in the final outcome."

For more information or to order a DNA sample kit for your dog or bird, contact Celera AgGen.

Canine services:
1-800-362- DOGG (3644)

Gene match registry:
1-800-995-BIRD (2473)

Reprinted with permission from PE Zoogen The ABCs of Animal Genetics. Copyright 1997. All rights reserved.

FIGURE 14

the sample yourself by simply rubbing the inside of your pet's mouth with the cotton swab provided in the DNA sample kit. All you have to do is mail it back to them. It's that simple. About two weeks later, you'll receive a DNA certificate that bears your name, your pet's name, and a DNA registration number.

Owners of exotic birds should request a kit from Celera AgGen or from one of the other avian services (See "Resources/DNA.") When your kit arrives, you carefully clip one of your pet's nails, draw a single drop of blood and place it in the small plastic test tube provided with the kit. You mail the sample back to the company where it will be stored until analysis may be needed in the future. It should be noted that even small amounts of blood loss from a tiny bird can be quite serious, therefore you may want to consider having this done by someone with experience, such as your veterinarian.

DNA Leaves No Doubt

In May of 1993, the *Newburyport Daily News* in Massachusetts reported that an animal control officer had captured a bright yellow and green Macaw. Within a few days, three people (ultimately five) stepped forward to claim the bird, which was valued at $2,500 dollars. All of the claimants offered various evidence: photos, lost bird reports that they had filed, etc. The first claimant showed up with photographs, and animal control confirmed that the woman had indeed reported her bird as missing some time before. A second claimant had, only a week prior, reported a bird stolen from the lobby of his hotel, and yet a third insisted that the bird belonged to him and that he could prove it beyond any doubt because he had a DNA profile on his bird. A sample of the bird's DNA was sent off to the lab. Meanwhile, two more people came forward claiming the bird belonged to them. When the DNA test results came back and were compared with the results of a DNA test the gentleman had done several years before, it was conclusive. There was no doubt that the bird belonged to him.

Cost of DNA Profiling

DNA profiling may be less expensive than you think. We were surprised to discover that the cost is around $50 for dogs and $15 for birds. Of course, prices vary from service to service, so call or write for exact prices. In addition, some kennel clubs offer discounted rates for members.

Animal Shelters

The central focus of this book is on lost and missing pets. So it is only fitting that we include a chapter on animal shelters, since they play such an important role in the care and management of stray animals, many of whom are people's lost and missing pets. The purpose of this topic is threefold. One, in terms of pet loss, there are important things you need to know, since if your pet is ever lost there is a good likelihood that it will be taken to one of your local animal shelters. The second is to present the shelter as a vital community resource, to encourage our readers to take advantage of the many services they provide, and to raise public awareness about the indispensable role that shelters play in the communities they serve. The third is to encourage people to get involved by supporting their local shelters financially and in other ways.

Any effective prevention strategy must include your having a thorough knowledge of how to recover a lost pet before that pet is ever lost. There are many important things you need to know about reclaiming your pet from an animal shelter. Much of this information can be found in the "Recovery" section of this book. (See "Check the Animal Shelters.") Here are a few things that are particularly important:

Know Where They Are Located

An animal shelter is the best place to search for your lost pet. It's the place animal control workers will take stray animals they pick up, and it's the place the majority of people will look for when they've found a lost animal that they can't take in while they're searching for its owner.

There may be several shelters, both municipal and private, where you live. It's important to know this, since your pet may be lost in one town but picked up in another. Our own county is a perfect example of what can be a very confusing situation. Strays picked up in our town are taken to a humane society shelter. In the adjoining town (actually just a few hundred yards away from where we live), strays are taken to a different shelter. If one of our pets were to turn up missing, we would have to call at least two different shelters.

It is very important that you collect the numbers and addresses for all of the facilities that take in strays within 60 miles of your home. This is not as difficult as it sounds. (See "Critical Contacts.")

Know What to Do to Reclaim Your Pet

Since laws regarding reclaiming animals from shelters may vary from state to state and from municipality to municipality, you need to know the requirements for retrieving your animal from the shelters in the area where you live. Our local shelter requires proof of ownership in the form of a photograph or medical records, and the animal must also have a license. If a pet is unlicensed, the owner can still reclaim the animal by showing proof of ownership, in addition to agreeing in writing to obtain a license within five days. If the owner fails to obtain a license, however, a summons will be issued. It is also important to be aware that shelters may have separate areas for quarantined and injured animals. If your pet is ever lost, be sure to insist that the shelter workers look for your pet in these areas. Better yet, search all the kennel areas yourself (accompanied by shelter staff in restricted areas).

As one way of safeguarding your pet, we recommend developing a relationship with the people at your local animal shelter. Most shelter workers care deeply for the animals in their charge and many volunteer their time. This way if your pet ever goes missing, you will already have established a relationship with the people at the shelter. There are many ways to get involved with your local shelter, from volunteering time to contributing money and supplies. (See figure 15.) Contributing much-needed supplies or volunteering your time at a shelter is a very rewarding experience.

How You Can Help Homeless Animals at Your Local Animal Shelter

The following is a list of ways you can support your local humane shelter:

• **Give a Little Bit**—Donate food, old blankets and towels, or other needed supplies to your local shelter. Contribute to one of its special programs.

• **Lend a Hand**—Volunteer your time at your local shelter. Bathe and groom the animals, walk dogs, or play with cats. Stuff envelopes for a mailing. Help publicize an event.

• **Find That Special Someone**—Choose your next pet from your local shelter. The shelter has many wonderful dogs and cats of different shapes and sizes just waiting for a permanent, loving home.

• **Help Spread the Word**—Tell your friends about your local shelter's services. Promote animal safety and responsible pet ownership. Celebrate "National Animal Shelter Appreciation Week," the first full week of November.

• **Be a Responsible Pet Owner**—Keep current identification on your dog or cat at all times. Spay or neuter your pet. Always keep your dog or cat properly confined or supervised. In addition to the basics (food, water, shelter, and veterinary care), give your pet lots of love and attention.

• **Vote for the Animals**—Support legislation to protect animals. Contact government officials about animal issues and urge them to support pro-animal legislation (and oppose legislation that harms animals).

• **Be a Hero**—Report animal cruelty and neglect, as well as injured or stray animals. You may prevent suffering and even save a life.

• **Teach Your Children Well**—Instruct children in how to care for animals properly and how to treat them with kindness. Set an example by doing the same.

FIGURE 15

Your Local Animal Shelter: A Vital Community Resource

Many people believe the animal shelter's role is limited to taking in strays and then trying to get them adopted. In the March/April 2000 issue of *Animal Sheltering*, The Humane Society of the United States reported that a survey by the American Pet Products Manufacturers' Association showed that when seeking information about their pets, "Pet owners turn to almost any other source—including veterinarians, pet store personnel, magazines, breeders, friends, and relatives—before they knock on the doors of their local humane societies or municipal agencies." According to The HSUS, "Fewer than five percent of pet owners approach shelters for information and advice."

Things are changing, however, as animal shelters all around the country have begun taking a more proactive stance and are becoming community resource centers that offer a variety of programs and services to the public. We read recently how the Humane Society of Indianapolis, a very proactive shelter, hosts an annual Valentine's Day Party, which they call *Heavy Petting Into the Night.* Many shelters are now opening their doors for tours of their facilities, providing space for grief support groups for those who have lost a pet, teaching pet parenting and obedience classes, and offering behavior advice and assistance; many even operate behavior hotlines. In terms of pet loss, these services can be invaluable to pet owners since not only can obedience training solve many behavior problems, it also happens to be one of the most effective ways of preventing pet loss. Call your local shelter; ask if they provide these kinds of services. Take advantage of this valuable but underutilized resource.

Support Your Local Shelter

Contrary to popular perception, many shelters are not tax-dollar supported but instead rely on the financial and volunteer support of people like you. Sadly, the majority of public and private shelters alike are woefully underfunded. If more people got involved, facilities would have the resources they need to deal with the overwhelming numbers of strays. This would go a long way toward reducing the immediate need to euthanize animals. We urge you to support your local animal shelter. Make them a part of your annual charitable contributions. We can hardly think of a better charity to support than one that cares for the homeless, sick, injured, abused, and stray animals in your community. Remember, that might be your pet someday if it were ever lost.

Pet Clubs and Breed Rescue Groups

Pet Clubs

Pet clubs are made up of enthusiasts for animals within a particular breed or species. Not only are pet clubs a great resource for the care and general maintenance of pets, they can also be invaluable when trying to recover a missing pet. (See figure 16.) What makes them particularly helpful in lost pet prevention and recovery is that they are part of a greater network of people who are similarly devoted to animals of a particular breed.

There are literally thousands of pet clubs across America, their memberships numbering in the millions. When you lose a pet you want to have as many allies as possible, and where better to turn for help and advice when you lose your Irish Setter than a group of people who love Irish Setters! You may even be able to enlist other club members to help you in your search. This is especially helpful when you're traveling far from home, because when you have to return, you will still have someone lending long-distance support. If your pet is a member of a recognized breed, we urge you to join a pet club, or at least compile a list of clubs before your pet is ever lost.

Having your child join a pet club is also a wonderful way of teaching your youngster about

---

Pet Clubs/Rescue Groups and Lost Pet Prevention and Recovery

As part of your overall prevention strategy, put together a list of these organizations before your pet turns up missing. Contacting these groups when attempting to recover a missing pet is very important, and could prove critical; consider the following:

• They have many members in their network.

• Many run facilities.

• They are made up of people who have more than a casual interest in a particular breed or species, and these folks will probably be willing to lend you assistance.

• Veterinarians, animal hospitals, and shelters call on breed rescue groups all the time to take in stray purebreds. Your lost purebred may not be in a local shelter because it was, in fact, placed with a rescue group.

• Club and rescue group members are a good source of information about the general care of a particular breed and may help you gain the knowledge you need to keep your pet safe at home.

• A club or group member may have heard of someone trying to sell your pet. Some purebreds are worth a lot of money. Some parrots, African Greys for example, can cost several thousand dollars.

• A club or group member may lend you long-distance support if you are traveling in another state, lose your pet, and are forced to give up the search and return home. Even if you don't own a purebred or an exotic animal, there is still a good chance that you will find a rescue group member willing to assist, as these are people who are devoted to improving the lives of all animals.

FIGURE 16

responsible pet ownership and about the proper care and maintenance of their chosen pet. Too often, animals such as hamsters, gerbils, mice, and reptiles, or "critters," as they are affectionately known, are purchased for children with little thought given to the care these animals will require. It is almost as though they are purchased as toys; without proper education about their care and handling, they are often treated as such. This lack of knowledge is a leading cause of escapes. Thousands of hamsters, gerbils, mice, reptiles, etc., are lost every year. Joining a pet club is a good place for your children to start learning about responsible pet ownership. Besides, pet clubs are just plain fun! (See figure 17.)

Rescue Groups

The fact that approximately one-fourth of all dogs that are brought to animal shelters are purebreds has led to the formation of literally hundreds of breed rescue groups. These are people who care so deeply for animals within a particular breed or species that they are willing to put their time, money, and efforts into saving animals that have been abused, neglected, abandoned, and may need to be euthanized at a shelter. Rescue groups are a great place to turn when trying to recover a lost animal. From Harriers to Hamsters, from Ferrets to Flat-coated Retrievers, from African Greys to Persian Cats, there are rescue groups for almost every breed and species of animal.

When we began writing this book, we admittedly had very limited knowledge about some pets. For example, we needed to know more about ferrets and so we called on the expertise of various ferret rescue groups. They were more than willing to help. Through them we learned much about ferret habits, the general care and protection of ferrets, and more importantly, how to prevent the loss of and how to recover a missing ferret.

If your ferret, exotic bird, or purebred dog or cat is ever lost, contact the appropriate rescue groups right away. You may also be able to find allies among rescue groups to assist you in your recovery efforts. As with pet clubs, if you lose your pet while traveling, a rescue group can offer continuing support even after you return home.

It's also important for you to know that veterinarians and animal hospitals frequently call the local rescue groups when an injured

Two Great Web Sites Just for Kids

Educating your child about proper pet care can significantly reduce the risk of escape or worse. Having your child join a pet club is a great place to start teaching them about responsible pet ownership. Both the American Society for the Prevention of Cruelty to Animals (ASPCA) and The Humane Society of the United States (HSUS) have web sites designed especially for young pet owners. They're really cool interactive sites filled with games, news stories, and lots of helpful information about proper pet care.

Visit the ASPCA's *Animaland* web site at **www.animaland.org.**

Be sure to also check out the HSUS's youth education division web site (*Kind News*) online at **www.kindnews.org.**

FIGURE 17

purebred animal is brought to them. This is also true for animal shelters. If a purebred comes in as a stray and is not adopted out, they will often call a rescue group to take it. In fact, if you were unable to locate your Afghan Hound or Siamese Cat at the local shelter, it might have been because it was placed with a rescue group. Maybe it was adopted, not euthanized.

Rescue group members will take these animals into their homes and feed, care for, and provide for them until they are adopted out. Many rescue groups run their own shelter and adoption facilities. As with pet clubs, compile a list of rescue groups prior to your pet's being lost. If you are so inclined, get involved in rescue work: you will find it to be one of the most rewarding experiences of your life.

How to Locate Them

There are literally thousands of pet clubs and rescue groups, and they're easy to locate. You can find them in pet magazines—especially breed-specific magazines—and your local library should have a book called the *Encyclopedia of Associations* in which there is a section, although very limited, on pet organizations. The best resource, however, is the Internet, where you can easily access the names, addresses, and phone numbers of the various pet clubs and rescue groups in your area. Many of these also have message boards for posting comments and asking and answering questions, as well as chat rooms for interacting with people who share your enthusiasm for whatever breed or species of pet you own. (See "Critical Contacts.")

Rabies

Many pet owners probably dismiss rabies as a problem of past generations. Indeed, the most popular image of rabies surely stems from the classic Disney film *Old Yeller*, a story set in the Texas hill country in the 1860s, a time when rabies was endemic throughout many parts of the United States.

Thanks to aggressive vaccination programs, rabies in canines is now quite rare. According to the National Association of State Public Health Veterinarians' (NASPHV) *2000 Compendium of Animal Rabies Prevention and Control*, "Cases of laboratory-confirmed rabies in dogs declined from 6,949 in 1947 to only 111 in 1996." (See figure 18.) The efforts to eradicate rabies have been so successful that many pet owners never get around to vaccinating their animals, even though many communities offer free vaccinations. This is quite a shift in

For Additional Information on Rabies Contact the CDC

To view the *Compendium of Animal Rabies Prevention and Control*, visit the Centers for Disease Control and Prevention's (CDC) web site at **www.cdc.gov** and search using the keyword "rabies."
Or contact the CDC:
U.S. Centers for Disease Control and Prevention
Mail Stop A-26
1600 Clifton Road, N.E.
Atlanta, GA 30333
(888) 232-3228

FIGURE 18

public perception toward this disease. It wasn't that many years ago that rabies was considered so terrifying that an animal even suspected of carrying it was shot on sight.

Nevertheless, the National Institutes of Health report that as many as "18,000 Americans receive post-rabies exposure treatment each year because of contact with animals suspected of being rabid." Most of these cases can be attributed to the rabies virus in wild animal populations, primarily raccoons, skunks, and bats. As their habitats have gotten smaller and their normal food supply has diminished, the dumpster and the backyard garbage can have become a tempting dietary supplement for wild animals such as raccoons. This is important to know, since it is here that your lost dog or cat is most likely to become involved in an altercation with a rabid wild animal.

Rabies and Lost Pet Prevention and Preparedness

Canine rabies is a rare occurrence and for the most part not a major threat. Until quite recently, very few communities required rabies vaccinations for cats, which is why today reported cases of rabies in felines far outnumber those in their canine counterparts. Ferrets, too, are susceptible, and many communities are beginning to require rabies vaccinations for them as well. Having your pet vaccinated against rabies and keeping vaccinations current is most important in terms of preparing for pet loss and recovery for several reasons.

- You may need a license in order to reclaim your pet from a shelter, and a current rabies vaccination is a prerequisite to obtaining a license.

What Should I Do if I Think I've Been Exposed to Rabies?

According to the National Institutes of Health, if you have been bitten or scratched by any animal who you do not know for a fact has been vaccinated against rabies, you should:

- Clean the wound immediately with soap and water to remove saliva from the area.
- Call a doctor right away.
- Notify the state or local health department.
- If soap is not available (when hiking, for example), you can use water alone, but be sure to wash with soap and water as soon as possible—and allow the wound to bleed, which also will help to clean it.

- You will need proof of current vaccination if you travel with your pet.

- Your lost pet could be subjected to an extended quarantine (at your expense) if it arrives at a shelter, is suspected of having been exposed to rabies, and its vaccination is not current.

If your pet is brought into a shelter, without rabies tags, and there is evidence of it having tangled with a wild animal, and the offending animal is not available for testing, the *Compendium Report* states that "the animal should be regarded as having been exposed to rabies." The recommendations set forth in the report are quite severe: "Unvaccinated dogs, cats, and ferrets exposed to a rabid animal should be euthanized immediately. If the owner is unwilling to have this done, the animal should be placed in strict isolation for six months and vaccinated one month before being released." According to Tufts University School of Veterinary Medicine's newsletter, *Your Dog*, the six-month quarantine period and the cost associated with boarding an animal for that period of time are the responsibility of the pet owner. "In some cases," the newsletter reports, "owners have had their dogs euthanized because of their inability to pay this expense." This should be incentive enough to keep your pet's rabies shots current.

Many communities use door-to-door canvassing as a way to enforce the vaccination and licensing requirements, and pet owners can be issued a summons for noncompliance. In many places, city officials will automatically issue a summons to pet owners whose animals are picked up by animal control and discovered to be unlicensed.

Where Do I Get My Pet Vaccinated?

As with all things where your pet's health is concerned, your veterinarian is a good place to start. Community health departments regularly sponsor free vaccination clinics at firehouses, community centers, and animal shelters. To find out where such clinics may be held in your area, call your animal control agency or local health department. You can also find these clinics advertised in the community section of your local newspaper. Two of the largest pet supply superstores, PETCO and PETsMART, offer low-cost vaccinations in many of their stores. (See "Resources/Rabies.")

Once your pet has been vaccinated, you will receive a proof of vaccination certificate for your pet records, which will also serve to obtain a license. Many veterinarians issue rabies tags, which frequently include the vet's name and phone number. Although this is helpful, it should not be relied upon for identification purposes. What is important is that these types of tags show shelter workers that your pet is indeed vaccinated. One major drawback to rabies tags, as with municipal license tags, is that calls to the vaccinating veterinarian are only answered during business hours. Rabies tags and municipal licenses should only be used to supplement more proper forms of pet identification. (See "ID Tags.")

Roaming and Escaping

As Americans, we cherish freedom above all else. Unfortunately, too many people extend the concept of freedom to their pets. In many places, especially in rural America, there has always existed a free-roaming attitude toward pets. That attitude persists today even though the dangers inherent in allowing pets to run free are common knowledge. It's not always just the pet who is at risk. Domesticated cats allowed to run loose can sometimes pose a serious threat to wildlife. In many places, it is illegal to allow your pets to roam.

What is Roaming?

We're not talking about a pet simply getting loose. By roaming, we are talking about a deliberate act on the part of pet owners to allow their pets to come and go as they please. It may be that they've simply given in to their animal's annoying behavior and persistent escape attempts.

No responsible parents would ever consider allowing their young children to run free and unsupervised. Children rely on the adults around them to guide, protect, and care for them. So do our pets. Every time you allow your pet to run free, you are risking its life, for a pet permitted to roam outside unsupervised faces a great number of mortal dangers.

The Many Hazards of Roaming

The most obvious hazard is, of course, being hit by cars. Some less obvious hazards include:

- Ingesting antifreeze or other toxic substances.
- Being killed, mauled, or maimed by wild animals. In states like Florida, for example, many pets are killed and eaten by alligators every year. Depending on what part of the country you live in, your pet may be at risk of attacks by wild dogs, coyotes, owls, and even eagles, not to mention exposure to rabies from raccoons, skunks, and other wild animals.
- Receiving abuse from humans, pranksters, or just plain sadists who deliberately harm animals and take pleasure in it.
- Being harmed by neighbors who get angry about people's pets invading their yards, digging in their flowerbeds, and going to the bathroom. Some have resorted to physically harming the animals (shooting them with pellet guns, poisoning, pet-napping, and even killing them).
- Being picked up by a pet thief and sold to a research facility, a dog fighting ring, or a puppy mill.
- Being caught in a hunter's trap. A New Jersey shelter recorded over 1,000 incidents of trapped pets in one three-year period.

• Being exposed to communicable diseases; roaming cats are at particularly high risk. (See figure 19.)

Keeping Indoor Pets Happy and Content

Many indoor pets are quite happy with their sedentary lives, while others are not. It's these animals who constantly yearn for the out-of-doors and stage persistent and repeated escape attempts. They constantly complain, meow, bark, destroy furniture, etc. Such behavior has led many a frustrated pet owner to simply give up and allow their pets to roam (or to relinquish them to the local animal shelter).

Many of these behavioral problems can be easily traced to separation anxiety or just plain boredom, the result of being left alone all day in an apartment or enclosure with little or no stimulation. Cats and dogs are complex creatures. Like us, they have physical, emotional, and psychological needs. It's quite likely that your pet's behavioral problems are its way of letting you know its needs are not being met.

Fortunately, there are many strategies for dealing with these situations. Providing your indoor, caged, or kenneled pet with an environment that is rich in stimulating activity can greatly reduce escaping behavior. It can also reduce and possibly eliminate other undesirable behaviors associated

Roaming Cats: At High Risk

Roaming cats run a great risk of contracting communicable diseases such as Feline Leukemia. Although there's a vaccine for this disease now, it's not 100% effective. Feline Immunodeficiency Virus (FIV) is a more serious danger since there is no vaccine and no known cure. FIV can be transmitted easily via the bite of another cat. It attacks the cat's immune system and is eventually fatal. According to Bruce Lawhorn, Associate Professor of Small Animal Medicine and Surgery at Texas A&M University, "Free-roaming cats and mixed-breed cats are at highest risk for contracting FIV infection. The disease is rare in cats housed strictly indoors." He offers the following advice, "You can reduce the risk by neutering your cat to reduce roaming and territorial fighting behavior, and by keeping your cat indoors."

FIGURE 19

with loneliness, boredom, and separation anxiety. Even if your pet has access to the out-of-doors via a kennel or enclosure, it is your responsibility to provide it with physical and mental stimulation. The all-too-common practice of leaving a dog in an empty kennel for many hours at a time can increase isolation and aggression, and also motivate your dog to attempt an escape.

Environmental Enrichment

Karen Commings defines environmental enrichment in a June 1998 article in *Cat Fancy* magazine as seeking "to turn a wild animal's unnatural habitat into an environment that satisfies its natural instincts and desires." According to Ms. Commings, "Although the domestic cat is not a wild animal, it retains instinctive behavior inherited from its wild ancestors."

The same can be said for dogs. The challenge for pet owners is to fill their pet's environment with a variety of stimulating and challenging activities, activities that not only provide physical exercise but also exercise the animal's intellectual muscles. The ideal environment is one which is both complex and unpredictable, one that offers the animal choice and a variety of sensory experiences, as well as regular interaction with people and/or other animals. This can include, but is certainly not limited to, objects to climb on and various safe chew toys for your dog, and scratching posts and window perches for your cat. There's a great book for working cat owners *(Cat Home Alone: Fifty Ways to Keep Your Cat Happy and Safe While You're Away)* by Regen Dennis. It can be purchased at bookstores or through various online book retailers.

Some Excuses for Letting Pets Roam

- *It's the Way I Was Raised*—Like so many things in our adult lives, we learn from our childhood experiences. Many of us grew up in homes where it was the accepted practice to just open the door and let the dog out or to allow the cat to come and go as it pleased. Unfortunately, many people never question these behaviors: that's just the way they've always done it. This is why humane education should begin early. The way we care for animals will most certainly affect the actions and attitudes of our children.

- *It's Just Easier*—Sometimes people feel it's just too much trouble to deal with undesirable behaviors such as constant meowing or barking, destroying furniture, tearing through the garbage when left alone, persistent escape attempts, etc., and just let their animals run free or relinquish them to the shelter. One of the main reasons cited for shelter relinquishments is owner frustration over behavior problems. While frustration is understandable, allowing pets to roam freely or dropping them off at the shelter is not.

Why Pet Containment Often Fails

According to an *HSUS News* article titled "Electronic Aid" by Leslie Sinclair, DVM, "Many pet owners focus their efforts on…preventing escape, without first determining why the dog is behaving the way he is." When bad behavior is ignored or creative ways to redirect the animal's energies are not explored, patterns of undesirable behavior continue. Often attempts are made to deal with escaping behavior. The typical pet owner's reaction is to build a fence or take extra care when opening doors and gates. These are only strategies to physically block the animal from escaping. These tactics often fail because they treat the symptoms and do nothing to address the real issue of why their pet wants to roam.

Why Pets Desire to Roam

It is probably safe to say that the greatest contributor to the roaming impulse in pets is the desire to mate. Too many people put off sterilizing their pets until the pets are older or ignore it altogether, even though it is common knowledge that unsterilized pets are much more likely to attempt to escape than pets that have been altered. Each pet is unique, however, and there are many reasons why pets desire to roam. The first step in solving the problem is to identify the motivating factor behind your pet's escape attempts. We are all for installing fences, constructing good solid enclosures and kennels. In fact, much of this section is dedicated to giving pet owners the information they need to make informed decisions about these things. However, building a fence will do nothing to curb your dog or cat's instinctual desire to mate, but neutering him will. Having a kennel built will not alleviate your dog's boredom (and can even exaggerate it), but providing environmental enrichment will, and so will teaching him tricks and practicing obedience skills. Constructing a good solid enclosure will not satisfy your cat's curiosity or hunting instinct, but providing her with frequent opportunities to play with a feather on a string, or anything else that involves stalking an object, will. (See "Training.")

- *Boredom*—When used properly, a kennel or enclosure is an excellent method of pet containment, even for a hardcore escape artist. However, there is hardly a crueler scenario than leaving an animal alone in a kennel or enclosure for long periods of time. How inhumane is it to make your pet live in an environment devoid of stimulation, with little or no human interaction, with the same dirty old chew toy, with no view of the outside world? Not only can it contribute to feelings of isolation (the underlying cause of many an escape attempt), but it can also lead to aggression and other behavioral problems (some of the very problems that frustrate pet owners to the point of allowing their pets to roam freely).

- *Separation Anxiety*—The dread of being away from their owners is another motivation for pets to escape and misbehave. Many people work long hours (something that should have been considered well in advance of taking on the awesome responsibility of pet ownership, by the way) and by the time they get home their pet's jumping for joy makes them anything but joyful. Many pets are fine being left alone in the house and simply sleep the day away. For a significant number of pets, however, long periods of separation can cause a variety of anxiety-related behavior problems, such as excessive barking, destroying furniture, etc.; the very things that have frustrated some pet owners to the point of throwing open the door and allowing their pets to roam freely. Let's be honest—most of us quickly become frustrated if we have to wait just a few seconds for an elevator or a couple of minutes for a bus. No one likes to wait. Consider then how your pet must feel. He loves you, but has to spend eight or nine hours every day alone, just waiting for you to return home. No one is suggesting that you quit your job, but we implore working pet owners to make their animals a priority, to schedule quality time with them each and every day. And when they are absent, we ask them to provide their animals with an environment that is rich in stimulating activity; a habitat that provides a variety of choices and sensory experiences.

- *Phobias*—Many pets are particularly sensitive to loud noises, so it is no jcoincidence that the busiest day of the year reported by animal shelters is July 5th. (See "Holidays and Parties.") Perhaps your pet is trying to escape the noise of a tractor at the construction site down the street or the taunting of the kid next door, or it may have developed a fear of thunder. Now any sound that even ap-proximates the sound he fears can induce flight. Many factors can contribute to an animal's phobias and subsequent escape attempts. Identifying them is one of the necessary steps in alleviating your pet's fears and phobias. (See "Training.")

What Can I Do?

Eliminating or greatly reducing your pet's urge to roam will take patience, persistence, perhaps a little money, the proper information, and a serious commitment on the part of you, the pet owner. One of the most successful and cost-effective things a pet owner can do to curb their pet's urge to roam, as well as to eliminate many of the undesirable behaviors associated with it, is to have their pet sterilized. This is especially true for male animals.

Spay and Neuter

Spaying is the surgical removal of a pet's ovaries and uterus; neutering is the surgical removal of the testicles.

Unless you are a professional breeder (not the backyard variety) or own purebreds that participate in certain competitive events (AKC Confirmation, for example) where the rules for eligibility preclude them from being sterilized, your animals should be spayed or neutered.

According to In Defense of Animals (IDA), an animal rights group dedicated to fighting animal cruelty, pets that have not been sterilized are at very high risk of running away, and so by not spaying and neutering your pets, you are putting them at risk of serious injury or death. Since spaying or neutering eliminates an animal's desire to mate, it makes your pet less likely to run off and subsequently less likely to be injured in a fight, stolen, or killed in traffic. It's no coincidence that a New Jersey animal shelter has reported that the majority of pets killed by motor vehicles are unaltered males. In addition, there are many health benefits associated with spaying and neutering. According to IDA, "Sterilized pets have twice the average life expectancy as unsterilized pets." This is partly because of a lower incidence of prostate, uterine, testicular, and breast cancers. The same IDA fact sheet states that "An unspayed female dog is 200 times more likely to develop mammary tumors than a dog spayed before her first heat, [and] an unspayed cat is seven times more likely to develop mammary tumors." It should also be noted that many municipalities have special lower licensing fees for sterilized animals.

Despite the obvious benefits, why are some otherwise well-intentioned pet lovers still reluctant to spay or neuter their animals? Generally, it is because they are misinformed.

Take the Quiz

The surgery is painful.
False—Animals undergoing the procedure are fully anesthetized. They may feel discomfort immediately following the operation, and complications, while they may occur, are rare.

Spaying/neutering causes pets to gain weight.
False—Given a proper diet and plenty of exercise, the effects should be minimal.

Spaying/neutering alters an animal's personality.
False—According to a 1998-99 *Puppies USA* article by Susan Easterly, "A pet's genetic makeup, along with the attention and training it receives, shapes its personality." Spaying/neutering may, however, decrease aggressiveness in males and the moodiness associated with heat cycles in females.

My pet is too young to be spayed.
False—Puppies and kittens can be sterilized as young as six weeks.

Spaying/neutering is expensive.
False—It's a lot cheaper to spay your pet than it is to raise a litter of puppies or to pay the medical bills if your pet gets hit by a car. Besides, many shelters offer spaying/neutering at a discounted rate when adopting an animal, and many veterinarians provide discounted or sliding-scale sterilizing services to the public. Call your local animal shelter, animal control agency, or talk to your veterinarian about discount spay and neuter services.

I have a male pet. He can't get pregnant, and therefore he does not need to be neutered.
False—While it may be true that he cannot get pregnant, it's a selfish attitude when you consider both the overwhelming numbers of unwanted animals and the risk of injury or loss.

It's a wonderful learning experience for children to see the miracle of birth.
False—There are overwhelming numbers of stray animals, many of which are eventually

humanely destroyed in the shelters because no one wants them. So this is the worst possible reason for not sterilizing your pet. If you want your children to see the miracle of birth, have them watch the *Discovery Channel* or *Animal Planet*. Or better yet, visit **www.allpets.com** and click on the "Petflicks" link. You and your children can view a video of an actual birth.

If you answered "true" to any of the above questions, you have been misinformed. The benefits of spaying and neutering in terms of lost pet prevention cannot be overstated. Besides the health benefits we've discussed, there is the issue of overpopulation. The statistics are truly heartbreaking. According to In Defense of Animals, "15 million dogs and cats are destroyed each year in the United States because there are not enough loving homes for all of them."

Where to Spay and Neuter

Your veterinarian can do the procedure. In addition, many animal shelters and humane societies are now offering the service and may even have free or discount clinics. You can easily locate a low-cost clinic near you by calling SPAY/USA. (See figure 20.)

Pet Containment

While spaying/neutering will certainly curb your animal's desire to roam, it is not a total solution. You still cannot simply allow your pet to come and go as it pleases. If you want your pet to have access to the out-of-doors, it is your responsibility to make sure it can do so safely.

Traditional Fencing

If you have a yard and want your pet to be able to run loose there, you really should have a fence. Chaining or tying an animal to an outside post (except in the case of an emergency) is both cruel and dangerous. Far too many dogs have become entangled and choked to death.

SPAY/USA

The goal of SPAY/USA is to reduce the number of unwanted cats and dogs and to put an end to animal suffering.

"SPAY/USA is a national referral service for affordable spay/neuter services. People who need assistance spaying and neutering their pets can call our toll-free number, (800) 248-SPAY (7729). They will be referred to a veterinarian or program in their area that provides affordable spay/neuter services. For some, affordable prices are an incentive to spay or neuter a pet. Callers are mailed a referral slip/certificate to obtain the low spay/neuter rate."

SPAY/USA operators are available Monday through Friday 9:00 a.m. to 5:00 p.m. EST.

For more information visit their web site at **www.spayusa.org**.

FIGURE 20

For most dogs, a properly-installed vinyl, wood, or chain-link fence will provide enough security. (Note: some dogs are able to climb up and over chain-link fences.) The quality of the gates and latches are as important as the material of the fence, since it is through open gates that many pets escape. A latch should be functional and easy to close, but not so easy to open. Childproof latches are ideal because they require a little effort to open. Spring-loaded gates that shut automatically offer the best protection of all, since guests, service people, and children may not always remember to close the gate. Locks are recommended since they offer a little more security, not only in terms of your pet getting loose, but also in keeping people (pet thieves and others) out. The height of a fence should also be proportionate to the size of your dog. Also, do not place objects, such as garbage containers, near the fence; many dogs have escaped by using them to climb up and over.

In selecting a fence company, check first with friends and neighbors who have had fencing installed (especially if they are pet owners). A reputable company will provide you with references, answer all of your questions, and address your concerns about your pet.

Electronic Fencing

There are several reasons why a pet owner might choose the electronic fence option. Perhaps you have a beautifully landscaped yard and don't want it obscured by a fence. There may be a municipal ordinance or homeowners' association rule against fencing off your property. For others, fencing off an entire yard is simply too costly. Still others may not want their pet to have access to the entire yard. When used properly an electronic fence can be a safe and effective alternative to traditional fencing. As with most things, there are pros and there are cons. (See figure 21.)

All of the electronic fencing systems on the market today basically operate on the same principle. A wire is buried or posts placed along the perimeter of your property. These are connected to a transmitter that transmits a steady, unbroken signal. Your pet wears a pronged, battery-operated radio collar that detects the signal if he approaches too close to the boundary. At first, the collar emits a warning sound. If the animal continues toward the perimeter of the yard, either a mild electric shock or a blast of citronella is applied.

Pets must be trained to the system in order for it to be effective. (Some systems come with a training video.) Marker flags are placed along the boundary so as to be visible to the pet. While wearing the collar along with a long lead, the pet is brought near the boundary, just to where it can hear the warning sound. At this point, the owner pulls back on the leash, bringing the animal to the safe area of the yard and offering praise. Once the animal has learned to run back to the safe area, it is brought just close enough to experience the shock or the citronella blast. Again, the animal is brought back to safety and praised. Once the pet has demonstrated that she respects the boundary, she is allowed to run free and the flag markers are taken away. Cats can be and have been trained to these systems. However, they were originally designed for dogs and while some, not all, manufacturers promote them as safe and effective for cat containment, this should be done with the utmost of caution. There are several manufacturers of electronic fencing. For a complete listing see "Resources/Pet Containment."

Some people object to the use of aversion-type training aids that shock animals into compliance. Many animal welfare organizations, however, approve of the use of electronic fencing, provided it is properly installed and pets are trained to the system. Pet owners must understand, however, that while an electronic fence can be very effective in preventing pet loss, it is in no way a substitute for a pet owner's time and attention. It is only containment and doesn't address your pet's roaming impulse. ***The best advice is to never leave your pet unsupervised in the yard.***

Electronic fencing can also be used to supplement standard fencing; for example, if there is an area where your dog constantly tries to tunnel under the fence, a strand of electronic fence can be buried at the base of the fence to keep your dog away from that area.

Electronic Fencing: Pros and Cons

Pros:

• **Allows Freedom**—Allows pets to have access to the out-of-doors with a reasonable assuredness of safety.

• **Cost-Effective**—The cost can be as low as $150 for a do-it-yourself fence, and up to several hundred dollars for more elaborate custom installations and home consultations and training. This is still quite cost-effective, considering that fencing off a large yard area with a traditional fence can cost many thousands of dollars.

• **Thwarts Tunnelers and Jumpers**—Electronic fencing also has the unique advantage of not being able to be tunneled under or jumped over.

• **Aesthetics**—Some people spend many thousands of dollars landscaping their yards. Electronic fencing is invisible and so preserves not only their view of the neighborhood but the beauty of their property as well, all while allowing their pets to enjoy the out-of-doors.

• **Ordinances**—Electronic fencing can be installed in places where local ordinances restrict fencing-off of property. This is one reason that many veterinarians and humane organizations approve of electronic fencing when used properly.

Cons:

• **Not 100% Effective**—Not even the boldest of the electronic fence manufacturers boasts complete success. Some animals have a very high pain threshold and will bridge the electronic barrier. With proper installation and training, however, these systems can be very effective.

• **Breeds**—Some dogs, especially those bred for hunting, may be particularly difficult to train to the system.

• **They Don't Keep People, Predators, or Other Pets Out**—An electronic fence may keep your pet in, but it won't keep anything or anyone else out. Someone wandering inside the perimeter of your yard could be bitten, exposing you to liability.

• **Not Maintenance-Free**—Because these systems rely on batteries in the pet's collar, they are not maintenance-free, although some systems provide a warning signal when the batteries are running low. Also, the underground wires are susceptible to damage from tree roots, freezing and thawing of the ground, etc.

FIGURE 21

So You're Gonna Let Your Cat Roam Anyway

The purpose of this chapter is to inform pet owners about the hazards faced by roaming pets and to offer our readers concrete solutions for curbing roaming and escaping behavior. While few people allow their dogs to roam freely anymore, many still feel it is fine to allow cats to roam. We respectfully but strongly disagree. The fact remains that many people will, despite the dangers, continue to permit their cats to come and go as they please. While we can empathize with pet owners whose cats may be particularly difficult to keep indoors, we cannot condone this practice. If you are going to allow your cat to roam, please, for your cat's sake, take the following precautions:

• **Secure Your Pet's Collar and Tags**–Before you open that door, be sure your cat's collar is fastened and its tags are securely attached.

• **Use Multiple Forms of Identification**–Including a registered ID tag and at least one form of permanent identification.

• **Do Not Delay Searching**–If your cat does not return around its usual time, do not delay actively searching for it. This is a serious problem with roaming cats. Many people wait days before searching for cats that have been allowed to roam; by then the holding time at the local animal shelter may have already passed, with tragic consequences.

Kennels

Either permanent or freestanding kennels can be customized to fit your specific needs. Permanent kennels set on a concrete slab are quite good at containing animals, but they can be costly. Freestanding kennels are easily assembled and are less expensive. Properly installed and with special attention paid to gates and latches, both types offer your dog access to the out-of-doors while still providing protection against pet loss. Modular kennels can be extended to meet your particular needs by purchasing additional panels. A rectangular kennel area is best because it can alleviate boredom by giving your dog room to exercise. It should be noted, however, that constant running and pacing in the kennel may be an indication that your dog is bored. There are solutions to this; see "Environmental Enrichment" above.

A kennel, when used properly, is a good alternative to traditional fencing, especially for those who cannot afford or who do not wish to fence off their property. Kennels, however, should not be employed as surrogate caretakers.

Cat Containment

The practice of allowing cats to roam freely, something that until quite recently was hardly ever questioned, is now considered unacceptable and even cruel. Despite the widespread knowledge of the dangers faced by loose felines, many cat owners still allow their animals to have free run of the neighborhood. The thrill of the great outdoors is available indoors, without the many risks: see "Keeping Indoor Pets Happy and Content," above. The traditional fencing prescribed above for dogs provides no security for cats. Fortunately, there are other options for cat owners.

Enclosures

Very popular today are the wire mesh units that offer a high degree of security against pet loss, while still allowing your cat to fully enjoy the out-of-doors. Modular enclosures that can be put together in various configurations are available in pet catalogs, magazines and on the Internet (keywords "cat enclosures," "pet enclosures," or "pet cages"), or you can easily build your own enclosure by simply framing out an area and covering it with wire mesh. Be sure to provide your pet with some protection against extreme weather, and position the enclosure away from tree limbs and power lines that might be knocked down during a storm.

One of the best resources we've found is the Safe Cat Outdoor Enclosures manual. This terrific do-it-yourself manual comes complete with 30 detailed drawings to help you build your own cat enclosure. Based on a modular design concept, the enclosures can easily be modified or expanded to meet your needs. The manual can be ordered online at **www.just4cats.com** or direct from the publisher. (See "Resources/Pet Containment.") Cat enclosures can be custom-designed to fit any yard, and then filled with all kinds of fun things to keep your kitty occupied. Just let your imagination go! This is what environmental enrichment is about—fill your cat's enclosure with scratching posts, tree limbs, plants, and shrubs. Be careful though. Some plants, such as oleanders and azaleas, can be toxic to cats and dogs, according to the American Society for the Prevention of Cruelty to Animals. For more information on pets and poisonous plants, visit their web site at **www.napcc.aspca.org.**

Cat Fencing

Cat Fence-In is a popular product for keeping your cat in your yard. Developed by a Nevada couple, the system has been on the market since 1990 and has won several awards, including being named one of *Cat Fancy* magazine's 1992 Editors' Choice Award Winners for best new cat products. Also, the highly-respected Tufts University School of Veterinary Medicine newsletter *CATNIP* gave Cat Fence-In a five paws rating. The system attaches to your existing fence, loops back in on itself, and prevents your cat from climbing up and over. Another model not only keeps your cat in your yard, it prevents other animals from coming into your yard.

This relatively inexpensive system has several advantages. It attaches to your existing fence and is easy to install, even for a novice. The system is made with a polypropylene mesh netting that won't rust or corrode, and there aren't any jagged edges that might injure your cat. It prevents cats from climbing up and over fences. Cat Fence-In also makes a tree guard to prevent your cat from scaling trees. It's ideal for feral cats and cats that have been used to roaming freely and have difficulty adjusting to an entirely indoor lifestyle.

When used properly, this type of cat fencing provides a good level of security against pet loss; however, you must still supervise your cat and check on it frequently. Cat fencing can be found in pet magazines, catalogs, and now on the Internet at **www.catfencein.com**. (See "Resources/Pet Containment.")

A Word about Feral Cats

The Humane Society of the United States defines feral cats as "unsocialized cats who are one or more generations removed from a home environment and who may subsist in a colony of similar cats living on the fringes of human existence." The HSUS points out that "feral cats rarely make suitable pets." The fact remains that many people take in feral or alley cats. In terms of preventing roaming, feral cats can be a real challenge. While acclimating feral cats to indoor living may be difficult, it is not impossible. We believe that anyone taking in a feral cat must educate himself or herself about how to care for them properly.

Fortunately, there is a lot of help available. There are dozens of feral cat groups all over the country that provide literature and even counsel people who have opened their homes to these needy animals. Doing a search of the Net, using the keywords "feral cats" will lead you to dozens of sites with lots of helpful information. Two sites we found to be particularly helpful are the Feral Cat Coalition of San Diego, California, at **www.feralcat.com,** and Safe Haven for Cats at **www.safehavenforcats.com.** Those without Internet access can call Safe Haven at (650) 802-9686. They will be glad to offer some advice.

Some Solutions to Behavior Problems

While frustration over behavioral problems is understandable, we must be willing to accept our part in our pet's having developed them. Are we perhaps working so many hours that our pets are not getting the time and attention they deserve? If so, then we must make time for them or accommodate them in some other way. (See "Pet Sitters, Boarding Kennels, and Caretakers.") Here are several ways to combat and alleviate behavior problems.

- *Scheduling*—Plan your pet's activities (walks, play, and feeding times, etc.). Doing so gives your pets a routine; something they will look forward to. This not only can alleviate boredom, it has the added benefit of setting your pet's biological clock. This can be very beneficial in terms of recovering a lost pet (e.g., a pet that was lost at 8:00 a.m. may scurry home on its own around its regular 3:00 p.m. feeding time).

- *Frequent Walks*—Both you and your pet will benefit from brisk early morning walks. Set your clock 15 minutes earlier and walk your dog or your cats, too, for that matter. Take your pet for a ten-minute walk each morning and watch your relationship thrive. (It is important to note that cats should only be walked on a leash attached to their harness, not to their collar.) Regular walks are a fundamental part of responsible dog ownership. If you can't walk your dog regularly, then consider hiring a professional dog walker or a responsible youngster from the neighborhood.

- *Playtime*—Ten minutes of play a day keeps the boredom away. Regular play sessions twice a day are a good start. A quick game of fetch can counteract an entire day's worth of separation anxiety. Supervised play with a feather or a string with knotted ends will not only satisfy your cat's hunting instinct, it's inexpensive and great fun. As you take a more active role in your pet's emotional wellbeing, you will see your relationship thrive and your pet's behavior problems decrease.

- *Tricks*—You can teach an old dog new tricks, and contrary to popular belief, cats can be taught to do tricks as well. This is one of the best ways to build a healthy relationship with your pet. Not only is it great fun, it also combats boredom, isolation, and loneliness. Also, it reinforces your position as the leader. There are many books, videos, and online resources for teaching and training pets. (See "Training.")

- *Family Affairs*—Recent surveys have shown that most people consider their pets to be members of their family. That's great because things like walking and playtime can be divided up among everyone, even in the busiest of families. Involve your children in age-appropriate parts of your pet's activities, and everyone will benefit!

- *Toy Variety*—Toys are a great way of enriching your pet's environment and can help alleviate behavior problems. There are interactive toys, toys that comfort, and distraction toys. Purchase a variety for playtime with your pet and for safe solitary play (it's not nearly as expensive as repairing damaged furniture or clothing!) Also, rotate your pet's toys regularly, preferably once a week, to combat boredom and give your pet a variety of sensory experiences. Two terrific articles, *Dog Toys and How to Use Them* and *Cat Toys and How to Use Them* can be found on the Dumb Friends League's web site at **www.ddfl.org**: just click on the "Behavior Info" link.

- *Digging Area*—Select an area in your yard where your dog is permitted to dig. You can even box off the area with 4x4s to create a border and make a digging area similar to a sandbox.

- *Window Perches*—Many cats are better able to cope with indoor life if they have a view of the outside world. A window perch where it can see birds, insects, a falling leaf, or passing traffic will entertain your cat for hours on end and is a great way of combating boredom.

- *Private Space*—Just as we do, pets need their own space. Provide your pets with a den or bedding area, where they can retreat to whenever they are feeling stressed or just need a break.

- *Training*—Training is one of the most effective methods of preventing pet loss. Training is not just sending your dog off to obedience school for a week or two. It involves specific obedience skills, various conditioning techniques, and even teaching your pet tricks. Training is something that needs to be continually taught and reinforced for the lifetime of your pet. (See "Training.")

The bottom line is that allowing your pet to roam is irresponsible. Even if it has returned a thousand times before, there will come a time when it doesn't (as thousands of grief-stricken and guilt-ridden pet owners will testify). Pet ownership is a major responsibility. It requires your time, money, effort, and commitment. If your lifestyle doesn't permit you to give a pet the time, care, and attention that it deserves, please reconsider your plans to bring a pet into your home. It is your responsibility to provide your pet with a safe, interesting, and stimulating environment. Until people begin taking pet ownership for the awesome responsibility that it is, animals will continue to suffer.

Training

Training Can Be a Big Help

Training your pet is one of the most effective ways of preventing pet loss, and may even aid in recovering your pet if it does turn up missing. A properly trained pet, one that has had its intellectual muscles exercised and its wits sharpened, is more likely to be content in its environment, and thus less likely to attempt to escape. A trained pet is also a better-behaved animal and thus a more welcome member of the family and the neighborhood.

According to animal trainer Larry Maynard of National Pet Detectives, "Dog obedience training is the easiest and best possible method to keep your pet from becoming missing or lost."

A dog obedient to your commands that happens to slip out of its lead is less likely to run off. And although a loud noise may still elicit fear, the fear will not translate into flight. Your dog will not run off, but instead will remain confidently by your side because you are its trusted leader. Because dogs are pack animals, they are happiest when they know their place in the social order, and training your dog establishes your position as the leader of the pack. Similarly, a well-trained cat that is getting the time, attention, and stimulation it deserves does not persistently meow to be let out, for it is content in the home environment.

A trained pet is eager for instruction and the loving praise that accompanies obeying your voice. Quite simply, a trained pet is a safer pet, a healthier pet, a happier pet, and a pet that is at much lower risk of becoming a missing pet statistic.

Training Methods

There are many different methods available for training your pet. For most people, the first idea is to take their pet to obedience school. There are many other options to consider, however. There are videos and books, and you can even hire a qualified professional instructor who will work with you in your home. The Humane Society of the United States believes that "group-training classes taught by an instructor using positive techniques is best. In a group, dogs learn how to socialize with other dogs and other people." For more information, visit The HSUS's *Pet Information Center* at **www.hsus.org.** Search keyword "Training" and choose the article ***Choosing a Dog Trainer***. This information sheet is also available in print form upon request. (See "Resources/Humane Organizations.")

There are different training techniques. Positive techniques encourage appropriate behaviors through reinforcement with food, play, attention, or praise. Training techniques that involve yelling, choking, shaking the scruff, jerking on the leash, forcing the dog onto its back, or frightening or inflicting pain are not humane and only serve to confuse and frighten your animal, and damage the bond between your pet and you.

Positive Conditioning

Conditioning is an integral part of training. The now famous Pavlov dog experiments were instrumental in the development of the whole field of behavioral psychology. Pavlov discovered that by coupling some stimulus (e.g., a bell) with a reward (e.g., food), he could cause his dogs to salivate. More importantly, he discovered that even when the reward was not offered, the dogs still reacted to the stimulus by salivating; a reaction he termed a "conditioned response." This concept can also work in reverse. Aversion conditioning, for example, is the principle on which electronic fencing is based. "Good training methods," however, "focus primarily on reinforcing good behavior," according to the Dumb Friends League, a humane society in Colorado. (See figure 22.)

Conditioning your pet through positive reinforcement can increase your chances of recovering your pet if it's ever lost. As mentioned earlier, feeding your pet on a set schedule may cause it to return home at the prescribed feeding time. Connecting its feeding time (i.e., reward) with the ringing of a bell, the blowing of a whistle, or the shaking of its dry food box (i.e., stimulus) may also aid in recovering your lost pet because it has been conditioned to respond to the sound that it knows means dinnertime. If your pet ever runs off, you can canvass the neighborhood making the sounds your pet associates with food. Clicker training has become very popular today. There are many books and even a clicker video and training kit. If your pet is ever lost you can bring your clicker along and click while you search. (See figure 23.)

Desensitization

Conditioning your pet may also involve various desensitization techniques designed to deal with a pet's fears and phobias, which are not always easily identifiable, and for which there can be a variety of possible causes. Before fearful behavior can be dealt with effectively, one must first discover the source of the problem. As with all things concerning your pet's health, it is best to consult your veterinarian as there may very well be a medical cause for your pet's fearful behavior. Escaping behavior can often be attributed to fear of

---

Selecting an Obedience Class

Here are some more tips from the Dumb Friends League to help you select an obedience class that's right for you:

• "Good obedience instructors are knowledgeable about many different types of training methods and use techniques that neither the dogs nor their owners find consistently unpleasant.

• "Good training methods focus primarily on reinforcing good behavior. Excessive use of choke chains or pinch collars or using collars to lift dogs off of the ground are not appropriate or humane training methods.

• "Good obedience instructors communicate well with people and with dogs. Remember that they're instructing you about how to train your dog.

• "Specific problems you may have with your dog may not be addressed in a basic obedience course. If you're seeking help with house soiling, barking, aggression, or separation anxiety, ask if the course covers these issues—don't assume it will.

• "Ask the instructor what training methods are used and how they (the instructor and staff) were trained. Also, ask to observe a class before you commit to one. If you're refused an observation or if your observation results in anything that makes you uncomfortable, look elsewhere.

• "Avoid anyone who: guarantees their work; whose primary methods focus on punishment; or who wants to take your dog and train him for you (effective training must include you and the environment in which you and your dog interact)."

The League is one of the most respected humane society/animal welfare organizations in Colorado and indeed the country. They publish a plethora of wonderful articles on pet training designed to help pet owners deal effectively with behavior problems. They ask that you first visit their web site at **www.ddfl.org**; the answers to most questions can be found there. If you need further assistance or do not have access to the Internet, call their behavior helpline at (303) 696-4941. If you live in Colorado outside of the Denver metro area or in Kansas, Nebraska, New Mexico, Wyoming, or Utah, call toll-free at (877) 738-0217.

FIGURE 22

thunderstorms or other loud noises. Unfortunately, many well-meaning pet owners reinforce their pet's fears by coddling and comforting them when they are frightened. This exacerbates the problem because the animal quickly begins to associate being comforted with its expression of fear.

One popular training technique for dealing with the fear of loud noises is to use a tape recording of whatever sound or noise is making your pet afraid. The noise is played at a low volume and coupled with feeding time, treats, or some other pleasurable activity. Over a period of days, the volume is gradually increased until the animal is no longer frightened by the sound. The Dumb Friends League regularly publishes helpful training and behavior articles online at **www.ddfl.org**. One exceptional article to check out on their site is "Helping Your Dog Overcome the Fear of Thunder and Other Startling Noises."

Training and Behavior Problems

Training is also beneficial in dealing with a variety of behavior problems such as constant barking or meowing, and persistent escape attempts—the very problems that frustrate so many pet owners. Such exasperation over behavioral problems is reported by shelter workers as being the major reason people cite for giving up their pets. Training your pet can eliminate many of these negative behaviors. While the initial training may take a bit of time, the ongoing practicing of commands and tricks can be done in a couple of short sessions a day.

Training Cats

While it's possible to teach cats specific skills, most cat owners would be happy if their cat simply knew the difference between the scratching post and the sofa.

Clicker Training
by Karen Pryor

Don't Shoot the Dog (1999 revised edition)
"This is the Bible on positive reinforcement training or operant conditioning and how it works. With over 300,000 copies in print, Karen Pryor's clear and entertaining explanation of behavioral training methods made *'Don't Shoot the Dog'* a best-selling classic!"

Getting Started Clicker Training for Dogs Kit
"This kit includes *The Getting Started Clicker Training for Dogs* book (approx. 50 pages), two clickers, an instruction booklet teaching how to use the clicker itself, and a sample of dog treats."

Visit **www.clickertraining.com** for these and many other clicker training resources. Be sure to check out Karen's *Clicker Magic* video. Items can be ordered by phone at (800) 47-CLICK (472-5425).

FIGURE 23

Gwen Bohnenkamp, author of *From the Cat's Point of View*, in one of her terrific online articles, "Basic Training for Your Cat," says, "Before we can train or teach our cats to do something or to stop doing something, we need to look at how cats learn." She goes on to say, "The key to training is to make sure that whatever you want your cat to do is exceedingly rewarding and pleasurable. Whatever you don't want your cat to indulge in must never be rewarding or fun; in fact, it must be unpleasant." The fact is that cats are cats and not dogs, and their "cathood" should be respected. Any training you put your cat through should be specifically geared toward cats. Visit Gwen's *Perfect Paws* web site at **www.perfectpaws.com,** and you will find many helpful training articles for both cats and dogs. Also check out Cats International (formerly the Wisconsin Cat Club); they publish a wonderful booklet titled "How to Live Happily Ever After with Your Cat." It addresses many cat behavior problems and how to deal with them using various training methods that are geared specifically toward cats, and it's free. Visit their web site at **www.catsinternational.org**. Even ferrets can be trained. Barron's publishes a guide with training methods geared specifically toward ferrets. (See "Resources/Training.")

Where to Find Training Help

There are many different methods used in training animals, so exercise some caution when considering a class or a trainer, or when buying books and videos. Make certain that the training techniques are positive and humane. The best training methods rely on rewarding good behavior, not punishing unacceptable responses. There are several training sources you should investigate.

- *Shelters*—One underutilized resource is your local animal shelter or humane society. Many shelters offer group obedience skills and socialization classes. Group-training classes are preferred because your dog will learn to socialize with other dogs and other people. Teaching your dog to socialize with other dogs is as important as learning specific obedience skills. Many shelters offer free classes or charge a nominal fee. Call your local animal shelter and ask what is available in your area. (See "Animal Shelters.")

- *Pet Supply Stores*—Two of the largest pet supply superstores offer pet training courses in their stores. For details, contact your local PETsMART or PETCO, or visit them on the web at **www.petsmart.com** and **www.petco.com**.

- *Obedience Schools*—A good thing to do when considering a school is to ask for references. Any good school will be delighted to provide you with references from humane societies, pet care professionals, and former students.

- *Your Veterinarian*—As with everything concerning the health and wellbeing of your pet, talk with your veterinarian. She or he may be able to direct you to a qualified school or training program in your area.

- *In-Home Training*—Many obedience schools have trainers available for instruction right in your own home, or they may be able to direct you to someone who does offer it in your area. The Association of Pet Dog Trainers (APDT) maintains an extensive directory of professional dog trainers on their web site at **www.apdt.com**. Just type in your two-digit state abbreviation. APDT also provides a host of other helpful resources including a list of books and videos. (See "Resources/Training.")

- ***Videos, Books, and Internet Resources***—There are many helpful books and videos available in pet supply stores, bookstores, pet magazines, and catalogs, as well as many Internet resources available for help in training your pet. (See "Resources/ Training.")

How Learning Tricks Can Help

Teaching your pet tricks is an informal method of training. Not only is it great fun, but it also enriches your relationship and helps you bond even more closely with your animal. Teaching your pet tricks, even for a few minutes a day, can have a positive effect on some of the underlying causes of misbehavior. Although it is best to start young, no dog or cat is too old to benefit from learning tricks (or from more formal training, for that matter).

Teaching your pet tricks, especially an unusual trick coupled with an equally unusual command, can actually be another method of positively identifying your pet if it is lost or stolen. Teach your pet to do at least one trick to a unique command. For example, one of our birds, Kiska, will hang upside down from your finger when she hears the command, "Do your Batman." This is something probably only our bird does! If she is ever lost or stolen, this trick alone could prove that she is our bird. You could teach your dog to roll over in response to the command "hippopotamus." It may sound silly but it would be something that only your pet would do.

Although a lot of people don't believe it, cats can be trained and learn tricks. Some people have even potty-trained their cats! It may require a slightly different approach and a bit more patience than working with dogs, but cats can be taught many tricks. Since very few people take the time to teach tricks to their cats, the fact that your cat has learned some tricks is another way of proving it is your cat. You can find trick training books and videos in pet supply stores, pet magazines, catalogs, and by searching the Internet. (See "Resources/ Training.")

Birds represent a similar situation. Not only does teaching your bird to do special tricks or to speak enrich your relationship and help you bond with your bird, it is another way of proving ownership. There are documented reports of people who have actually located the owner of a lost bird because it could repeat its phone number or address.

Traveling with Pets

Traveling, vacationing, and moving with pets present many challenges in terms of preventing pet loss and being prepared for it should it happen. Although many of the same strategies for thwarting and preparing for pet loss at home are the same, losing your pet a thousand miles from home or in transit will certainly complicate matters and make recovering your pet quickly even more critical. The simple fact is that if you lose your pet away from home, eventually you will be forced to return home with or without your pet. Apply what you've learned already about prevention, and prepare your recovery plan in advance.

Whether you are going on a weekend trip, or vacationing several hundred miles away, for pet owners the first thing to decide is, do I travel with or without my pet?

Some Things to Consider

- Is your pet a good candidate for traveling? If your pet is either very young or very old, pregnant, or recovering from surgery, traveling is not a good idea.

- If your dog is a biter or an incessant barker or does not respond to basic obedience commands, do everyone a favor and do not bring your pet along.

- Research whether your destination requires a quarantine period for your pet.

- Depending on what type of pet you have, it may be illegal in the area you wish to travel (e.g., it is illegal to own a ferret in California, Hawaii, and New York City). You could be fined, your ferret could be confiscated, and in a worst case scenario it could be euthanized. For a comprehensive list of places where ferrets are currently illegal, visit **www.especiallyferrets.org** and click on the "Legal Info link." If you plan to travel with an exotic bird or animal and cannot prove domestic origin, you may run into similar problems.

- If your travel plans do not specifically include time for pet involvement, then please consider the alternatives. (See "Pet Sitters, Boarding Kennels, and Caretakers.")

- You will no doubt be unable to take your pet with you everywhere you go on your trip. Leaving your pet in your hotel room, even if it is confined to a carrier, is not recommended. Call in advance of your trip and find out what boarding facilities and pet daycare is available in the area where you will be traveling.

- If you are moving, you are responsible for making the transportation arrangements for your pets. Regulations forbid moving companies to transport animals. They may, however, refer you to a professional animal shipper. The Humane Society of the United States has a terrific web site at **www.rentwithpets.org** for pet owners who are moving and looking for pet-friendly housing. (See "Transporting Your Pet.")

- How are you planning to travel? Buses and most trains make no accommodation for pets, leaving pet owners with basically three choices: flying with their pets, shipping them, or taking them along in a car or truck—all of which present their own challenges in terms of lost pet prevention and preparedness.

If proper precautions are taken, traveling with a pet who enjoys the road can be an enriching experience for both you and your pet. If, after reading the above items, you decide to travel alone and leave your pet at home, you then must decide on a boarding kennel or a professional pet sitter or caretaker. All of these require preparation and planning in order to ensure that your pet does not go missing, and having a clear plan for what you will do if it does.

Preparing for the Trip

If you've made the decision to travel with your pet, there is much to do to make certain you and your pet have a safe journey. (See "Transporting Your Pet.")

Consult Your Veterinarian

Discuss your plans with your veterinarian. Once it's been determined that your pet is fit to travel, there are several things you will need to consider. All states and countries have rules for animals crossing their borders. If you will be transporting your pet to another state or country, you need to find out ahead of time what the requirements are in your destination. (See figure 24.) You will most certainly need an up-to-date health certificate, including proof of current rabies vaccination (you may also need this documentation to reclaim your animal from a shelter, if your pet is lost during your trip).

If you and your pet will be going by air, be advised that animals may not be exposed to temperatures lower than 45°F unless you have a certificate signed by your veterinarian that states that your pet is acclimated to lower temperatures. Also, there may be other documentation requirements that can only be secured by a licensed veterinarian. (See "Transporting Your Pet.")

Also, should the need arise during your trip to board your pet, you may need additional vaccinations. (See "Pet Sitters, Boarding Kennels, and Caretakers.")

During your pre-trip veterinary visit, inquire if medication for carsickness or tranquilizers are appropriate for your pet. If you will be flying with your pet, be aware that "oversedation is the leading cause of animal deaths during airline transport," according to the *Journal of the American Veterinary Medical Association.*

USDA Voice Response Service

Finding out the animal requirements in your destination state or country is not as complicated as it sounds. The United States Department of Agriculture's Animal and Plant Health Inspection Service operates a 24-hour/365-day-a-year up-to-date Voice Response Service. Call them toll-free at (800) 545-USDA (8732). Simply follow the telephone prompts and enter the two-digit postal code of your destination state (e.g., PA for Pennsylvania).

FIGURE 24

Plan Your Itinerary around Your Pet

Don't just wing it and expect to find a pet-friendly hotel when you arrive in town. Do your research. Allow time in your schedule for exercise breaks. Have confirmed reservations at places you know welcome pets. Know where you will be staying each night of your trip.

Knowing your itinerary in advance also allows you to take the necessary preparedness steps to maximize your chance of a speedy recovery if your pet is lost. Read "Preparing for Recovery" in this book, and compile the necessary items in advance of your trip (paying special attention to the "Critical Contacts" list described in that section). Compiling your "Critical Contacts" list for a distant location is not as difficult as it sounds. Most larger public libraries have phone books for every major metropolitan area in the country. If you have access to the Internet, go to Yahoo yellow pages, simply type in your destination and a topic ("pets" or "dog walking"). If you will be staying with friends or relatives along the way, ask them to compile the necessary information for you in advance.

Maps can be critical to conducting an organized, systematic search for a lost pet, especially in an unfamiliar city, miles from home. Purchase a map of the area where you will be staying prior to your departure or as soon as you arrive. You can find maps for most locations at any of the large bookstores. This will save you precious time if your pet is ever lost.

Have Proper Pet Identification

Your pet's identification is the only link between you and your pet. Licenses and rabies tags won't be as helpful when you're away from home. Be sure to make temporary tags for each stopover, changing them each time you change hotels. Include your name along with the phone number and address of the hotel where you will be staying (if you have a cell phone, include that number, too), as well as a contact number back home just in case. (See "Pet Identification.")

If you plan on traveling with your pet, this should be reason enough to join a national tag registry. If you already use one, be sure to call and give them your itinerary and contact information. And it's also ample justification for using some form of permanent identification, such as a tattoo or microchip.

Purchase an Animal Carrier

If you have a pet, you definitely should own a carrier. In many different situations, a carrier is the best way to safely confine your pet. If you will be transporting your pet by air, then you must have a USDA-approved carrier. In addition, individual airlines may have their own specifications. (See "Transporting Your Pet.")

Carriers are a must for safe automobile travel as well. It is not a good idea to allow pets to ride unrestrained in a moving vehicle, for your pet could become nervous and distract you and cause an accident. If you are traveling with small children, they may not always be mindful and when you stop to rest, they may throw open a door and off goes your pet. Also, most hotels, even if they allow pets, require that you have a carrier before you're allowed to check in.

The American Society for the Prevention of Cruelty to Animals recommends that "whatever kind of pet carrier you use, your pet should be able to stand, sit, lie down, and turn around in it. Do not attempt to cram him or her in too small a space. The carrier must have ample ventilation. This is assured by the mesh panels in soft-sided carriers." If your traveling companion is of the feathered variety, you will need a travel cage. Travel carriers and cages can be purchased through catalogs, online pet supply stores, or by searching the Internet (using the key words "pet cages," "bird cages," or "pet carriers").

Take Your Pet Records with You

Although vaccination records and current health certificates are a must when traveling, you will also need current photos and a detailed written description of your pet. (See "Pet Record Keeping.")

Educate Yourself

Being well-acquainted with lost pet prevention and recovery will dramatically increase your chances of a speedy recovery when you're on the road. Know exactly what you will do if your pet goes missing by reading and implementing the suggestions in "Preparing for Recovery."

Finding Lodging for You and Your Pet

Increasing numbers of people are taking their pets with them on vacation, and the travel and tourism industry has responded positively to the trend. Hotels, motels, and resorts are becoming much more accommodating to pets today, and the nation's interstate highways are now dotted with thousands of pet friendly establishments, all vying for the attention—and the vacation dollars—of these pet-toting tourists.

"Pet friendly" is a term that, in our opinion, is being too broadly used. We have found that many of these establishments are at best what we would describe as "pet tolerant." Many pet travel books simply list the various establishments that accept pets and do not differentiate between *pet friendly* and *pet tolerant*. Pets Welcome— **(www.petswelcome.com)** is a terrific site. Not only do they list over 25,000 pet friendly locations (many of which allow you to make reservations right from the site), they also use a special icon to distinguish those that are particularly pet friendly. Click on the icon and learn what other travelers had to say about their stay, or tell about your own lodging experience. There are also many books on traveling and vacationing with pets. The American Automobile Association's book *Traveling with Your Pet* contains listings for more than 10,000 establishments that welcome pets, and gives a little information about their requirements and accommodations. One problem with any pet travel book, however, is that the information is always changing, so be sure to call ahead. When it comes to locating pet friendly lodging, the Internet has some distinct advantages. (See figure 25.)

The only way to find out for sure whether your pet will be considered a welcome guest or a marginally tolerated nuisance is to call the hotel and ask, so that you can get a sense of how they really feel about pets as patrons. Many hotels will not let you check in with a pet unless you have a travel crate. Ask about their policy regarding pets. Are their employees—maids for example— instructed to be cautious about pets in people's rooms? Discuss your concerns about pet loss. Inquire about any additional pet-related services that may be available at the hotel or in the area (e.g., pet walking, pet sitting services, etc.).

Your pet's safety is ultimately your responsibility. You must take the necessary precautions. Follow the same procedures you would at home, such as making sure windows and doors are secured. Alert hotel staff that your pet is in the room. If you have not already compiled a list of important phone numbers and addresses ahead of time, do it as soon as you check in. (See "Critical Contacts.") Do not leave your pet for long periods of time, but if you must leave your pet, put out the "Do Not Disturb" sign and crate your pet. Include your pet in your travel activities to the greatest extent possible. When choosing a restaurant, for example, try to find one with outdoor seating that permits pets. And remember, many thieves prey on tourists, so pet theft is always a concern. (See "Stolen Pets.")

The Net is a Great Tool for Travelers

When it comes to locating pet friendly lodging, the Internet has the distinct advantage over travel books that information is easily updated and kept current. There are many pet travel sites online. The larger sites, **www.petswelcome.com, www.traveldog.com**, and **www.takeyourpet.com** also have travel clubs that offer a variety of perks for members, such as discounted lodging, airline tickets, and extensive listings of resources like pet sitting services and boarding facilities. One site, **www.dogfriendly.com**, even has a listing of dog friendly employers.

FIGURE 25

Transporting Your Pet

So you've decided to travel with your pet, and now many preparations need to be made. First and foremost, you must decide on a mode of transportation. The travel choices for your pet are limited—you can drive, fly, or hire a professional animal shipper.

Trains and Buses

The two major bus lines—Trailways and Greyhound—do not permit passengers to bring pets along. As for trains, only some commuter rails allow small pets confined to a carrier to travel. Amtrak makes no accommodations for animals of any kind other than assistance animals.

Air Travel

Safe air travel for pets took a small step forward recently when the Federal Aviation Administration Reauthorization Bill became law. Included in this legislation are portions of the "Safe Air Travel for Animals Act" (originally dubbed the "Boris Bill") designed to make air transportation of pets and other animals safer. (See figure 26.) Many organizations, including The Humane Society of the United States (HSUS), applauded the legislation, calling it, "A step toward providing long-overdue protection for pets and other animals traveling on our nation's airlines."

The law holds the airlines accountable to consumers by mandating that airlines provide monthly reports to the U.S. Department of Transportation on all incidents of loss, death, or injury of animals. These reports are to be made public through the Department of Transportation's monthly publication, "Air Travel Consumer Reports." More importantly, the legislation mandates improved training in animal care and safe transport techniques for baggage handlers. Lack of training for employees has always been a major concern among animal welfare organizations.

Even with the new regulations, there are still inherent risks for pets traveling as cargo by air. Just learning the regulations, which are frequently amended, is an arduous task and the reason that many pet owners turn to a professional animal shipper. Although there are limits as to what pet owners can do, air travel can be made safer if proper precautions are taken. Let us first look at some of the hazards.

The Dog Who Lobbied for a Law

"Boris the dog knows how to get politicians to sit up and listen. When he wanted to promote a pet project, the boxer mix appeared at a press conference in front of the Capitol in Washington, DC. The pooch soon had lawmakers eating out of his paw. This spring, the 'Boris Bill,' which protects animals aboard commercial airlines, was signed into law. Airlines will be required to report monthly on pets that are injured, lost or have died on planes and provide better training for employees who handle animals.

"The law grew out of Boris's own airplane horror story. In 1996, he and his owner, Barbara Listenik, were flying to New York City, when Delta staffers accidentally crushed his cage, breaking some of his teeth. Terrified, Boris ran off. Listenik found him six weeks later emaciated and living in an abandoned building.

"Listenik, who is suing Delta, and Boris joined forces with other animal rights advocates to crusade for the law. They convinced Sen. Frank Lautenberg and Rep. Robert Menendez (both D-New Jersey) to sponsor the 'Boris Bill,' which became part of a larger aviation law. Says Listenik, 'It's exciting to know a bark can be heard.' As for Boris, he won't be earning any frequent-flier miles—he now travels only by car."

FIGURE 26

Perils Facing Pets in Flight

"The skies are not so friendly for our animal companions," according to an HSUS fact sheet on the Safe Air Travel for Animals Act. "[Our pets] often face such risks as excessively hot or cold temperatures, poor ventilation, scarcity of oxygen, and rough handling. The airline industry treats live animals as mere baggage, transporting them in cargo holds not designed for life support." The fact sheet also points out that the number of animals lost, killed, or injured on commercial flights each year exceeds 5,000.

These are some frightening statistics indeed. The decision to put your pet in the cargo hold of a plane is not one that should be made lightly. In fact, due to the death of several pets, some airlines have even instituted a "pet embargo" during the summer months when hot temperatures in the cargo hold can reach life-threatening levels. Patricia Curtis, author of *Indoor Cat*, warns, "If the airline tells you that the cargo or baggage compartment is heated or air conditioned, it means it is when the plane is in flight."

Stopovers and Transfers

If you have to switch planes, then so does your pet. And if you have a layover, you'll spend that time in a comfortable, temperature-controlled environment. Meanwhile, your pet is likely to be waiting with other baggage on a sweltering hot or freezing cold tarmac. According to Ms. Curtis, "Sometimes animals have survived plane trips safely only to expire when left for a time with other baggage in the blazing sun on the runway."

Another serious situation occurs when a pet is loaded on the wrong plane and sent to a different destination. As many travelers know from firsthand experience, misplaced or incorrectly-routed luggage is not an uncommon occurrence. The mere thought of such a possibility should be enough to persuade you that shipping your pet by air should never be a casual decision.

Poorly Trained Employees

An increasingly pet-conscious public has forced the major U.S. airlines to be more "pet friendly." It is by government edict, however, that airlines have been forced to adhere to some standards for the humane transportation of animals. The lack of trained personnel with regard to the safe, humane handling of animals used to make flying with your pet particularly hazardous. The training of baggage handlers is now mandated, and hopefully the situation will improve. It is hard to imagine how a pet could get loose in the cargo hold of a plane or in an airport terminal, but it can happen.

The story of Tabitha clearly demonstrates that if your pet is lost or injured while in the care of an airline, you may have to make a lot of noise in order to get any cooperation from them. (See figure 27.) You may have to contact the media and ultimately a lawyer. One good thing is that airlines hate bad press, and lawyers thrive on sensational cases where the media is involved. You can also file an Air Travel Incident Report. You can download the report form from the HSUS's *Pet Information Center* at **www.hsus.org**. Search keyword "Travel" and choose ***File a Complaint Against an Airline.*** If you have a bad experience when shipping your animal by air, contact the United States Department of Agriculture–APHIS–Animal Care (USDA) (See "Resources/Traveling With Pets") and the airline involved.

To be fair, no one is suggesting that airlines intentionally harm animals; it's just that animal safety has not been a priority. Many animal welfare advocates admit that the new regulations have made air transportation safer for our pets. What upsets people, however, is that when things have gone wrong, the airlines have generally attempted to minimize, deny, or avoid responsibility for their mistakes.

Things Have Improved

"Overall, the safety of pet travel aboard an aircraft has improved dramatically," according to Bridget Monrad, of Happy Tails Pet Services, in her online article, "Flying the (Furry) Friendly Skies." Fortunately, many airlines are beginning to heed the call for safer pet policies and are implementing programs to make certain that pets arrive safely at their destinations. According to a June 2000

The Story of Tabitha

Exactly how Tabitha escaped from her cage into the baggage compartment of the Tower Air flight that was carrying her and her owner, Carol Ann Timmel, from New York to LA is still a mystery. Upon landing, Miss Timmel went to claim her cat from baggage and was told that Tabitha, her American Tabby, had escaped from her cage. So began Tabitha's incredible odyssey trapped in the walls of the plane. It would be 12 days, 30,000 miles, an attorney, and a court injunction later before Tabitha was reunited with her owner.

The reason this story is important is that it demonstrates that when an airline loses a pet, you may have to make a lot of noise in order to get the airline to cooperate. According to the September/October 1994 issue of *Your Cat* magazine, Miss Timmel "held regular press conferences, accusing Tower Air of being more interested in profit than in Tabitha's welfare. One paper ran a daily 'Cat Watch' column."

Miss Timmel waged war with Tower Air through the media, eventually convincing a judge to grant an injunction forcing Tower to ground the plane for 24 hours so the plane could be thoroughly searched.

FIGURE 27

news release from the American Kennel Club, "Continental Airlines has announced a permanent change in their procedures for shipping live animals… Under the new 'pet safe' program, Continental will no longer accept pets as checked baggage. Pets will instead be accepted as cargo, and shipment will be coordinated through the carrier's QUICKPAK Live Animal Program. According to Continental, this program will allow the company's cargo service to offer same day, airport-to-airport delivery with features designed to ensure an animal's comfort and safety." According to the news release, "Continental will continue to accept small pets for travel in the cabin."

In-Cabin Pets

As does Continental, most major airlines allow smaller pets to fly in the passenger cabin as long as they can fit comfortably in an airline-approved carrier under the seat in front of you. As there is no industry standard for these carriers, you need to inquire about what is required by the airline you will be flying.

Flying in the cabin is, of course, much safer since the temperatures inside the passenger section are constantly controlled, and your pet will never leave your sight. Be sure to let the airline know when you are making reservations that you will be boarding with a pet. Also, the USDA recommends that you reconfirm with the airline, 24 to 48 hours prior to your departure, that you will be bringing your pet.

Many airlines restrict the number of pets per flight and the types of pets permitted to fly in the cabin. Certain pets—ferrets, rabbits, and iguanas, for example—may not be permitted. And there may be a fee, which can vary from airline to airline. You can get a list of individual airline pet policies at the **www.traveldog.com** web site.

Even the air in the passenger cabin can inhibit the breathing of certain breeds (e.g., short-nosed animals). If you have any doubts, ask your veterinarian. Since a visit to the veterinarian is a prerequisite to your pet's traveling by air, be sure to get everything you need during your visit all at the same time. (See figure 28.)

In the Aircraft Cabin

• Make sure the carrier is big enough to ensure the comfort of your pet (do not, for the sake of carrying your pet with you, attempt to cram your pet into a carrier that is too small). Flying is stressful in itself, and you want your pet to be as comfortable as possible.

• Use a thick, absorbent towel to line the bottom of your pet's carrier in case of accidents.

• Purchase a carrier that will fit securely underneath the seat in front of you.

• Be considerate of other passengers. For everyone's safety, your pet's as well as the other passengers', do not take your pet out of the carrier—not only is it unsafe, it's against FAA regulations.

• Bring along food and water for your pet if the flight will last more than a few hours.

• Let the person sitting next to you know that your pet is traveling with you, as he or she may have allergies and may prefer to exchange seats with someone else.

Air Travel Requirements for Pets

Once your veterinarian has given your pet a clean bill of health, there are certain regulations that you will have to comply with before the airline will accept your pet. Some are established by the government, while others are the policies of the individual airlines. The following information is from the United States Department of Agriculture.

- *Age*—Dogs and cats must be at least eight weeks old and must have been weaned before traveling by air.

- *Kennels*—Kennels must meet minimum standards for size, strength, sanitation, and ventilation. And kennels must be enclosed and allow room for the animal to stand, sit, and lie in a natural position. They must be easy to open, strong enough to withstand the normal rigors of transportation, and free of objects that could injure the animal.

- *Sanitation*—Kennels must have a solid, leak-proof floor that is covered with litter or absorbent lining. Wire or other ventilated subfloors are generally allowed (pegboard flooring is prohibited). These requirements provide the maximum cleanliness for the animal in travel.

At the Veterinarian

- Get your pet a complete physical exam.
- Get proof of up-to-date vaccinations; your pet may be turned away without this.
- Obtain a current health certificate from your veterinarian dated no earlier than ten days before departure.
- Get a letter from your vet that states that the animal is acclimated to lower temperatures. Animals may not be exposed to temperatures less than 45°F unless there is a certificate signed by a veterinarian stating that the animal has been acclimated to such temperatures.
- Avoid using tranquilizers. Tranquilizers should only be used when absolutely necessary. (Talk to your veterinarian about what is best for your pet.) The American Humane Association cautions veterinarians to "carefully consider the use of tranquilizers or sedatives for their clients who are considering air transportation for their family pet."
- Ask your veterinarian for advice concerning motion sickness and your pet.

FIGURE 28

- *Ventilation*—Kennels must be well-ventilated with openings that make up at least 14% of the total wall space. At least one-third of the openings must be located in the top half of the kennel. Kennels also must have rims to prevent ventilation openings from being blocked by other cargo. These rims—usually placed on the sides of the kennel—must provide at least three-quarters of an inch clearance.

- *Handles and Markings*—Kennels must have handles for lifting to prevent cargo personnel from having to place their fingers inside the kennel and risk being bitten. Kennels also must be marked "Live Animals" or "Wild Animals" on the top and one side with directional arrows indicating proper position of the kennel. Lettering must be at least one inch high.

- ***Animals per Kennel***—Each species must have its own kennel with the exception of compatible cats and dogs of similar size. Maximum numbers include two puppies or kittens under six months old and 20 pounds each and of similar size, 15 guinea pigs or rabbits, and 50 hamsters. Airlines may have more restrictive requirements, such as allowing only one adult animal per kennel. Be sure to check with the airline you are using.

- ***Feeding and Watering while Traveling***—Instructions for feeding and watering the animal over a 24-hour period must be attached to the kennel. The schedule will assist the airline in providing care for your animal in case it is diverted from its original destination. You, as a pet owner or shipper, are required to document that the animal was offered food and water within four hours of transport, and the documentation must include the time and date of feeding. Food and water dishes must be securely attached and be accessible to caretakers without opening the kennel. Food and water must be provided to puppies and kittens every 12 hours if they are eight to 16 weeks old. Mature animals must be fed every 24 hours and given water every 12 hours.

Airlines may also have additional requirements as well: removing or disabling wheels and not locking carrier doors are two examples. It is best to call and check with the individual airline you will be flying with.

Air Travel and Lost Pet Prevention

There are inherent risks involved anytime you entrust your pet to the care of another, whether it is a caretaker, a pet sitter, a kennel, or an airline. There is also a certain amount of trust you must place in the person or persons responsible for your pet. The difference when leaving your pet with a sitter, a caretaker, or even a kennel, is that you have more direct control over the care your pet will receive. You will also be able to screen the individual and go over your prevention and recovery plan in detail. These opportunities are not afforded you when you place your pet in the care of an airline. Of course, it wouldn't be possible to go over your plans regarding prevention/recovery with every airline employee who may handle your pet. Although your options are limited, there are some things you should do:

- Call the airline yourself, and inquire what you can expect from them, especially as it relates to losing your pet. Do they have a plan in place if your pet is lost? Have they ever lost a pet or sent it to the wrong destination? If something like this were to happen, what would the airline do to retrieve your animal?

- Double-check all the tickets. Never assume your animal's ticket is correct simply because yours is. Make sure everything on it is correct.

- Make sure your pet is wearing a collar and an identification tag. If your pet will be flying as cargo, appendage-type tags are not recommended and can be dangerous; they get hooked on things like the metal grating used on crates and cages. Nameplate tags that are attached to the collar with rivets are much safer and can't fall off or get caught on things. Travel tags that slip on the collar are also available and embroidered collars are good as well. Also, use more than one type of identification, such as a tattoo or a microchip. (See "Pet Identification.")

- Make sure that your pet has been loaded. Before you board, do everything you can to physically check on your pet. Ask the flight attendant if it's possible to check that your pet is safely onboard the aircraft.

Flight plans that require changing planes present the greatest opportunity for things to go awry. Try your best to schedule a non-stop flight, or at the very least, a direct flight. If you are forced, for whatever reason, to schedule a flight with long layovers and/or connecting flights, it would probably be best to consider some other way of transporting your pet. If you have no other choice and decide to go ahead with the trip, there are some more things you should consider.

Ask about your airline's tracking system. Many airlines have procedures in place to trace a pet placed aboard the wrong aircraft.

Be sure your pet's carrier has all of the proper markings on it. On a large double-wide piece of masking tape, write in indelible fluorescent ink the address and phone number of your pet's final destination. Include all of your personal contact information, including your cell phone number, if you have one, and the number for your pet's identification tag registry. Cover the masking tape with a wide piece of clear tape to prevent smudging (packing tape works really well). Be sure the carrier door is secured with a leash snap (locks are not permitted).

Are you feeling overwhelmed yet? We don't blame you! Fortunately, there is an alternative. There are companies that specialize in the transportation of pets.

Professional Pet Transportation

Professional animal shippers transport a variety of animals ranging from zoo creatures to exotic animals to livestock. Many companies, however, specialize in the transportation of pets. Of these, some only provide services for relocation while others will make arrangements for people vacationing with their pets.

It is best to select a company that belongs to an association, because such organizations often set minimum standards and their members are accountable to the association for meeting those standards. Also, with an association, consumers have additional recourse if things go wrong. The Independent Pet and Animal Transportation Association International Inc. (IPATA), for example, requires that all of its members be registered as Intermediate Air Carriers with the Federal Aviation Administration and that they be bonded and insured.

While IPATA members are primarily involved in the permanent relocation of clients, some of their associate members (e.g., Happy Tails Pet Services Inc.) provide for transporting pets for those traveling for leisure or vacation.

Another good reason for using an association is easy referrals. On the IPATA web site (**www.ipata.com**), shippers are listed by state. It took us all of two minutes to locate five professional pet shippers in the state of New Jersey. Many pet travel web sites also have listings of shippers (e.g., **www.traveldog.com**).

If you decide to use the services of a professional animal shipper, discuss your concerns about pet loss. Ask what they would be prepared to do in the event your pet was lost during transit, and insist that you be contacted immediately if your pet is lost or injured. Make certain that they are registered with the FAA as an Intermediate Air Carrier and are bonded and insured. And always ask for references. (For a list of pet transportation companies, see "Resources/Transporting Your Pet.") The services each company offers may vary, but all reputable companies will:

- Gladly answer all your questions.
- Understand and address your concerns about pet loss and the risks involved in shipping animals on commercial airlines.
- Be fully informed regarding all the latest requirements and rules governing the transportation of animals via commercial airlines, as well as rules set by individual airlines.
- Make all of your pet's flight arrangements.
- Be able to identify non-stop and direct flights, or flights with the shortest layovers.
- Be knowledgeable regarding the latest quarantine information.
- Secure a veterinary health and inoculation certificate for your pet.
- Make ground transportation arrangements, if necessary, both to and from the departure and arrival airports.
- Clear your pet through customs.
- Provide you with a carrier that meets all government regulations and any requirements set by the individual airline.
- Be registered with the FAA as an Intermediate Air Carrier and be bonded and insured.

Using a professional animal shipper may make things easier for you, but it does not by any means eliminate all the risks. Although the new rules governing the commercial air transport of animals are a positive step in the right direction, they have only slightly improved the safety of pet flight. There will always be an element of risk when pets are shipped as cargo. At the risk of repetition, if you are traveling for leisure and cannot carry on your pet, it may be best to leave your pet with someone. (See "Pet Sitters, Boarding Kennels, and Caretakers.") On the other hand, how about a road trip instead?

Taking Your Pet on the Road

Traveling with pets in a motor vehicle, while safer in our opinion than shipping them by air, still presents many of its own challenges in terms of lost pet prevention and preparedness. Recovering a pet lost on the road is obviously more complicated than trying to find one who wandered away at home. Also, you need to be prepared in the event of an accident while traveling. One of the major themes of this book is preparedness. The ability to quickly recover your pet lost far from home is extremely important. Therefore, prior to your trip, there are some things you need to do to be prepared. (See "Traveling With Pets.")

Keeping your pet confined to its carrier is a must when traveling. If your pet is not accustomed to being in a carrier, take the time to acclimate it to its carrier in the weeks prior to your trip. Harness restraints, which are basically seat belts, are not quite as safe, but most people are more likely to use these on short trips around town. Our point is to encourage you to always use one of these methods to help protect your pet.

If your pet isn't used to traveling in a car, it's important that you take the time to make it feel safe in a moving vehicle. A nervous pet is at greater risk of loss than a calm one. Long before your trip, take your dog on frequent, gradually longer car trips to a park or someplace where the two of you can play. Your pet will quickly associate a car ride with something pleasurable. Here are some things you should pack for your trip and some things to do right before you leave.

- *Prepare for Recovery*—Carefully go over your "Preparing for Recovery" items and gather your pet records, recovery kit, and your list of important phone numbers and addresses. (See "Critical Contacts.")

- *Accident Pouch*—Keep your pet information in your glove box any time you are traveling in a vehicle. This will alert police or emergency medical personnel that your pet was traveling with you. It should also contain contact information, instructions for the care and/or placement of your pet and a photograph of your pet. There are products and services available for just this sort of thing; wallet alert cards and window decals for example. (See "Accidents.")

- *General Travel Supplies*—While you are packing, don't forget your pet's food and drinking water, as well as dishes for both, plus your pet's bedding, litter and litter box, any medications your pet may be taking, and a first aid kit.

- *Toys and Treats*—Bring along several of your pet's favorites.

- *Instruct Children*—If you are also traveling with children, talk to them about your pet's safety and reinforce this lesson throughout the trip (e.g., children should be let out of the car by an adult whenever you stop, rather than allowing them to just throw open the doors).

- *Feed Your Pet*—About two or three hours before you leave on your trip, give your pet some food and water so that it has time to digest it and do its "business" *before* getting into your car.

- *Exercise Your Pet*—Just before departing, take a nice long walk, or better yet, a run or a good game of fetch, so your pet can release any built-up tension and be nice and tired when you start out.

Following a few simple rules will go a long way toward keeping you and your pet safe on the road.

- *Flatbeds and Pickups*—DO NOT transport your pet in the bed of a truck; not only is it unsafe, it's illegal in several states.

- *Keep Your Windows Rolled Up*—The sight of another dog or cat outside your car can incite your pet to leap through an open window in pursuit of its new friend. Flying debris could also injure your pet.

- *Rest Stops*—Although frequent rest breaks are a necessary part of any long road trip, pay particularly close attention to your pet whenever you stop (rest stops are where many travelers lose their pets). We know from personal experience that rest stops are prime hunting grounds for pet thieves. A close friend of ours had a dog stolen while just running in at a rest stop for a quick cup of coffee.

More Travel Tips from The Humane Society of the United States

Visit the HSUS's *Pet Information Center* at **www.hsus.org.** Click on Pet Care Link and read several informative travel articles from *Preparing Your Pet's Travel Supplies* to *Tips for Safe Pet Air Travel.* You can even view a short video clip, "Pet Minute," on traveling by car with pets. Not everyone has access to the Internet. Fortunately, many HSUS pamphlets can be ordered in print form. Contact HSUS at (202) 452-1100 to request a publication catalog free of charge.

- *Collar and Leash*—Do not under any circumstances permit your pet to leave the car without a collar and leash, even if you are comfortable doing so at home.

- *Walking Your Pet*—Never allow young children to walk the pets. Even if they do so at home, it's just too risky.

- *Identification*—Always have your pet wear its collar and visible identification, both inside and outside the car.

- *Use Temporary Tags*—In addition to its regular tags, make sure your pet is wearing temporary identification tags that will tell anyone who finds it how to reach you while you're on the road. (Using a tag and/or tattoo registry is the best way to be sure someone will be reachable in the event your pet is found.)

- *Never Leave Your Pet Alone in the Car*—Leaving an animal unattended in a car is an open invitation to pet thieves, and it is also quite dangerous. On a hot day, the temperature inside your car can quickly rise to well over 100° F—*even with the windows open slightly*—and your pet could die in just a matter of minutes.

- *Note Landmarks*—One of the most important things you can do is to know where you are anytime you stop. Take note of landmarks, street or highway signs, and the exit number you took off of the interstate, so that if you lose your pet, you can tell others exactly where it occurred.

- *Take Your Time*—Pull over every once in a while just to cuddle with your pet and talk to it (also, many pets—especially birds—are comforted by familiar music).

Traveling with Birds

More and more, people are traveling with their birds. As with all animals, anything you can do to reduce the travel-related stress on your bird is a good idea. The safest thing you can do to prevent bird loss—at home or while on a trip—is to clip its flight feathers. If for some reason you're against clipping your bird's wings, leave your pet with someone else while you travel. Be certain that whoever will be caring for your "unclipped" bird while you are away is instructed to exercise the utmost of caution, and has experience caring for birds. If you hire a professional sitter, don't simply take their word for it; ask for references from other bird owners that they have sat for.

Another serious threat facing birds on the road is theft. Exotic birds, as you are probably well aware, are very expensive and the prime target of someone wanting to make some illegal profit. Never leave your bird unattended, not even for a second. Take along plenty of treats and fresh water and as mentioned above, make frequent stops just to play with and calm your pet. Be sure to have all of your bird's paperwork in order, and seriously consider having your bird implanted with a microchip prior to your trip.

Traveling with Ferrets and Other Critters

Follow the general rules for cats and dogs. Keep your ferret, guinea pig, hamster, or any other kind of pet confined to its cage or carrier. If you walk your ferret, always use a proper harness. Be aware that ferrets are illegal in several cities and states, and your ferret could be confiscated by the authorities, or worse.

Accidents

Planning Ahead is the Best Protection

Plan ahead to safeguard your pet not just against loss, but also to provide for its temporary or possibly permanent care or placement in the event of an accident (whether you're on a cross-country road trip or driving in your own neighborhood).

With the flashing lights and sound of sirens, not to mention the trauma of the impact, your pet could easily run off in the confusion. If you are unconscious, you won't be able to alert emergency workers that your pet was in the vehicle with you. Even if you're conscious, you may be injured and therefore unable to search for your pet. How do you tell others to look for your pet?

What if your pet is alone at home and you have an accident and are hospitalized? Who will care for your pet? A cat or a dog may be fine for a day or two until arrangements can be made, but birds must eat daily to survive and ferrets need a lot of water or they'll dehydrate very quickly.

There are precautionary measures you can take to protect your pet in each of these circumstances:

- Set up a "Pet Partner" arrangement with a friend, a family member, or close neighbor; someone who could assist you if you were injured and unable to search for your lost pet yourself. (See "Pet Partners.")

- Use static cling window decals and an emergency notification wallet card to let emergency workers know that you have pets, and to let them know who to contact if you are seriously injured. These items are available in pet catalogs, pet magazines, and pet supply stores.

- Create two emergency envelopes. Each envelope should contain specific instructions and contact information to be kept in your glove box—one envelope is for

PetAlert

PetAlert was developed by Pet Guardian Angels of America (PGAA) to help identify you as a pet owner so that your pet's welfare can be attended to if you are in an accident or otherwise become unable to provide the care yourself. A series of identification items (e.g., wallet identification card, glove compartment notice, house display notice, and a car decal) link your designated caregiver and your pet via PGAA's database through their round-the-clock toll-free number. One great thing about this service is that PGAA has extensive contacts with various pet rescue groups and animal shelters. In the event that your designated caregiver is unable to care for your pet, PGAA can place your pet, temporarily or permanently. To find out more about PGAA PetAlert visit their web site at **www.pgaa.com**.

FIGURE 29

when your pet is traveling with you in the vehicle, and the other is for when you leave your pet at home.

- Use proper pet identification, including some type of permanent identification, a tattoo or microchip, and consider using a national tag registry. ("See Registries and Recovery Services.")

- Use a registry that provides additional recovery services (i.e., contacting shelters for you, mailing lost pet postcards, etc.). This can make the difference between recovering or not recovering your pet if you are in an accident and unable to search for your pet yourself. They do many of the things that need to be done when a pet is lost. (See "Registries and Recovery Services.")

- Use a pet emergency service (PetAlert is an example) that provides comprehensive support for just such emergency situations. (See figure 29.)

- Prepare a list of rescue groups in your area or in the area where you plan to travel, since you may find a rescue group member willing to lend you assistance. (See "Critical Contacts.")

- Provide for your pet in your will. Make arrangements with your executor for permanent placement of your pet and make arrangements for temporary care, since it can take some weeks to find a permanent home for your pet. Authorize that funds from your estate be used for this purpose.

Planning for Your Pet's Future without You

The Humane Society of the United States, in an article titled *Planning for Your Pet's Future Without You*, suggests that you "find at least two responsible friends or relatives who agree to serve as temporary emergency caregivers in the event that something unexpected happens to you. Provide them with keys to your home; feeding and care instructions; the name of your veterinarian; and information about the permanent care provisions you have made for your pet."

To read the entire pamphlet, visit The HSUS's Pet Information Center at **www.hsus.org**. Those without Internet access can call to request a copy. HSUS also makes a kit, "Providing for Your Pet's Future Without You," which is available for a few dollars and can also be requested when you call. (See "Resources/ Humane Organizations.")

Pet Sitters, Boarding Kennels, and Caretakers

Somewhere along the line, a situation will no doubt arise when you have to rely on someone else to care for your pet. Some people hire caretakers to walk their dogs or to check in on their pets while they're at work. Professional pet sitting is a huge business, and there are even doggie daycare centers. Whether it is a trusted friend, a family member, or a professional, it is important to understand that there is always a risk of pet loss when you entrust the care of your pet to someone else. It is your responsibility to equip them with the knowledge and the tools they need to prevent the loss of your pet, and to recover it quickly should your pet get away.

Many prefer a family member or close friend because they are simply uncomfortable having strangers in their homes, even if they are professionals and come with references and insurance. (It should be noted, however, that simply being a friend or family member does not automatically qualify someone to care for your pet.) While kennels rarely lose pets, a lot of folks are understandably uneasy about subjecting their animals to what can be, for many pets, especially cats, a traumatic experience. They are also concerned about possibly exposing their pets to communicable diseases that are not all that uncommon in facilities that house multiple animals.

The most important thing to remember before you entrust the care of your pet to another is that you must insist that they agree to follow the basic rules of lost pet prevention. More importantly, they must assure you that if your pet is lost while in their charge, they will do everything in their power to recover your pet. While many pet care professionals already have a basic understanding of lost pet prevention and recovery, it is your job to discuss the various aspects with them. Leave no room for ambiguity. Give them specific instructions that will help prevent the loss of your pet, and provide guidelines for what to do in the event that loss occurs anyway.

Advantages of Professional Pet Sitters

When it comes to pet sitting, there are many advantages to hiring a professional instead of relying on a friend or family member. They are, after all, professionals; caring for animals is what they do. If the sitter is an association member, he or she in most cases will have taken and passed courses in pet sitting. Regardless of your choice, however, keep in mind that they are not likely to be as vigilant and conscientious as you are about lost pet prevention.

Professional pet sitting is a big business today. There are literally thousands of pet sitters, both independent and associated. Unless an independent sitter comes to you with excellent recommendations from someone you know and trust, we would suggest you go through an association. Two of the largest of these are the National Association of Professional Pet Sitters and Pet Sitters International. (See "Resources/Pet Sitters, Boarding Kennels, and Caretakers.")

Boarding Your Pet

If you're considering this option, keep in mind there is an alternative to a boarding kennel. Many veterinarians and animal hospitals also board pets. For many, this is preferable since they may already have an established relationship with them, and medical help is right there on hand.

Although it is difficult to imagine how a pet could be lost from a boarding facility, it does happen, and the standard precautions we've discussed throughout this book need to be taken.

Tips for Choosing a Pet Sitter from Pet Sitters International

- "Make sure the sitter is bonded and insured.
- Have the sitter provide references.
- Determine that the sitter has experience in caring for pets and is clearly mindful of their safety and wellbeing.
- Does the sitter provide written literature describing services and stating fees?
- Have the sitter visit your home before the first pet sitting assignment to meet the pets and get detailed information about their care.
- Watch to make sure the sitter shows a positive attitude during the initial meeting, and seems comfortable and competent dealing with animals (watch your animal's reaction as well).
- Does the sitter want to learn as much as possible about the animals in his or her care?
- Does the sitter provide a service contract which specifies services and fees?
- Is the sitter courteous, interested, and well-informed?
- Will the sitter take precautions to make sure your absence from home is not detected by others through any careless actions or disclosures by the sitter?
- Does the sitter conduct business with honesty and integrity, and observe all federal, state, and local laws pertaining to business operations and animal care?
- Make sure the sitter has a veterinarian to call for emergency services.
- What is the sitter's contingency plan for pet care in case of inclement weather or personal illness?
- Does the sitting service provide initial and ongoing training for its sitters?
- Does the sitting service screen applicants for employment carefully?
- Make sure the sitter calls to confirm that you have returned home as scheduled.
- Does the sitter refrain from criticizing competitors?"

To locate a professional sitter near you, visit the PSI web site at **www.petsit.com** or call their Locator Services at (336) 983-9222.

Reprinted with permission from Pet Sitters International. Copyright 1994. All rights reserved.

Dogs especially are at risk since they need to be exercised, and it is these times that provide the greatest opportunity to escape. Also, with all the other barking and meowing, boarding your pet can be a stressful experience for your animal. Finding a boarding kennel or boarder is very easy: finding a good one requires some homework. Boarding kennels are listed in the telephone directory. Here again, using the services of an association is probably preferable. Calling or visiting the web site (**www.abka.com**) of the American Boarding Kennels Association (ABKA) makes locating a qualified kennel near you very easy. All ABKA members agree to adhere to a high standard of ethical conduct set by ABKA. Members found to be in violation risk having their membership revoked. ABKA also has a Voluntary Facilities Accreditation Program (VFA Program). According to ABKA, "Boarding kennels which participate in the VFA Program must submit detailed information about their animal care procedures and business policies and submit to an on-site inspection by trained VFA evaluators. The VFA Program offers pet owners the assurance that accredited facilities have earned the ABKA 'stamp of approval' by successfully completing this comprehensive program." In all instances, we highly recommend that you inspect the facility yourself.

Be aware that communicable diseases are an obvious concern, and many kennels will require additional vaccinations before accepting your pet. The Humane Society of the United States publishes a helpful info sheet titled "Choosing a Boarding Kennel" which you can view by visiting their *Pet Information Center* online at **www.hsus.org** or by calling or writing to request one. (See "Resources/Humane Organizations.")

Walking Services

One of the main reasons that people allow their pets to roam is frustration over behavior problems, which can often be traced to things like separation anxiety, boredom, and lack of attention, including lack of regular walks and exercise. Walking your dog is simply a part of being a responsible pet owner. Many dog owners, however, work long hours and are simply unable to walk their dogs often enough, and so turn instead to professional walking services. Dog walking services are very popular today, especially in big cities.

In terms of pet loss, one of the greatest risks is "pack-walking" (it is not uncommon for professionals to walk as many as 15 animals at a time). Those who practice this argue that it is safe, explaining that dogs are naturally pack animals and are happier when walked in groups. We respectfully but strongly disagree. Another argument they make is that walking several animals at a time saves the consumer money. This is undoubtedly so, but we agree with Pet Mates Professional Pet Care Services of New York City that claims the risks far outweigh the benefits. (See figure 30.)

Doggie Daycare

For many working parents, daycare is an absolute necessity for their children. The same is true for many millions of American pet owners whose pets are as important to them as their children. These busy dog owners understand the negative consequences of leaving their pets home alone all day. They appreciate the fact that dogs can suffer from stress, loneliness, and separation anxiety— all causes of escape attempts and a number of other behavioral problems. Doggie daycare can be a godsend for both the dogs and their owners.

Doggie daycare facilities generally provide a wide variety of stimulating activities and sensory experiences that channel a dog's energy in a positive direction. They also help your dog to socialize with other dogs. By the time you pick up your dog in the evening, it may be too tired to try an escape attempt! Doggie daycare facilities can be located in most metropolitan areas. They can be found in the local Yellow Pages. Yahoo online yellow pages at **www.yahoo.com** are a good source, and another is the Doggie Directory at **www.doggiedirectory.com**. Or try your favorite search engine using the key words "doggie daycare" or "pet daycare." Your veterinarian may also be able to direct you.

Preparing Your Pet's Caretaker

These general guidelines apply to anyone who is charged with the care of your pet, be they a friend, a family member, a professional sitter,

The Disadvantages of Pack-walking Dogs

• "The probability that your pet will get loose and run from the group is always possible. The walker will never be able to go after your dog with all the other dogs in tow.

• Dogs in packs become more aggressive to a dog that is being walked near them individually, thus increasing the chance of someone breaking free.

• The walker can actually become a human maypole when dogs are riled up.

• Dogs are not able to do their business leisurely when they have to keep up with the group.

• Dogs are tied up outside (unattended many times) while walker is getting the next dog to add to the group.

• In the extreme heat of summer, pack-walking can be a dangerous activity since dogs can quickly become overheated. It is also a dangerous activity in the extreme cold when there is ice and salt on the ground.

• During the walk, dogs who are older, smaller, or not as fit may be literally dragged behind, causing them to overexert themselves in an effort to keep up.

• Dogs are piled up in local dog runs (a fenced in area for dogs to run free and get exercise) where they are left waiting with one or two attendants while the main walker goes and gets more dogs.

"The only advantage of pack-walking that we can think of is that the walker makes a lot of money. According to an article in the June 14, 1998 edition of *The New York Times*, 'Pack walking keeps prices down for the pet owner and increases income for the business.' There are rates offered to pet owners for as low as $8 for an hour for a two-hour walk. This means that the walker can make anywhere from $32 to $120 an hour. What a deal! But it's not a good deal for Fido."

If you're in New York City and need a walking service or just want someone to drop by during the day and play with your pup or kitty, contact Pet Mates Inc. at (212) 414-5158 or visit their web site at **www.petmates.com**. Hey, they'll even feed the fish.

Reprinted with permission from Pet Mates Inc. Copyright 1999. All rights reserved.

FIGURE 30

a dog walker, a doggie daycare facility, and even a neighbor who checks in on your pet during the day while you are at work.

- Be sure that you can always be contacted (a cell phone works well). If you are traveling, let them know your itinerary, and insist that there be no delay in contacting you if your pet is lost, or in the event of any other emergency.

- Go over everything, and insist that the normal rules for lost pet prevention be strictly followed (e.g., keeping windows closed, gates securely latched, etc.). Insist that your pet always be leash-walked and never be without its visible identification inside or outside of the house. (One more time: purchasing identification tags through a national registry is indispensable, since someone will always be able to contact you whether you are ten or ten thousand miles from home.)

- Equip them with everything they need to recover your pet quickly. Leave them a copy of this book. Go over the "Preparing for Recovery" section in detail. They will need your pet records, copies of photos, your list of "Critical Contacts," etc. If you have a Pet Partner arrangement, be sure they know how to contact them. (See "Pet Partners.")

- Give them the names, phone numbers, and addresses of your veterinarian and an alternative veterinarian, as well as emergency clinics in the area.

- Call daily to check on your pet.

- When hiring a professional, express your concerns about pet loss, and ask what specifically they would do if your pet turned up missing while in their care. Inquire if they have ever, in fact, lost someone's pet.

- When hiring a professional sitter or boarding your dog at a kennel, go through an association such as the National Association of Professional Pet Sitters, Pet Sitters International, or the American Boarding Kennels Association.

- Screen them thoroughly, and ask a lot of questions. Any professional caretaker will answer all of your questions to your satisfaction, and will not take offense nor trivialize your concerns. By asking questions you will also get a sense of how they care for animals. Trust your gut feeling.

- Get references, and be sure to check them out yourself.

- Make an appointment to check out the facility in person when considering a kennel for your pet.

- If you do decide to ask a family member or friend, go over everything with them in detail, and insist they hold to the same standards you would expect from a professional.

- When hiring a dog walking service, be sure they do not pack-walk the animals. Pack-walking may save you a couple of dollars, but it is simply too dangerous.

• Your veterinarian is a good source for many things that involve pet care. Talk to your veterinarian. She/he will likely be able to make referrals for quality pet care services.

Pet Partners

What is a Pet Partner?

A "Pet Partner" is a person (but not necessarily another pet owner) with whom you've entered into an agreement. It could be a friend, a relative, or a neighbor. Both of you agree in advance to help one another if your pet is ever lost. Having a Pet Partner can be critical in a variety of situations.

Benefits of Having a Pet Partner

There's not a pet owner reading this who wouldn't benefit from having a Pet Partner arrangement. There is so much that needs to be done in order to recover a lost pet. Besides physically searching for it, you must visit shelter facilities, distribute flyers, make a thousand phone calls, etc. Having a Pet Partner means tasks can be divided up, and when your pet is lost it helps to know that you are not alone. There are so many situations where having a Pet Partner could literally make the difference between recovering and not recovering your pet, for example:

How to Set Up a Pet Partnership

Your Pet Partner should be someone you absolutely trust. Both of you should have keys to each other's homes, copies of each other's pet records, and instructions for the proper care of your pet (detailing any medical needs, special diet, etc.).

Arrangements should be made between the two of you for temporary, long-term, permanent care or placement. Your veterinarian should be made aware of this agreement and should have a permission slip signed by both of you authorizing both Pet Partners to get any necessary emergency treatment for your animals. Both Pet Partners should be fully informed about lost pet prevention and recovery.

- If you are away on vacation and your pet's caretaker loses your pet.
- If your pet were lost during a disaster, or if a disaster struck while you were not at home.
- If you are elderly, disabled, or housebound.
- If you were in an automobile accident or became ill and were unable to care for your pet.
- If you lost your pet on moving day and were unable to delay the move.
- If you need an alternative contact to give to your ID registry, your Pet Partner could be one of your alternative contacts.
- If your Pet Partner loses their pet, you get to be there for them. There is hardly a more rewarding feeling in the whole world than to help reunite a distraught pet owner with his/her beloved pet.

Moving

Moving is stressful for everyone concerned, your pets included. There is so much that has to be done—showing your home to prospective buyers, choosing a moving company, making all of the arrangements at your new address and on top of it all, making the transportation arrangements for your pet (moving companies are prohibited by regulations from transporting animals). With all the hustle and bustle, it's easy to overlook your pet's needs. Your pet should be one of your primary concerns. Fortunately, there is help available. (See figure 31.)

More Moving Tips

The Dumb Friends League publishes a helpful pamphlet ("Moving With Your Pet"). It is easily accessible on their web site at **www.ddfl.org**.

Also visit **www.rentwithpets.org**, a site created by The Humane Society of the United States, with lots of helpful information on moving and renting with pets.

FIGURE 31

Making the Preparations

In the days and weeks leading up to a major move, there will be a lot of changes in your pet's environment, with boxes stacked high, your pet's favorite chair covered in plastic moving wrap, carpets rolled up, and there will be a lot more activity. Understandably, these changes can make your pet anxious, and an anxious pet is a pet at risk of flight. People may be coming over to look at the house (often while you're not at home) and others may be helping you pack up, all adding to your pet's opportunities to escape. There are several things you can do to make the transition safe and less stressful for your pet.

- *Create a Safe Place*—Setting aside a spare room where your pet can be temporarily confined can provide him with much-needed security. Put your pet's bedding and some of his favorite toys in the room. It will also help to play a little soft music (this is especially comforting to birds, who can be particularly sensitive to extra activity). Post a sign on the door alerting people to your pet's presence, and alert movers and friends that your pet is not to be disturbed. If you don't have a spare room, then crate your pet when needed. Confining your pet to its carrier or to a safe room is the best protection. And find the time to give your pet at least a portion of its normal attention, even if it's difficult.

- *Be Aware of Increased Activity*—Whether it's the packers, real estate agents, or neighbors coming to say their good-byes, there will be a lot going on in the days leading up to your move. Even pets that are not normally prone to escape attempts may attempt to bolt out an open door or window as a result of the stress. Besides, you're no doubt going to be distracted yourself. You must strive to remain vigilant regarding your pet's safety.

- *Alert Real Estate Agents*—Talk to your agent about your concerns for your pet's safety. Set down some rules. Make sure they alert all other real estate agents who might show your home that there is a pet in the house and that you expect every precaution be taken to ensure your pet's safety. Insist that all windows and doors be shut, and gates securely latched after each showing. Tell them that your pet will be confined to its carrier or to a room, and that this area is strictly off-limits. Of course, any serious buyer will want to see every room in the house, but if someone is truly interested in purchasing your home, they will make a second appointment to see it while you are there.

- *Alert Packers*—When it comes time for the moving company to start packing your household goods, plan to be there or at least arrange for a friend or family member to be there. The packers are there to pack, not to look after your pet. That's your responsibility. Keep your pet confined to its safe room or crate, and let the packers know that there are pets in the house and that your pet's room is off limits. Note: Be sure not to pack your pet records, as you'll need them while traveling. Owners of small animals have to consider the danger of their pet's accidentally being packed up. This happens more often than you might think! The chaotic atmosphere, all the packing and stacking, and strangers moving about may cause your animal to seek out a hiding spot to escape all the confusion. (See figure 32.)

What do you do if, despite all your preparations, your animal turns up missing? Being prepared for pet loss at any time is important. If your pet is lost while you are in the middle

---

Cat Survives Three Weeks in Box

August 10, 1997 Associated Press

NEWPORT, RI–Rebecca Hampton feared she'd lost the family cat when he vanished last month after movers packed up their belongings at their home in Oklahoma.

Simon, an 11-year-old Russian blue, was actually trapped under a box spring and sealed in a crate. He stayed there for 22 days without food or water until her husband opened the crate Wednesday at their new military home at Fort Adams, RI. Silver-gray Simon was still alive, although weak at a bony six pounds.

"This is like a miracle," Mrs. Hampton said. "I thought he was going to die. I really did. He looked that bad."

She rushed Simon to the Newport Animal Clinic, where veterinarian Randal Wirth gave him intravenous liquids. "The cat was very perky, very bright and alert, purring about, jumping out of the cage to get at the food we were serving him," Wirth said. "Despite dehydration and weight loss, Simon appears to be in good shape," said Wirth. "It's really quite surprising," Wirth said. "The body has enormous mechanisms for reserving fluid and using other body tissues for energy."

Mrs. Hampton believes Simon crawled into the box spring to get away from the commotion caused by the movers. "Simon probably survived because he had been plump, about 12 pounds, before his ordeal," she said.

FIGURE 32

---

of a move, however, you have a real mess. If the move is still days away, there is some time to search. If it happens on the day of the move, it could be disastrous if you're caught unprepared. All of the prevention and preparedness strategies we outline in this book will prove crucial to your recovery efforts. Here are some key strategies to safeguard your pet during the moving process:

- Set up a Pet Partner arrangement. (See "Pet Partners.")
- Use proper identification. We hate to beat this to death, but it can never be stressed enough: have multiple forms of identification for your pet. (See "Pet Identification.")
- Speak with the moving company ahead of time about your options should you lose your pet during the move. Do they have storage facilities in case you have to stay behind and no one can meet them at your new address? Can the move be delayed without your suffering a financial penalty?

Moving Day

A house on moving day is no place for a pet to be roaming about freely. Not only could your pet escape, it could easily be injured. You will be distracted with many things such as watching the movers, making sure that nothing is damaged, making last minute arrangements, etc. Once again, alert the movers to the fact that you have pets, and require the movers to be cautious. It is an absolute must that you confine your pet on moving day. If you do not have a carrier or a spare room, consider leaving your pet with a trusted friend or relative for the day, or even boarding it overnight.

You and Your Pet's New Home

Pets are comfortable in familiar surroundings. In the new neighborhood, your pet's usual reference points are gone. Familiar sights, sounds, and smells are all different now. The change can be quite disorienting for pets. Be extra cautious the first several days, because your pet could be easily spooked by the new mailman, by a strange lawnmower, or by the kids in the new neighborhood. Respect the fact that your pet needs time to get acclimated to its new environment. One great way to help your pet along is to begin regular walks immediately, a half-mile in each direction (less if your dog is not used to longer walks), until your dog is thoroughly acquainted with the new neighborhood.

As soon as possible, update your list of Critical Contacts. Get the numbers and addresses of the animal shelters, rescue groups, etc., in the area. Do not put off getting new ID tags for your pet. Use temporary tags in the interim, and license your pet in your new city right away. Also, contact any identification registries to which you belong, and give them your new address and phone number. Of course, you'll need to locate a new veterinarian as well. Why wait? Many of these things can be done prior to your move. Locating a new veterinarian, for example, is as simple as visiting **www.vetweb.net**. Vet Web maintains an extensive directory of veterinarians listed by state. Bird owners can locate an avian vet by visiting the Association of Avian Veterinarians' web site at **www.aav.org**. It's that simple. Locating shelters and breed rescue groups is just as easy. (See "Critical Contacts.")

Moving is stressful to say the least. Being aware of certain hazards inherent in moving, taking extra precautions to protect your pet, and having a plan in place should the unthinkable happen, is your best protection against pet loss and will maximize your chances of recovering your pet quickly if it is lost during a move.

Stolen Pets

According to the organization In Defense of Animals, an estimated 1.5 million dogs and cats are stolen from households across the United States every year and sold to the highest bidder. Supplying animals for use in experimentation is big business, a well-financed and highly-organized industry whose key players include licensed animal dealers, major universities, government laboratories, and the biomedical, cosmetics, and chemical industries. The use of animals for research is an emotionally charged and controversial subject, one that is outside the scope of this book. No matter one's view on it, everyone can agree that people's pets should never be used for this purpose. Unfortunately, the above-mentioned industries require a regular supply of research animals. Many animals are raised specifically for use in experimentation (so-called "purpose-bred" animals). Most people are unaware, however, that many are acquired through "pound seizures" (the reprehensible practice of selling surplus shelter animals [often people's pets] for a variety of purposes, including experimentation). The very nature of collecting "Random Source" animals (animals acquired from a variety of sources, including outright theft) lends itself to abuse. The risk of discovery is low, the risk of meaningful prosecution even lower. Considering that a dog can fetch as much as $700, the trade in illicitly-acquired animals is very profitable. Organized pet theft aside, there are basically three reasons why pets are stolen.

Some of the Frightening Reasons behind Pet Theft

- *Impulsive Stealing*—We recently read the story of a teenage boy who stole someone's pet chicken for no particular reason at all. It is the perfect example of an impulsive act of pet thievery. Perhaps the boy thought it was just a cool thing to do. Fortunately, the animal was recovered.

- *Revenge*—Getting back at someone is one of the chief motivating factors behind pet theft. Your pet could be stolen by an ex-spouse or jilted lover, an angry coworker or neighbor who just doesn't like you. We read a story recently on **www.pet-detectives.com**, titled "One Kitty's Nightmare," about a pair of feuding neighbors, one of which ultimately resorted to cat nabbing.

- *Money*—Most pet thieves are motivated by money. Your pet is a commodity. Purebred animals and exotic birds and reptiles can be sold to shady pet stores, crooked breeders, or directly to individuals who don't want to pay a high price. The biggest market, however, are laboratories that use the animals for research and experimental purposes. It isn't just purebred animals that these facilities are after. Your mutt or mixed breed is no safer. Depending on the type of research being done, they are often looking for animals of a certain size, weight, sex, or age, regardless of breed.

Tips for Thwarting Burglars

- Purchase a home security system, and plainly advertise its presence around your property. Even if you don't have a security system, create the illusion that you do by putting up signs that say something to the effect of "This Home Protected by XYZ Security Company, Inc."
- Display a "Beware of Dog" sign or, better yet, "Guard Dog on Premises."
- Leave the radio or television on when you are not at home.
- Make it difficult for burglars to get at exotic pets. Keep a lock on the cage and secure it to something that cannot be carried away.
- Never leave spare keys outside (e.g., under a plant, doormat, or in a mailbox) where burglars can easily find them.
- Don't leave notes on your door, as they indicate that you may not be at home.
- Keep trees, shrubs, and bushes trimmed so thieves don't have any place to hide.
- Join your neighborhood watch program.

For more information on burglary prevention, visit the National Crime Prevention Council web site at **www.ncpc.org**, or call or write them. (See "Resources/Stolen Pets.")

FIGURE 33

The odds of recovering a pet that has been stolen are significantly lower than recovering one that has simply run off. The best protection against pet theft is preventing it in the first place. Being aware of the ways pets are stolen will help you take the necessary steps to prevent it.

- *Stolen During Burglaries*—Pets are seldom the prime targets of a burglary; they are more often taken by the criminals as an afterthought. Make the burglars' job as difficult as possible. (See figure 33.) According to the National Crime Prevention Council, "Many burglars will spend no longer than 60 seconds trying to break into a home. Good locks—and good neighbors who watch out for each other—can be big deterrents to burglars."

- *Stolen from Vehicles*—It is *always* a bad idea to leave your animal unattended in a car, even for just a few minutes. In addition to being a serious health risk, especially in either very hot or very cold weather, it's also an open invitation to pet thieves. When you know you will be running errands and will have to leave your pet in the vehicle unattended, do not bring it along.

• ***Stolen from Yards***—Pet thieves are bold. Many pets are stolen right out of their owners' backyards. Have fencing installed that's high enough not only to keep your dog in, but also hopefully to keep pet thieves out. (See "Roaming and Escaping.") And be sure to keep the gate to your yard padlocked. Don't leave your

---

Research Dog Saved by Tattoo

"Unconscious, just moments from the beginning incision, an eight-month old American Staffordshire Terrier lay on the operating table of a mid-western research laboratory. As the researcher shaved the dog's abdomen (preparing it for surgery from which it would never awaken), tattooed numbers were uncovered on the skin of the dog's inner thigh! The surgery was instantly aborted.

"The doctor performing the research went right to the phone and called a toll-free number he had used several times before. Within minutes, a comprehensive nationwide search began for the owner of the tattooed pet. The number the researcher called was a 24-hour pet identification hotline operated by the National Dog Registry, the oldest and largest missing pet recovery system in the world, which is headquartered in Woodstock, New York.

"When the operator at NDR ran a database search for the pet's ID number with no successful match, she began the arduous task of networking with all other cooperating organizations that might have records on the number. The operator knew that without a registration in a national database (such as NDR's), the tattoo was virtually worthless as an identification and recovery tool, and the dog on the table at the research laboratory would surely die.

"NDR's operator persisted in her efforts. One of the calls she placed was to the Breeder's Action Board (BAB) in Michigan, a group that regularly works with NDR. (BAB is a non-profit organization promoting responsible dog ownership and public education.) Believing that the tattoo number might be part of their state pet ID system, BAB's Betty Melia called the Michigan Department of Agriculture. The Department had the number on file, but had no current information on the owner. Persevering, Betty called the veterinarian listed as the dog's tattooer and uncovered more recent information.

"When she contacted Miron Duncan of Detroit, his shock and amazement confirmed that Roxanne, his AmStaff, had disappeared from his back yard three months earlier. Although he had searched the neighborhood and put up signs, Miron despaired of ever seeing Roxanne again. He almost could not believe that she had been found in a research lab hundreds of miles away, in another state.

"BAB called NDR with Miron's name and phone number. NDR notified the doctor at the research lab that the owner had been located. Roxanne was saved!"

pet unattended in the yard for long periods of time, and never go away (even for a ten-minute trip to the convenience store) and leave your pet in the yard.

- *Stolen from Outside Enclosures*—Outside enclosures such as aviaries, kennels, cat enclosures, and pens should be kept locked. Please remember that these are not surrogate caretakers. You always need to check on your pet regularly; once every half-hour is generally a good rule.

- *Stolen from Outside a Store*—Never leave your dog tied up outside a store while you go in and shop. This is probably a carryover from an earlier and safer time in small town America. Today? Don't do it! This is very dangerous for your pet and completely irresponsible.

- *Stolen while Roaming the Neighborhood*—Besides all the other hazards we've discussed that will be faced by pets permitted to run loose, roaming pets are prime targets for pet thieves. These crooks are known to cruise neighborhoods looking for stray animals, and some go as far as to employ a bitch in heat to attract stray males.

Additional Tips for Preventing Pet Theft

- *Use Proper and Multiple Forms of Identification*—Hopefully a Good Samaritan will find your loose animal before a pet thief does. The multiple ID approach is the best way to protect your pet: an ID tag, a tattoo, and a microchip. Of these, tattoos can be an especially good deterrent to thieves planning to sell your animal to a research facility, because pet thieves know that labs will not accept tattooed animals. Funding requirements are beginning to force many labs to scan for microchips as well.

- *Be Aware of Strangers*—Take special notice of people you don't know, or strange vehicles in your neighborhood. Professional pet thieves often drive vans or trucks with darkened windows. They may have out-of-state license plates. Burglars usually spend some time casing neighborhoods looking for vulnerable homes. Trust your instincts. Write down the license plate number, and report any suspicious activity to the police.

- *Prepare a List*—As a preventive measure, write down all the places you can think of where a pet thief might try to sell your animal. Include pet stores, bird jungles, reptile and exotic animal stores, etc. You can also write (and should do so before your pet is stolen) to the United States Department of Agriculture (USDA) for a list of research facilities and registered animal dealers in your area. (See "Resources/Stolen Pets.")

- ***Know Who to Contact***—Write down important phone numbers, such as the In Defense of Animals' Pet Theft Hotline (800-STOLEN PET). National Pet Detective's Larry Maynard facilitates a lost and stolen pet e-group at **www.groups.yahoo.com** search National Pet Detectives. This group is for those who have registered their pets with NPD. (See "Resources/Stolen Pets.")

A Little History

Award-winning author Judith Reitman, in her book *Stolen for Profit*, exposes the key players in this horrible business that can only be described as trafficking in animal cruelty. Pet stealing is very organized, and there is never a shortage of eager buyers willing to pay top dollar for animals, no questions asked. Recent holding-period and record-keeping requirement amendments to the "Animal Welfare Act" were intended to put a stop to the trade in pets. While these improvements are welcome, they have made the situation only marginally better. While the USDA is responsible for overseeing animal dealers and enforcing these new regulations, many people have complained that too few resources have been allocated to make much of a difference. Some have gone even further, accusing the USDA of being in collaboration with the research industry. Few pet thieves have been caught and fewer prosecuted in any meaningful way.

Who's Selling?

Some animal shelters, many of them government-run facilities, sell stray pets to animal dealers. In most instances, these dealers turn around and sell the animals to research facilities. Federal regulations require shelters to hold stray animals for a minimum of five days before being allowed to sell them. Several states have banned this practice of "pound seizure," but too many others still permit this reprehensible practice. To find out if your state permits pound seizure and what you can do to stop it, contact In Defense of Animals. (See "Resources/Stolen Pets.")

There are two types of animal dealers licensed by the USDA:

- ***"Class A" Dealers***—These are people who breed and raise animals to sell to retail pet stores, research institutions, and to other animal dealers.
- ***"Class B" Dealers***—People in this category obtain dogs and/or cats from a variety of sources (sometimes referred to as "random source" animals), some of them legal and some of them no doubt illegal.

Who's Buying?

According to Last Chance for Animals, in their "Pet Theft Report" to Congress, "Dogs sell from $150 to $700 and cats from $50 to $200. Documentation exists which reveals dealers are literally making millions of dollars by selling their random source animals to research facilities."

Research facilities are not the only customers for stolen pets. There are many eager buyers out there who use animals for a variety of purposes. According to *Pet Theft What You Can Do* published by In Defense of Animals (**www.idausa.org**), "Dogs and cats are sold to many different clients for many uses, including dog-fighting rings as fighters or as bait." They are also sold "to puppy-mills, for breeding, as meat for human consumption, as prey for exotic animals, as fur for clothing or accessories, as protective guard dogs, or for cult rituals. The most consistent and highest-paying client, however, is often the research industry."

Isn't Anybody Watching?

The job of overseeing animal dealers and research facilities falls to the Animal and Plant Health Inspection Service (APHIS) of the United States Department of Agriculture. APHIS is in charge of inspecting facilities, investigating reports of noncompliance, levying fines, and has the power to suspend or even revoke the licenses of dealers and research facilities that violate the law. This oversight process is rarely initiated, however, and can take years to complete.

According to an article written by Janice Sparhawk Gardner that appeared in the February 2000 issue of *Dog World* magazine, "Despite these negatives, there have been improvements." She points out that "around 1980,…rodents were discovered to be much more susceptible to toxins that affected humans, so the use of dogs and cats in these tests was practically eliminated." She points out that a combination of rule amendments and scientific breakthroughs have drastically reduced the demand for animals in many types of research that had previously relied on them. Another positive which she points to is the fact that "new licensing and grant procedures have compelled many labs to check for tattoos or microchips and make attempts to get an identified animal back to its owners." She adds, "Experts in enforcement and in humane organizations…claim the purposeful and organized theft of pets for ultimate use in education (surgery and anatomy) or in research is enormously diminished from even three years ago."

The federal government has shut down some pet theft rings, but so much more needs to be done. We suggest you write to your senators and representatives, and insist that more money be allocated for enforcement of federal regulations and for investigations, and that violators be vigorously prosecuted. You can add your voice to those of others by supporting such groups as In Defense of Animals and Last Chance for Animals. It is worth repeating that the prospects of recovering a stolen pet are not very good. The best advice we can offer is prevention, prevention, prevention.

Mishaps

Sometimes pets aren't really lost. In fact, they simply may be hiding in a box or napping in a pile of clothing, as cats and other small animals love to do. Or it may be that your pet is trapped or injured somewhere nearby. This is why it is important to do your best to eliminate the possibility of a mishap. Your pet could die while you are out searching for it, and all the time it was right beneath your feet. (See figure 34.) Become aware of the things that could go wrong.

Knowing about Mishaps Can be Crucial

Time is always an important factor in recovering a lost pet. In the case of mishaps, it is even more important. For our feathered friends, a mishap could easily spell disaster. Some

---

Nelly's Story

A two-year-old Golden Retriever, Nelly, disappeared from her owner's 11,000-acre ranch in Texas. After a thorough search of the area was conducted, not a trace of Nelly could be found. The next day the distraught owner contacted Chad Harris's Bloodhound Pet Investigations Pet Search and Rescue, which uses bloodhounds to investigate lost or missing pets.

Mr. Harris arrived just a couple of days after Nelly was discovered missing. Like any good investigator, he started asking questions. Two and two was not making four. If Nelly had run away, Fred (the stray who had shown up a few days earlier), would almost certainly have gone with her. Chad's first thought was that someone "had picked her up in the parking lot while they were in the meeting, thinking she was a stray."

While they were discussing the disappearance, a repairman arrived and began working on the cable which had gone out on Thursday. Chad had barely begun his investigation when the cable guy crawled backward from under the deck and said, "There's a dog under there!" Nelly was right under their feet the whole time, tangled in the cable wire. The circulation to her hind leg had been cut off and she was wounded, but alive. She had been trapped for 48 hours and never made so much as a peep. If it had been much longer, Nelly might have lost her leg.

This story is a perfect example of a mishap that could have been avoided had the owner surveyed the area around his home with the possibility of mishaps in mind. He could then have identified this potential danger area, and eliminated it by simply blocking access to underneath the deck. This story also clearly illustrates why time can be critical when it comes to mishaps.

FIGURE 34

birds have a very high metabolism and can literally starve to death in 24 hours! Your pet may be stuck in a heating vent, or someone may have inadvertently closed it in the dryer. Parakeets have been known to crawl inside a paper towel roll, get tangled in the drapes, or get stuck inside a vase.

The possibility of a mishap is the very reason why, when trying to recover a lost pet, you should always search your home and property first, unless you actually saw your pet take off running or flying down the street.

Survey Your Home and Property

Take a careful look around your house. Try to spot as many potential pet hazards as you can. Think of the many ways and unusual places where your pet could hide or get trapped. Make a list of what you see, and begin to eliminate these potential hazards. Each property is unique, so only you can determine what dangers are present in your home. Here are a few tips for mishap-proofing your home:

Inside

- Seal off access to all crawl spaces.
- Check behind sinks. The openings in the wall made to accommodate the pipes are often cut too large, leaving a space large enough for a small pet to crawl into and get trapped behind the sheet rock wall. Caulk, fill, or otherwise seal any holes.
- Keep cabinets, doors, and closets closed at all times.
- Be mindful of odd ways that pets can be "lost," and take extra precaution when you have visitors. I recently read of a ferret inadvertently being taken home by a visitor in a shopping bag.
- Post little pet reminders on appliances—something like STOP! CHECK FOR PETS!
- Keep the toilet lid down.
- Don't leave standing water unattended in sinks or tubs. Soap bubbles are particularly dangerous. A bird trying to land on the bubbles can easily drown.
- Fill empty vases, beer steins, and other ornamental knickknacks with sand to prevent birds and other small animals from sliding in and being unable to get back out.
- Block your pet's access to the insides of appliances, and check them all carefully

Poison-Proof Your House and Garage

For advice on poison-proofing your home, visit the American Society for the Prevention of Cruelty to Animals' National Animal Poison Control Center web site at **www.napcc.aspca.org** and click on the "Virtual Tour" link. If your pet has ingested a toxic substance, call NAPCC at 888-4ANI-HELP (888-426-4435). There is a fee for this service. Ferret owners should visit **www.ferretsfirst.com** for an extensive list of plants that are poisonous to ferrets. (See "Resources/Additional Resources.")

before turning them on. And check laundry before tossing it in the washing machine. Small animals, such as ferrets, like to curl up and sleep in piles of clothes.

- Use strips of wood to prevent pets from crawling underneath or behind appliances. Older appliances, especially refrigerators with open motors, are particularly dangerous.

- Make sure you keep all windows closed that do not have screens.

- Keep window screens secured. Check them regularly. If you have a ferret, be aware that standard metal screening is no match for your pet's teeth and claws. Use heavy-duty hardware cloth to cover screens.

- Sew the hems of curtains and draperies shut or use a safety pin. They often have open spaces where birds can get caught.

- Always dispose of cardboard paper towel rolls when finished. They are hazardous to small birds.

- Fill and caulk all holes along baseboards: even a hole the size of a quarter is large enough for some critters such as mice, gerbils, etc., to crawl through.

> **CatFinder**
>
> Here's a unique product for locating a pet in the home. While marketed to cat owners, it can be used for any pet. A tiny receiver attaches to your pet's collar. If your cat, small dog, or ferret were to be trapped somewhere in your home, all you have to do is click and hold the transmitter for a few seconds, and listen for the beeping sound. This can save a lot of time and unnecessary searching.
>
> This product is available online at **www.housecat.com**. Simply search for the product by name, CatFinder. (See "Resources/ID Tags.")

Outside

- Keep shed and garage doors closed at all times.

- Keep garbage can lids on securely.

- Eliminate yard junk (building materials, spare parts, etc.) where your pet can be trapped.

- Seal off access to the areas beneath the house, decks, and porches.

- Seal drainage pipes with hardware cloth to keep pets out, yet still allow water to flow freely.

- Always try to be present when someone will be doing repairs at your home. If you can't be there, be mindful to check that no crawl spaces are left open.

Some types of pets are at much higher risk of mishaps than of escaping. It's hard to imagine your pet mouse getting very far; the fact is that most small critters that are lost are victims of mishaps right in the home. Ferrets, unless picked up and carried, rarely go more than a house or two away. They are more likely to be trapped, injured, poisoned, or accosted by a neighbor's dog than to run away. Educating everybody in the family is the key to preventing the loss of these critters. (See "Prevention: Ferrets and Other Critters.")

There are probably hundreds of ways your pet could fall victim to a mishap in and around your home. The above lists are admittedly incomplete, but they are a good place to start. Only you can assess what dangers are present where you live. Because your pet may be trapped or injured, remember to search your own home and property first.

Holidays and Parties

For many people, their pets are full-fledged family members. And when holidays and celebrations roll around, it is only natural to want to include pets in the festivities. When it comes to pet loss, however, holidays can be an extremely hazardous time.

According to Pat Miller in a May 1999 article in *The Whole Pet Journal*, "January 1st and July 5th are universally reported to be the busiest days for animal shelters." It is no coincidence that these two days directly follow the two loudest and most intoxicating holidays of the calendar year. For many people, alcohol is simply part of the celebration. Even people who do not normally drink may have a little glass of holiday cheer when December 31st rolls around. Alcohol, however, can make people less attentive to things like latching the gate or closing the door behind them.

Also, the increased numbers of people coming and going, and doors opening and closing, quickly create many more opportunities for your pet to escape. It's likely that there will also be several nieces, nephews, and cousins all running around playing games with your children. Understandably, the last thing they will be thinking of is pet loss.

There also may be more strangers—company, drop-in visitors, mail carriers, delivery people, etc.—in and around your house during holiday times. Depending upon your pet's comfort level, they can make your pet anxious, and an anxious pet is a pet at risk of flight.

Special holiday celebrations can create especially dangerous situations for your pets. Independence Day fireworks probably top the list. The noise of fireworks exploding every few minutes can frighten the mellowest of pets. And what's a party without music? (Your pet would probably say that it would make for a better party!) Loud music can frighten your animals, and the general party atmosphere can make the whole scene appear to your pet as horrifying chaos.

Making Festive Times Safer for Your Pets

With a little planning and a good dose of vigilance, you and your pet can both enjoy the festivities. Here are a few tips on how to make your holidays and parties safer for your pets.

Prepare a Safe Room

Set aside a room where your pet can go to get away. (This will be useful in many other situations where you need to confine your pet, such as during a disaster or on moving day.) Your pet should associate this space with something pleasant; it should never be used as punishment. Your pet's safe room should have something such as soothing music to mask the party sounds, bedding, food and fresh water, and several of your pet's favorite toys. If you are having people over for a holiday party, be especially sensitive to your pet's anxiety level. If you notice your pet acting nervously, then don't hesitate to use the safe room. Make sure you pay several visits to comfort and reassure your pet.

Another approach is to use desensitization training. Sound-effect tapes that mimic fireworks, thunder, or almost any sound that might frighten pets are one method used by trainers to recondition pets that are frightened by loud noises. Even so, we recommend the use of the safe room as your best and most loving tactic. Whatever you do, do not take your pet to see the fireworks display!

Some Additional Ways to Protect Your Pet

- *Use Proper Identification*—How many times have we said this already? There's a reason we keep repeating it. It's one of the best ways to protect your pet. Use proper and multiple forms of identification.

- *Designate a Sober Person*—If there will be drinking at your party or holiday festivities, designate one sober person who can be responsible for taking over if pet loss does occur (and who can drive people to their homes, if needed).

- *Inform Your Guests*—Let your guests know that you have pets, and tell them about the safe room that is off-limits. Also, place a sign on the door to remind them. If your pet will be present at the festivities, regularly remind people to close doors behind them, to latch the gate, and to not open windows.

- *Post Colorful Signs*—Place notices around the house as reminders to people about your pet's needs. This may seem paranoid; however, the danger is real, and you need to do everything you can to protect your animals. A year-round notice on your front door is also a good idea. The Humane Society of the United States cautions pet owners, when posting permanent notices, to use the static-cling type or handwritten ones, for good reason. Emergency personnel, such as firefighters, are hesitant to attempt to rescue animals listed on permanent stickers, because too often previous tenants leave the stickers behind and the pets are no longer in the home.

- *Keep Your Dog Safe at Home*—Do not take your dog to fireworks displays. They always take place after dark, with hundreds and sometimes thousands of people in attendance, many from far away. If your dog was lost under these circumstances, it could be tragic. Also, your dog could be picked up and taken far away, perhaps to another state, and you might never see it again.

Halloween Hazards

Halloween can be a particularly dangerous time. Here are some common Halloween hazards along with some tips to keep your pet safe:

- *Trick or Treaters*—Put yourself in your pet's place, and try to imagine what your pet must think when halfway through what had been an ordinary day, the doorbell suddenly begins ringing every five minutes. Then when the door is opened, groups of children in scary masks and costumes all begin shouting, "Trick or Treat!" This is a recipe for disaster: frequently opening doors, children in costumes, noise, and confusion—all these combined can easily induce a fright-to-flight response. Be kind to your pets, and put them in their safe room with music playing to mask the sounds of Halloween.

Mischief Night

When people are out and up to mischief, it is a very dangerous time for pets. You now know enough not to allow your pets to roam freely. But even if you have an outside enclosure or kennel, don't use it on Halloween. Keep your pets indoors.

- *Animal Abuse*—In the weeks leading up to Halloween, there is always a marked increase in reports of animal abuse (especially abuse of cats, and black cats in particular). Some have suggested satanic cults are responsible. However, whether it's cultists, wild teenagers, pranksters, or just plain sadists, your pet could become the target of an abuser. So real is this danger, that many shelters and pet stores refuse to adopt out or sell black cats around Halloween. Keep your pet in the house, and do not allow it outside.

Statistically, holidays are a very hazardous time for pets. If, however, certain precautions are taken, both you and your pet can enjoy the festivities with assurance. Remember, your pet's safety is your responsibility, not that of your guests. If you want to have your pet join in the festivities, take every precaution to ensure your pet's safety and comfort. The Dumb Friends League has produced several terrific articles on keeping pets safe during the holidays. (See figure 35.)

┌───┐
│   │
│ ***Holiday Safety Tips from the Dumb Friends League***   │
│   │
│   For additional tips on keeping your pets safe during holidays, visit   │
│ the League's web site at **www.ddfl.org**. The answers to most of your   │
│ questions can be found there. If you don't have Internet access, call   │
│ or write to request printed materials. (See "Resources/Humane   │
│ Organizations.")   │
│   • *Holiday Hazards: Keeping Your Pet Safe this Holiday Season*   │
│   • *Keep Your Pet Safe on Halloween*   │
│   • *Keep Your Pet Safe on the Fourth of July*   │
│   • *Helping Your Dog Overcome the Fear of Thunder and Other Startling Noises* │
│   │
└───┘

FIGURE 35

Disasters

As you've learned throughout this book, being prepared and being informed are the keys to lost pet prevention and recovery. At no time is that more true than before, during, and after a disaster.

There is much valuable information that has already been published on this topic. Information for pet owners is available through books, government agencies—the Federal Emergency Management Agency (FEMA), for example—and various humane organizations involved in disaster rescue and relief. We will focus on disasters as they relate to preventing and preparing for pet loss.

Billions of dollars and untold hours are expended annually to both avert and prepare for disasters. Governments at the national, regional, and city level set aside resources for preventing and preparing for disasters, from the designing of roads and bridges, to enforcing building codes that prevent or minimize loss of life and damage to property in the event of a fire, flood, or earthquake. Until quite recently, however, pets and other animals were an afterthought when it came to disaster preparation.

Media coverage about the plight of pets following several recent disasters has finally prompted communities all over the United States to begin including pets in their disaster planning. When Hurricane Andrew plowed through the state of Florida in 1992, killing, injuring, and displacing many thousands of pets, it was a real wake-up call. Soon, communities across the country were finally beginning to incorporate into their disaster plans the importance of animals.

Pet Disaster Relief and Rescue Organizations

While many communities still have not established disaster plans for evacuating animals, the good thing for both pets and their owners is that several private emergency pet rescue organizations do exist. These groups advise community leaders, and educate the public about animal disaster preparation. They also help set up temporary shelters and veterinary facilities in the event of a disaster, and even go door-to-door if necessary to evacuate pets. In November 2000, the Federal Emergency Management Agency (FEMA) signed an agreement with The Humane Society of the United States. The partnership is part of FEMA's new Project Impact program, in which HSUS will provide both technical expertise and assistance in helping communities to develop disaster plans that include both companion and farm animals.

Alliances among various humane organizations are common. The American Humane Association (AHA) has actually been rescuing animals since the First World War. Founded in 1917, the AHA's disaster relief program is called Emergency Animal Relief (EAR). More recently, the AHA has teamed up with Animal Planet to form Animal Planet Rescue, in order to prevent a lack of supplies and resources during a disaster. (See figure 36.) Emergency Animal Rescue Services, better known as EARS, is part of United Animal Nations, founded by Terri Crisp, author of *Out of Harm's Way: The Extraordinary True Story of One Woman's Lifelong Devotion to Animal Rescue*. Together, these groups provide preparedness workshops to train volunteers, who can then respond in an emergency by working with government and animal welfare agencies to assist communities during major disasters. If you'd like more information, all of these organizations provide literature for disaster planning and preparation for companion and other animals. There is even a group (Ferret Friends Disaster Response International) that specializes in disaster preparation for ferrets. (See "Resources/Disasters.")

Keys to Survival

From hurricanes to chemical spills, disasters can strike suddenly and with little warning. While it is impossible to come up with a single plan that will cover all emergencies, here are some basic steps you can take to improve the chances that you and your pet will survive unscathed:

Animal Planet Rescue (APR)

"The aim of APR is to rescue animals during times of disaster, and to provide information to the public about how to protect animals before, during and after a disaster strikes. The 80-foot long Animal Planet Rescue vehicle is equipped with the necessary items to provide emergency animal care during disasters, and can house 12 rescue personnel as well as carry 40 tons of equipment.

"The truck is also a mobile veterinary clinic and comes equipped with a 4-wheel-drive Chevy Blazer, as well as rescue rafts. The command center is equipped with fax machines, cellular phones, computers, and satellite mapping technology. It is capable of holding 300 gallons of potable water as well as a portable corral for temporary care of livestock and horses."

FIGURE 36

- **Prepare**—More than any other situation we've discussed, disasters demonstrate the absolutely crucial need for preparedness. Preparedness can make a chaotic situation much less stressful, and thus minimize the risk to your pet in the event of a disaster.

- **Remain Calm**—Animals are extraordinarily perceptive. They can instantly read your emotions, and panicking will only make a dangerous situation that much more perilous for both you and your pet.

- **Confine Your Pet**—If you have some advance warning, place your pet in a closed room or in its carrier while you prepare to evacuate. Many people believe that animals have a sort of sixth sense about disasters, and some say that increased numbers of lost pet reports are a predictor of earthquakes. Regardless, don't take any chances. Confine your pet.

- **Don't Wait, Evacuate**—The Humane Society of the United States cautions pet owners: "Don't wait until the last minute to evacuate if you have pets. Once the disaster is imminent, if the only way out is by official rescue transport, emergency officials may not allow you to take your pets when they bring you out."

- **Provide Proper and Multiple Forms of Identification**—Proper identification will enable rescue workers to reunite you with your pet in the event you get separated.

- **Don't Leave Your Pets Behind**—Hopefully, you will have some advance warning and, barring risk to your physical safety and the safety of your family, you will be able to do everything in your power to bring your pet with you if you are forced to evacuate. The more prepared you are, the less likely it is that you will ever have to make the awful decision to leave your pet behind. One way to prepare is to sign up with the Emergency Email Network's e-mail notification service at **www.emergencyemailnetwork.com**. They will notify you in the event of an impending emergency such as severe weather. Unfortunately, some disasters give little warning. (See "If You Have to Leave Your Pets Behind" below.)

- **Have a Plan**—Or better yet, have three. In his book *Operation Pet Rescue*, Gregory N. Zompolis suggests you have three plans: a 5-minute plan, a 15-minute plan, and a 45-minute plan. This is because some disasters, such as hurricanes, normally give you quite a bit of time to prepare. Other emergencies, however, are more sudden. He also suggests that you write out your evacuation plan in big bold letters, which will allow you to read it easily with a flashlight or candle.

Help for Those with Disabilities and Their Service Animals

The Independent Living Resource Center of San Francisco, in cooperation with the American Red Cross, has produced a series of tip sheets for people with disabilities and their service animals to improve their emergency preparedness in an earthquake. Copies of these tip sheets (four in all) can be requested free of charge by sending a self-addressed, stamped envelope to the Independent Living Resource Center San Francisco, 649 Mission Street, San Francisco, CA 94105. For more information, e-mail Herb Levine at **herb@ilrcsf.org**. (See "Resources/Disasters.")

Basic Pet Survival Kit

Here are some items that could prove vital in caring for your pet during a disaster:

- *Pet Records*—Keep a copy of your pet's records accessible and sealed in a watertight plastic bag. Keep another copy at a safe location away from home (e.g., with a friend or family member, or in a safe deposit box).

- *Photographs*—Photographs can be particularly useful in disaster situations. Your pet's photos will aid rescue personnel in identifying your pet.

- *Phone Numbers*—Make a list of the following numbers: local animal shelters; your veterinarian as well as an alternate veterinarian; animal hospitals; animal rescue groups; humane organizations, especially those involved in disaster relief; state, county, and municipal governments; disaster relief organizations such as the Red Cross, FEMA, etc. (See "Critical Contacts.")

- *Information on Pet Friendly Lodging*—Most emergency shelters will not accept pets other than assistance animals for people with disabilities. Therefore, it's important to compile a list of names, numbers, and addresses of pet friendly hotels, motels, etc., where you could evacuate to, if necessary. It's best to leave nothing to chance. Contact them, and find out their pet policies before disaster strikes. The American Automobile Association publishes a book with thousands of listings, and you can easily locate and make reservations for pet friendly lodging on the Internet. (See "Resources/Traveling With Pets.")

- *Collars, Leashes, and Harnesses*—Carry spare collars, leashes, and harnesses for each of your pets so that you can keep them safely under control when moving them.

- *Animal Carrier*—Carriers are useful in many situations where your pet needs to be confined. In the event of a disaster, a carrier is indispensable. Buy a pet carrier that allows your pet to stand up and turn around inside. Train your pet to become comfortable with the carrier. Since carriers are multipurpose, purchase a USDA-approved carrier that you could use if you were to fly with your pet. Purchase a spare travel cage for birds. (See "Transporting Your Pet.")

- *Food and Water*—At a minimum, keep a week's supply of food and potable water for your pet. Have both dry and canned pet food. Store pellets and seed foods in a cool, dry place and keep water in sanitized, non-breakable containers. Remember to replenish these supplies, as needed, with fresh food and water.

Additional Tips

- *Pet Partnerships*—Having a friend or neighbor who can help out is always a good idea; in a disaster situation, it can be crucial. (See "Pet Partners.")

- *Boarding*—If you have advance warning, consider boarding your pet at a kennel, your veterinarian's office, or with friends or relatives as long as they, too, aren't in the evacuation area. Nearly all boarding facilities will require proof of current rabies vaccinations, and may have several other vaccination requirements. (See "Pet Record Keeping.")

Survival Tips for Birds and Other Pets from The Humane Society of the United States and the American Red Cross

Caring for Birds in an Emergency

Birds should be transported in a secure travel cage or carrier. In cold weather, wrap a blanket over the carrier and warm up the car before placing birds inside. During warm weather, carry a plant mister to mist the birds' feathers periodically. Do not put water inside the carrier during transport. Provide a few slices of fresh fruit and vegetables with high water content. Have a photo for identification and leg bands. If the carrier does not have a perch, line it with paper towels and change them frequently. Try to keep the carrier in a quiet area. Do not let the birds out of the cage or carrier.

Reptiles

Snakes can be transported in a pillowcase, but they must be transferred to more secure housing when they reach the evacuation site. If your snakes require frequent feedings, carry food with you. Take a water bowl large enough for soaking, as well as a heating pad. When transporting house lizards, follow the same directions as for birds.

Pocket Pets

Small mammals (hamsters, gerbils, etc.) should be transported in secure carriers suitable for maintaining the animals while sheltered. Take bedding materials, food bowls, and water bottles.

This entire brochure ("Pets and Disasters: Get Prepared") can be obtained free of charge by sending a business-size, self-addressed, stamped envelope to HSUS Disaster Services, 2100 L St. NW, Washington, DC 20037.

For in-depth, expert assistance, community planners and animal care professionals may contact The HSUS's Disaster Services Program, 2100 L St., NW, Washington, DC 20037; Phone: (Disaster Services) (301) 258-3103 or (301) 258-3063, e-mail: disaster@hsus.org.

Reprinted with permission from The Humane Society of the United States and the American Red Cross.

- ***Outside Kennels and Enclosures***—It's generally not a good idea to put your pet in an outside kennel or enclosure during a disaster situation, especially in a serious storm (unless your house itself is not safe), as falling debris could injure your pet. This is why it's important, when constructing outside kennels or enclosures, that you build them in clear areas, away from tree limbs and power lines. Also, have on hand a heavy-duty wire cutter, in case something were to fall and trap your pet inside the enclosure.

- ***Regular Reassurance***—Remember that your pet is frightened and anxious. Talk to it frequently in an upbeat, confident voice during the chaos. Try distracting your pet with a toy or its favorite game.

- ***Keep Cats and Dogs Separated***—Even if they're the friendliest of playmates, keep your cats and dogs separated during the emergency.

- ***Safe Place***—While waiting to evacuate, keep your pets confined to a carrier or to a room away from windows, wall units, hanging plants, etc. In some instances, a ground floor bathroom is a good location since the walls are reinforced with plumbing, although a ground floor bathroom may become flooded during a hurricane. These are the types of decisions you need to make on a case-by-case basis.

So You're Not Going to Evacuate?

Not all disasters require evacuations. In other situations, people are just plain stubborn and refuse to evacuate, believing that they've ridden out a thousand storms and they'll ride this one out, too. This is foolhardy in more ways than one. If the situation worsens, these folks may be forced to evacuate, and they might not be permitted to take their animals with them at the eleventh hour. We strongly urge that if the call goes out to evacuate, leave with your pets while it's still safe.

If You Have to Leave Your Pets Behind

The unfortunate reality is that there could be a situation where you may be forced to evacuate and leave your pets behind. Here are some vitally important steps to take to keep your animals safe until you can be reunited:

- Set up separate locations if you have different types of pets (dogs, cats, birds, etc.).

- Leave familiar items to comfort your pet, such as the pet's normal bedding and favorite toys.

- Leave enough dry food for at least three or four days (not moistened food, as it can quickly turn rancid). Young puppies may overeat and become sick. If you know a brand that your pup is *not* particularly fond of, use this.

- Purchase a no-spill container for water. If you use a bathroom with a tub, open the cold faucet slightly to allow your pet to drink, but make sure the drain is clear so the water will drain out to keep your pet from accidentally drowning. If you have a large dog, you can partially fill the tub.

- Post a picture of your pet along with a note alerting rescue workers to your pet's location in your house. Be sure to include contact numbers where rescue workers can reach you.

Rescuers Help Reunite Animal Disaster Victims With Families Following Tornadoes

May 7, 1999

MOORE, Oklahoma—A small black poodle walked happily out of the Moore Animal Shelter this morning with his owner, an elderly man who was separated from his companion during the tornadoes and who had been desperately searching for him ever since. Not long afterwards, a boy and his father showed up looking for their three dogs and the reunion between the boy, who was sporting some cuts and bruises from his bout with the tornadoes, and his three Rottweilers, brought tears to the eyes of animal rescuers.

With an unknown number of dogs and cats separated from their families earlier this week when tornadoes hit the Oklahoma City area, many families are now desperately searching for their beloved companions. At the animal shelter in Moore, a suburb south of Oklahoma City that was hit hard by the tornadoes, volunteers with the Emergency Animal Rescue Service, a national disaster response team, are helping rescue any dogs and cats still wandering in the streets and are bringing these animals to the shelter for care and comfort. The animals also are photographed and information is entered into a binder for those looking for lost pets.

EARS volunteers also have visited all local veterinarians in the area and have photographed the injured animals now housed at the clinics. This system has helped several families track down their dogs and cats, including a young boy who found a photo of his Basset Hound in the binder.

EARS Director Terri Crisp, a veteran of more than 45 disasters, said the heartwarming reunions are the best reward for animal rescuers who have seen so many animals left unclaimed following a disaster. "Our goal is to reunite as many as possible of these animals with their families," said Crisp. "The people and the animals have gone through so much in this disaster and they need each other. For some, it's all they have left."

For more rescue stories or for more information on EARS visit the United Animal Nations' web site at **www.uan.org.**

• Birds must eat daily to survive. The Federal Emergency Management Agency recommends talking "with your veterinarian or local pet store about special food dispensers that regulate the amount of food a bird is given. Make sure that the bird is caged and the cage is covered by a thin cloth or sheet to provide security and filtered light." It's also a good idea to leave several seed or treat sticks.

After the Disaster is Over

In many situations, you won't be permitted to return home right away, not until the disaster area is deemed safe. After you are allowed back in, you might find your pet missing. Don't panic. There is a good chance it was evacuated by rescue personnel. Check with emergency operation leaders first, and then follow the normal recovery procedures outlined in this book, as closely as the situation allows.

Two messages of encouragement: One, never assume the worst. An animal's survival instinct is extremely strong, and you may be happily surprised. Two, don't give up hope. It may take a long period of time to find your pet. Following the October 1991 firestorm in Oakland, California, for example, pet owners were still being reunited with their pets in the early months of 1993.

Home Sweet Home

Once you and your pets have made it safely back home, there are still a few simple things you should do to make sure everything goes smoothly and safely:

• Inspect your house to make certain it's free of hazards and that it's safe to keep your pet indoors.

• Even if your yard is fenced in, don't let pets off-leash right away. You want to make sure it's safe, and you want to allow your pet time to reacquaint itself with its environment, which may look quite different (trees might have been damaged, power lines may still be down, familiar scents may have changed, etc.). There also may be a danger of contaminated water or wild animals that have sought refuge in your yard.

• Outside kennels, cat enclosures, and aviaries should be examined thoroughly to be sure they are safe and secure.

• Get things back to normal as quickly as possible, as pets are comforted by familiar surroundings. Play your pet's favorite game and its favorite music (this is especially comforting for birds), and give your pet a sense that everything is okay.

• Exercise extreme caution if you come upon a stray animal. It may be frightened, confused, or otherwise traumatized by the events and could bite or scratch. It is probably best not to try to capture it. Call your local animal control since they are expert at capturing stray animals and have the proper equipment.

Prevention: Birds

Keep Your Bird Safe—Clip Its Wings!

Nearly every bird that has turned up missing was able to escape because its owner failed to keep its wings clipped. Flight feathers often grow back unnoticed, which is why a regular clipping schedule is so important. Not only is clipping safe and humane, it's by far the most effective method of bird loss prevention. If your bird can't fly, it won't get very far. It's not always a matter of escape either. Many birds have been seriously injured or killed by flying into ceiling fans and windows.

Clipping wings is a relatively easy and pain-free procedure that bird owners can learn to do themselves. (See figure 37.) Yet many people still put it off or forego clipping altogether, and as a result, many thousands of birds escape every year. Sadly, most are never recovered, instead falling prey to wild birds and other animals, succumbing to the elements, or being kept by those who find them.

Wing Clipping Tips

Planned Parrothood operates one of the finest sites on the entire Internet for all things concerning birds. You'll find many helpful links from "Stolen Birds/Lost and Found" to "Ask the Vets" where you can submit non-emergency questions that will be answered by an avian veterinarian; visit them at **www.plannedparrothood.com**.

Here is some helpful advice from Planned Parrothood on the subject of wing clipping:

"The best way to learn to clip wings is to watch someone do it for the first time. Before clipping any bird's wings, each wing must be lifted to examine for 'blood feathers.' These are new feathers that are coming in that still have a supply of blood through the shaft. If they are cut, profuse bleeding can occur. Cornstarch or flour can stop a broken feather from bleeding, but the safest measure is to firmly grab the feather as close to the skin as possible and pull it out. You should then squeeze the skin shut and put some pressure on it for a minute until all bleeding stops. Generally, the first ten primary feathers on both wings are cut back (i.e., to the bend in the wing). Cockatiels may need extra feathers clipped, as they can get good lift with an insufficient wing clip. NEVER leave one or more feathers for 'show clips.' Without the other feathers to protect them, they are very vulnerable to being broken. Never clip up underneath the secondary tier of feathers. You will permanently damage the feather follicle. Clip both wings evenly."

FIGURE 37

Check your bird's wings frequently. Because clipped wing feathers grow back gradually, your bird may not give you any indication that it has regained its flying ability. And even clipped birds can, in the right wind, be carried many hundreds of yards away.

Why the Reluctance?

- *Fear*—Some people are simply afraid to do it themselves. No problem, as long as they have it done by a veterinarian or bird professional on a regular basis.

- *Lack of Research*—Many people get birds without investigating all the care and maintenance that is involved with responsible bird ownership.

- *Philosophical Opposition*—There are those who believe all birds are meant to fly, without fully considering the dangers that face free-flying pet birds.

More Bird Safety Tips

- Did we mention this? CLIP WINGS! CLIP WINGS! CLIP WINGS!

- Check regularly for new primary flight feathers.

- Do not allow your bird to fly freely in the house.

- Do not take birds outside unless they are caged. That is the advice that *Bird Talk* magazine regularly gives its readers. They do, however, acknowledge that many people do take their birds outside and do so responsibly. However, they always caution bird owners about the dangers (e.g., predators, disease, etc.). There have been many instances of pet birds being attacked by wild birds even with their owners standing right next to them.

- Do not take your unclipped bird outside on your shoulder. Even if its wings are clipped, hold on to it carefully with your fingers or better yet, use a bird harness. Bird harnesses are available in pet magazines or can be purchased online at **www.petsmart.com**, under the brand name Feather Tether Bird Harness, or at **www.flightquarters.com** and **www.fredbird.net.**

- Keep cage doors securely fastened. Birds, especially parrots, are expert at figuring out how to open cage doors. Consider this prior to purchasing a cage. Leash snaps are very good for keeping cage doors secured. Our editor has an African Grey parrot who has even figured out how to open leash snaps!

- Theft is a real concern. Do not leave your bird in a window facing the street where it might attract the attention of a thief. Also, use a good lock for your cage, and secure it to some solid structure. (See "Stolen Pets.")

- Use extra caution when changing the catch pans, slide-out trays, external feeders, and water dispensers in your pet's cage, as birds can slip through the openings.

- Check screens regularly to make certain they're securely fastened and free of holes.

- Do not rely on venetian blinds in front of an open window to keep your bird from escaping.

- If the doorbell rings while your bird is out of its cage, put it back before opening the door.

- Monitor the activities of children and friends around your bird.

- If possible, teach your bird to say its address and phone number.

- Teach your bird an unusual trick as one more way of proving the bird is yours.

- Train your bird to come when you call.

- Make tape recordings of your bird's own call (and its mate's call, if it has a mate) to attract it if it does get loose outside.

Plan Ahead—Have These Items on Hand

- Color photos of your bird.

- A travel cage for recapture. If you take the time to familiarize your bird with his travel cage, you'll have a far better chance of coaxing him into the cage after you've found him.

- A tall ladder for high trees and a shorter one for roofs and hedges. If your bird is resting on a power line, DO NOT attempt the rescue yourself. Call the police or fire department.

- A net with a very long handle. These can be found in pet magazines and catalogs or purchased online at **www.pythonproducts.com**.

- Gloves, binoculars, and a flashlight.

- Keep a spare pillowcase beneath your bird's cage. This can be used for transporting your bird after it is found and could prove critical in an emergency where you have to evacuate quickly (in a fire, for example).

- A list of bird clubs in your area (many bird lovers keep feeders and might see your bird in their yard). You may also be able to enlist some allies among club members.

- A list of the phone numbers and/or addresses of veterinarians (especially if they specialize in avian care), animal hospitals, and emergency clinics in your area. (See figure 38.) Other important numbers include pet stores, bird jungles, and rescue groups in your area. There are also the web sites **www.plannedparrothood.com** and **www.birdhotline.com,** for posting lost bird advertisements, that have had

Locating a Bird Vet near You

You can easily locate a listing of avian veterinarians in your area by visiting the Association of Avian Veterinarians' web site at **www.aav.org** and searching by zip code. Compile a list of avian vets in your area ahead of time, since if someone finds your lost bird and they try to keep it, there is a good chance they will eventually take it to an avian veterinarian.

FIGURE 38

some great success stories. (See "Critical Contacts.")

Bird Identification Options

- *Microchip Implants*—We strongly urge you to take advantage of this technology. More and more veterinarians and animal shelters have the scanning devices necessary to detect a microchip.

- *Leg Bands*—Bird bands are important and can prove ownership. Write down the numbers, and keep them with your pet records. Unfortunately, there is no national identification registry for leg bands that we are aware of. A leg band can be traced to a breeder or, if the bird was imported, to a quarantine facility. From a leg band, you can even determine the date the bird was hatched. But because birds may change hands many times before they are ultimately sold, a band will not necessarily lead the finder of your lost bird to you. Another drawback to leg bands is that a bird may outgrow its band.

- *DNA*—DNA, as an ID method, will not help a finder of your lost bird to locate you. If, however, someone else tries to lay claim to your lost bird and refuses to return it, or if your bird is ever stolen, having a record of your bird's DNA profile is proof positive that the bird belongs to you; proof that will stand up in court. (See "DNA.")

The Story of "Pepe the Gambler"

Birds are particularly susceptible to mishaps, those unforeseen events that by their very nature are unpredictable. You can minimize the risk of mishaps by surveying your home and identifying and eliminating potential hazards. (See "Mishaps.")

Donna Eaker of California shared her mishap story (which fortunately had a happy ending) in the January 1999 issue of *Bird Talk* magazine. Donna owned several slot machines, which she kept directly across from her bird's cage. Her maroon-bellied conure named Pepe had always shown a keen interest in the machines, bobbing, screaming, and trying every conceivable way to get to them any time someone would play them.

One day while she was vacuuming, Donna moved Pepe's cage up against one of the slot machines. This was the opportunity that this extremely curious bird had been waiting for, and Pepe wasted no time exploring the machine that had fascinated him for so long. An hour and a half passed before Donna realized that Pepe was no longer on top of his cage.

A 45-minute search ensued, but to no avail. It was then that faint scratching sounds were heard coming from the area of the slot machines. Apparently, Pepe had managed to crawl up the shoot where the coins are released and had gotten himself trapped inside the machine. Even though she had the key to the machine, Donna soon realized that the entire machine had to be removed from its case. It took nearly another hour and a half to rescue the bird. Fortunately, she was able to find an opening just large enough for Pepe to squeeze through. His heart was racing and he was covered with grease, but he was safe and back in Donna's arms again.

Prevention: Ferrets and Other Critters

While much of the following information is specific to ferrets, much of it can be applied to other critters as well. Pocket pets, as they are affectionately called, are lost in the home all the time and often meet with horrible ends, being squashed, burned, or swallowed up by the dog or cat. Prevention is always best, whatever your chosen pet, but it is even more so when it comes to these particularly vulnerable creatures.

In the September/October 2000 issue of *Ferrets* magazine, Troy Lynn Eckart writes, "Predictably, preventative measures are the best way to keep your ferret from getting lost. Regardless of how careful you are." She also cautions that "ferrets are very clever little animals and are always extremely curious about what lies beyond the front door."

Ferrets are very affectionate and playful. This has no doubt contributed to the fact that they've become one of the most popular pets today. According to Angela Espinet, of For Ferrets Only (**www.craftycreatures.com**), "A ferret always wants to be anywhere other than where it is at any given moment, which is why caging is essential, unless the ferret is under supervision (the kind you would give a two-year-old child)."

Ferrets are by nature very inquisitive animals. It is this curious nature that makes them susceptible to becoming lost, and they also face many dangers right in the home. Household appliances, furniture, and poisoning are just a few of the hazards faced by unsupervised ferrets in the home. This is why ferret-proofing your house is a must. (See "Mishaps.") Ferrets are also very clever creatures and are particularly adept at learning how to open the doors to their cages. They are geniuses when it comes to devising escape plans!

Ferrets are adorable creatures and make great pets, but one must be vigilant to prevent them from getting away and getting hurt. It is hard to say just how many ferrets are lost each year. One need only look at the lost pet classifieds to know it is no small number.

Some Additional Hazards Escaped Ferrets Face

- *Canine Distemper*—If your ferret escapes and is unvaccinated, or you are not sure if it is, it is at risk of contracting canine distemper from dogs, skunks, raccoons, etc. This disease is almost always fatal.

- *Deafness*—Loss of hearing is common among ferrets, which obviously puts them at particularly high risk if they ever escape, since they wouldn't be able to hear such threats as cars or predators. You can train your deaf ferret to come to you by using "light switch training" (switch the light off and on, and each time your ferret responds favorably, give it a treat and lots of praise). It is also possible to teach your deaf ferrets to respond to hand signals.

- *Heatstroke*—Although they can tolerate cold temperatures fairly well, ferrets are highly susceptible to heatstroke. Ferrets also dehydrate quickly and need to drink water as frequently as 15 times a day. These facts are important in terms of pet loss, and especially with mishaps, because if your ferret is lost or trapped somewhere, it could easily die if you do not recover it quickly.

Impulse Buying

Many people fall in love with ferrets at first sight and purchase them with little thought given to the care these creatures require. These impulse buyers quickly learn that they are ill-prepared for ferret ownership.

Many people believe ferrets to be similar to cats. While there are some common traits (ferrets and cats both being very playful, curious, and often quite independent), the similarities end there. Ferrets are more like perpetual kittens, and while most people enjoy the kitten stage, they are only too happy when it passes and their kitten mellows into a mature cat. Without doing your homework and learning all you can about their true nature and what is required in the way of proper care, purchasing any animal on a whim is a bad idea, and, quite frankly, a cruel thing to do. Loss aside, every year thousands of ferrets are turned over to ferret rescue shelters because their owners were unprepared for ferret ownership and all it entails.

Some Thoughts about Children and Pets...

We recently saw a young girl walking down the sidewalk with her friends. When we saw that she was carrying a small lizard, we told her it wasn't a good idea to carry it around like that because it could easily slip away. She simply skipped off and ignored our plea. Did her parents know about, or perhaps even permit, this irresponsible behavior?

It's debatable whether or not lizards, reptiles, and other exotics should even be kept as pets, an issue that, while important, is simply outside the scope of this book. The fact remains, however, that millions of people do keep such animals as pets. While the issue excites strong emotion on both sides, everyone agrees that any animal, once purchased as a pet, deserves to be treated humanely and to be properly cared for and loved. Unfortunately, the loss of a lizard does not excite the same emotion as the loss of a dog or cat. The attitude that some animals are more deserving of proper care and treatment simply because of their status in society is simply wrong.

Children learn by example. Your attitudes and actions about responsible pet ownership will do much to shape the thoughts and behavior of your children and their friends. With proper adult guidance, pets can be a wonderful vehicle for teaching children a respect for animals that will last a lifetime. Children without proper guidance, however, too often treat these vulnerable creatures more like toys, handling them too roughly and taking them outside to play. Children—and a lot of adults, too—need to be taught that each animal is a unique creature and requires its own special type of care.

As with any pet, purchasing or adopting one should be a thoughtful decision. It should never be done on impulse, and the whole family should be involved in the discussion. The purchase of any pet should be accompanied with the purchase of educational materials about the general care of your chosen pet. Education is one of the most effective ways of preventing pet loss (or worse).

One of the most important things a pet owner can do to reduce the risk of pet loss is to purchase educational materials, books, magazines, videos, etc., on the general care and maintenance of their chosen pets. Talk to your veterinarian, other owners of similar pets, and research information on the Internet. This holds true for all pets, but it is particularly important when it comes to ferrets and other critters, since the average person simply has less experience with them than they do with cats and dogs. Such education is especially important for children who have expressed an interest in having a pet. It is also important for us parents to understand that we are not acquiring a pet "for the kids". Even the most enthusiastic child may not, as time passes, sustain their interest in the pet. As adults, we must not only want the pet as well, but also be prepared to assume full responsibility for its care.

Things You Can Do to Prevent the Loss of Ferrets and Other Critters

Unlike dogs and cats, sterilizing your ferret will not decrease the risk of loss, according to Jeanne Carley, of The Ferret Company (**www.ferretcompany.com**). Ms. Carley has been doing ferret rescue work in California for over ten years and in consulting with her on this topic she pointed out that "approximately 92% of ferrets are sterilized at a young age for health and sanitary reasons. Female ferrets die of anemia and male ferrets (females too, but not as much) are pretty stinky if not neutered or spayed. But sterilizing ferrets will not have any effect on their interest in checking out the great outdoors or the next room for that matter. Ferrets are naturally curious and sterilization has no impact on that natural tendency. Ferrets should be sterilized, absolutely, but one should not assume that by sterilizing a ferret they've decreased the possibility that it might escape." Fortunately, there are many things ferret owners can do to prevent and prepare for escape. Here are several things you can do:

- Train your ferret to come to the sound of a squeaky toy or a whistle, and reward him with a treat. Clicker training has become very popular, and there is even a book on training ferrets. (See "Resources/Training.") Light switch training can be very helpful since deafness is not uncommon in ferrets.

- Attach a bell to your ferret's collar.

- Alert your neighbors to the fact that you own a ferret. Ferrets don't tend to wander very far. There is a good chance that if your ferret ever escaped, it would show up at the door of a neighbor. Show your neighbors a photo (many people don't know what a ferret looks like) and let them know what to do if your ferret ever shows up at their door.

- Use multiple identification methods, including having your ferret tattooed and microchipped. Just about any animal can be tattooed, and there are tiny microchips made especially for birds and smaller pets.

- Create a designated "ferret-proofed" room for when company comes or when kids are in and out with friends; put a sign on the door to alert people or simply cage your ferret.

- Post additional signs around your home alerting guests that there is a ferret in the house and to be cautious. While signs can be helpful as an extra precaution, they should not be relied upon. No guest, unless a ferret owner themselves, can possibly know how easily a ferret can slip by them and escape. The only sure way to protect your ferret is to have a separate "ferret-proofed" room or to cage your ferret when you have company.

- Purchase an adjustable harness (special harnesses are available for ferrets), and teach your ferret to walk on a leash. Make sure your harness is secured with a clasp or fastener. Velcro closures are not recommended as they can too easily come undone.

- Purchase a proper cage or tank for your particular pet. Pet care books and pet supply store employees should be able to give you some guidance here. Ferrets are expert cage door openers, so secure the door with a leash clasp.

- Keep furniture a few feet from windows, if at all possible.

- Be aware of the animal's habits. Some critters are more prone to biting or nipping, which could cause someone to drop the animal and off it could run. Purchase gloves for handling if necessary.

Humane Traps Can Help

Although ferrets are domesticated creatures and rarely need to be trapped, it is still a good idea to be prepared. Humane animal traps, such as those made by Havahart, can be used to safely capture your ferret, as well as other critters, hamsters, gerbils, rats, etc. They can be purchased at feed stores, pet supply stores, or you may even be able to borrow one in a pinch from a shelter or animal control. You can also purchase them directly from the manufacturer at **www.havahart.com.**

- Use hardware cloth, and attach it over your regular screen (be sure it is secured to the screen frame and not just to the screen material). Inspect window screens regularly to determine if your ferret has been clawing them.

- Secure cabinets with good quality safety latches, as ferrets can easily open cabinets, even those equipped with child safety locks.

- Use a check rule. If you allow your ferret access to the house, some have suggested a one-hour check rule, others a twenty-minute check rule. If you have not seen your ferret in that time, go and find it. Others believe caging is essential, that it is simply too dangerous to allow ferrets unsupervised access to the house at all, and strongly advise against it.

- Know the laws regarding ferret ownership at your destination point prior to traveling with your ferret. Ferrets are illegal in some states and in several individual counties and cities. Your ferret could be confiscated. (See "Traveling With Pets.")

- Make use of the Internet. Many good critter-specific web sites are included in our resource section. (See "Resources/Ferrets and Other Critters.")

- Update your list of important phone numbers and addresses. Your list should include veterinarians, animal clinics, clubs and rescue groups, and pet stores in your area. (See "Critical Contacts.") Rescue groups are particularly important here as many operate private shelters. If your ferret is picked up by animal control they may, as a rule, contact local ferret rescue. These are not difficult to locate. The American Ferret Association maintains an extensive list of ferret shelters, by state, on their web site at **www.ferret.org**.

The Pocket Pet Video Series

We can't say enough about these videos. Whether you are a new pet owner or have owned your pocket pet for years, these high-quality instructional video guides are a must-see.

Complete with professional actors, animation, and original music, the Pocket Pet Series is not only great fun to watch with the whole family, it is also a great way of teaching your children and their friends about responsible pet ownership.

Not only will these videos make your Pet Pal, as they are affectionately referred to in the video, healthier and happier, your pocket pet will also be at much less risk of becoming lost.

The Pocket Pet Series of instructional video guides includes Chinchillas, Ferrets, Gerbils, Guinea Pigs, Hamsters, Pet Rats, and Rabbits.

We agree with the producer of these videos that "The videos are the most informative, entertaining, educational, and family-oriented small pet instructional video guides available anywhere."

To order these wonderful videos see "Resources/ Ferrets and Other Critters" or visit their web site at **www.pocket-pet-series.com.**

FIGURE 39

Teach Your Children about Responsible Pet Ownership

Ferrets (as well as too many other animals) are often purchased for children as though they were a toy or a game. True, ferrets can make wonderful pets for kids. Unlike toys and games, however, ferrets and other critters do not come with instructions. It is the responsibility of the adults to provide youngsters with the guidance and education they need. This lack of instructing children about proper pet care is directly responsible for the escape of countless hamsters, mice, gerbils, lizards, etc., each year. These escaped pets often meet terrible fates right in the home. Purchase educational materials for your children; books, videos, etc. One of the greatest educational resources we have found is the Pocket Pet Series of educational videos. (See figure 39.) They are terrific, and we highly recommend them. Also check out Pet Care Guides for Kids from the American Society for the Prevention of Cruelty to Animals (ASPCA). They are designed specifically for young children and cost around $10. They can be purchased at bookstores or directly from the ASPCA. (See "Resources/Humane Organizations.")

- Make sure your child's desire to have a ferret or other critter isn't a fad. If one of their friends owns a ferret, have them take care of their friend's pet for at least a weekend. This will give them a better idea of all that ferret or critter ownership entails. You must be prepared, however, to assume full responsibility for the care of the animal if your child's interest in it begins to wane with time.

- Supervise your children's activities with their pets.

- Have children join a ferret or critter club, and get them a subscription to critter-specific newsletters and magazines.

- Make use of the Internet. There are chat rooms where kids can meet other kids who love ferrets, mice, rats, hamsters, gerbils, etc. There are also educational web sites with lots of helpful pet care information. (See "Resources/Ferrets and Other Critters.") The American Society for the Prevention of Cruelty to Animals has created a wonderful web site just for kids. Check it out at **www.animaland.org**.

- Never allow children to take their ferret outside without a leash and secure harness. Other critters should be kept indoors.

Section II

RECOVERY

How to Find Your Lost Pet

Check Close to Home First!

When your pet is missing, time is the most important factor. Most lost pets that are recovered are reunited with their owners quickly, and in close proximity to the area where they were lost. Unless you saw your pet take off, search around your own property first.

Before you do anything else, look in every nook and cranny in your house, around your yard, and throughout your immediate neighborhood. Remember, many pets that are thought to be lost are merely hiding (or sleeping) somewhere on your own property. Perhaps your pet is nearby, but it's trapped or injured; this could have tragic consequences.

If this initial search effort is unsuccessful, or if your pet has been missing for some time, don't despair. Pets can and have been recovered long after they have gone missing—in some cases, months and even years.

While being prepared is important in finding your pet quickly, our recovery tips will help anyone whose pet has turned up missing. There are some items you need to gather that will be critical in recovering your pet. (See "Preparing for Recovery.") The key thing is not to panic. Take a deep breath, and read all the way through this section. We won't waste your time. Together, we'll do everything we can to help you find your lost pet!

Your Pet May Be Closer than You Think

Search inside Your House

- Cabinets, boxes, and closets are excellent hiding places for cats and ferrets.

- Laundry baskets and piles of clothing make for a nice warm napping spot for your ferret.

- Beneath blankets is another spot to look for your cat or ferret.

- Furnaces and hot water heaters are very dangerous for critters, hamsters, gerbils, etc., which will seek out a warm dark area to hide and end up seriously injured or even killed.

- Openings in sheet rock walls, often beneath sinks or anywhere that plumbing goes into the wall, are ideal hiding places for snakes, lizards, and various critters.

- Holes in baseboards are another attractive hiding place for snakes and critters.

- Reclining chairs and sofa beds are accessible and cats, ferrets, critters, and even some smaller-breed dogs may find themselves a hiding place here (be very careful opening furniture so as not to injure the animal).

- Appliances are particularly hazardous for ferrets (especially refrigerators with open motors). Washers, dryers, and dishwashers are often left with the door ajar, and a curious kitty or mischievous ferret can find their way inside.

- Curtains with hemmed bottoms; birds can get caught in these.

- Birds can easily climb in and be unable to get back out of empty vases, beer steins, and other large knickknacks (they have been known to die from heart failure in the panic).

- Anywhere and everywhere in your home where your pet could possibly hide or be trapped.

Search outside Your House

- Many houses have crawl spaces between the foundation and the floor where pets can easily crawl into and become trapped.

- Dogs and cats can easily crawl beneath decks and porches and become tangled in wires.

- Garages present many opportunities for pets to get into dangerous situations.

- Cats, especially house cats not used to the out-of-doors, can easily climb up trees but often cannot climb back down. Trees right in the immediate area are often the first place caged birds will perch if they escape.

- On the roof.
- In car engines and wheel wells (cats are notorious for hiding here).
- Tool sheds.
- Debris piles.
- Drainage pipes.
- Anywhere and everywhere your pet could possibly hide or be trapped on your property.

Preparing for Recovery

It is crucial that you keep your pet records organized; simple file folders work well for this. Create at least two copies of everything, and, as a safeguard against disasters, such as hurricanes, floods, etc., keep them in watertight containers and keep one copy at a location away from your home. Prepare your pet record folders before your pet is ever lost. This will save you valuable time and make your search better organized and more likely to succeed. (See "Pet Record Keeping.")

Your Pet Records

If you haven't kept good pet records, it is not too late. Gather as many of the following items as you can and proceed to "Organizing the Search."

- *Medical History*—Any and all vaccination records and a record of your pet's veterinary visits (both check-ups and emergency visits) should be included, as well as any special dietary needs. X-rays can positively establish ownership.
- *Purchase Receipts*—Include these if you purchased your pet from a breeder, or adoption documentation if you got it from a shelter.
- *Photographs*—Have several photographs, preferably in color, taken from various angles. Keep replacing these with up-to-date photographs as your pet grows. (See "Photographing Your Pet.")
- *Written Description of Your Pet*—Human memory can sometimes be faulty, especially when stress is involved. Write a description before your pet is lost. Include as many physical details about your pet as possible:

- Markings (patches, spots, tattoos, etc.)
- Color patterns
- Coat texture (rough, silky, smooth)
- Hair length (long or short)
- Tail (long, short, cut, bushy, corkscrew, etc.)
- Ear set (erect, cropped, tipped, etc.)
- Eye color
- Breed (Husky, Shepherd, etc.) and if mixed breed, the standard breed it most resembles.
- For birds, feather colors and patterns.

- *Tags*—You should always have spare identification tags and since they are small, keep them with your pet's records.

- *Tag/Tattoo/Microchip Registry Information*—Contact numbers and all the paperwork. Note: the contact numbers may be different from the ones for updating information.

- *Club Membership Information*—Organize all the contact numbers, membership cards, and information for any pet club to which you belong.

Recovery Kit

Next, assemble the following items ahead of time so if your pet does turn up missing, you can get right to work:

- Log sheets for keeping track of places you've hung flyers, received reported sightings of your pet, telephone calls you've made and received, etc. You can easily make these yourself with a word processing program, or there are terrific forms for this exact purpose that can be downloaded from our web site at **www.lostpetfoundpet.com**.

- Create a template for a "lost pet" flyer by scanning a photo of your pet and using a word processing or some other publishing program. Save this on a floppy disk that you place in your Recovery Kit. Also, since floppy disk errors are not uncommon, print out at least one copy to photocopy later if needed. If you don't have access to a computer, simply tape a clear color photograph to a blank sheet of paper and then, using a ruler, draw straight lines where information can later be filled in by hand. Use the sample flyer in the back of this book as your guide. Flyers can also be downloaded free of charge from our web site at **www.lostpetfoundpet.com**.

- Materials for making freestanding signs (the type you see along the road at election time): 1x2-inch pieces of wood cut into 2-foot lengths; poster board or sheets of cardboard; and clear plastic sheeting to protect your signs. Staple flyers to poster board and then staple poster board to both sides of each stake. Signs should be strategically placed at high visibility locations, like busy intersections and anywhere that traffic slows or stops.

- Rolls of tape, a stapler and staples, thumbtacks, and a hammer (for freestanding signs) for putting up flyers on a variety of surfaces.

- Maps of your town and colored highlighters.

- A spare collar and leash.

- A whistle, bell, and/or clicker (depending on which one you used to train your pet).

- A powerful flashlight, not only for searching at night but also for looking in dark places such as abandoned buildings, underneath porches, in drainage pipes, etc.

- A first aid kit because your pet may be injured when you locate it.

- A bottle of fresh water and, of course, some treats.

Critical Contacts

Preparing the following list of phone numbers and addresses is one of the most important things you can do to increase the chance of a successful recovery. We have only included phone numbers, e-mail addresses, and web sites here because for people who have just lost their pets, there is no time to mail. If you want these addresses, they can be found in "Resources." In addition, you can locate the links for the following Critical Contacts on our web site at **www.lostpetfoundpet.com**. Just log on and click the "For Our Readers" link.

- *Animal Shelters*—There are several important things you need to know about reclaiming your pet from an animal shelter, and several items you should bring along. Please read "Check the Animal Shelters." There may be several shelters, both private and municipal, near where you live. It is important to know where all of them are since each town's animal control may use a different facility. You can locate them in your phone directory where they may be listed under a variety of names ("animal shelter," "humane society," or "animal control"). Also check the city or county government pages. You can also call the nearest shelter and ask if they have a list of other facilities. One of the best ways, however, is online. Here are a few great sites for locating animal shelters by zip code.
  - *ASPCA National Shelter Directory—(www.aspca.org)*. The American Society for the Prevention of Cruelty to Animals maintains a national shelter directory on their web site. Simply click on "National Shelter Outreach Link."
  - *Pet Finder—(www.petfinder.org)*. On this site you can choose the "Shelter and Rescue Groups" link. They are listed by two-digit state abbreviation, or enter your zip code and click on the "Local Shelters" link.

- *Pets 911—(www.1888pets911.com).* On this site, just enter your zip code and choose "Local Animal Shelters." Their web site address is also their toll-free number: 1 (888) PETS911. They use a very easy prompt system, and you can quickly locate the two or three nearest animal care facilities in your area.
- *Pet Shelter.org—(www.petshelter.org).* Click on the "Shelters" link and search by state.

- *Veterinarians*—They can be located in a phone directory; you can call and ask your own veterinarian or search online. Here are sites that help you locate veterinarians by state and town:
  - *Association of Avian Veterinarians—(www.aav.org).* To locate veterinarians who specialize in avian care.
  - *Vet Web—(www.vetweb.net).* This is a fairly comprehensive list, but veterinarians not registered with the site will have only address and unconfirmed phone number (you may need directory assistance).

- *Animal Hospitals*—Your own or other area veterinarians should be able to direct you. Also try calling shelters in your area.
  - *American Animal Hospital Association (AAHA)—(www.healthypet.com).* The AAH maintains a listing by state and city. Phone: (800) 252-AAHA (2242).
  - *Pets911—(www.1888pets911.org).* Locate emergency veterinarian clinics.

- *Law Enforcement Agencies*—Local, county, and state agencies can all be located in the phone directory blue pages, or by dialing directory assistance.

- *Animal Control*—Some municipalities run their own animal control departments while others contract this service out. Call your local municipal government office to find out who handles animal control in your community. Also, get the numbers of the animal control facilities run by all the surrounding towns and/or suburbs.

- *Dead Animal Retrieval*—Sadly, many lost pets are located this way, underscoring even further the importance of prevention. You can get the number from your municipal government offices and from animal control. Again, each surrounding town may have different arrangements.

- *Identification Registries*—If you have joined one or more of these, then you have the contact information already. Be sure to also include it in your "Critical Contacts" list.

- *Pet Clubs and Breed Rescue Groups*—You can usually find these listed in the various pet magazines. Another way is online at these sites:
  - *Bird Clubs*—Bird Talk—*(www.birdtalk.com).*
  - *Breed Rescue Groups*—These can be located in pet breed magazines, but the best place is again on the Internet at Pet Guardian Angels of America

(**www.pgaa.com**), which lists breed rescue and adoption groups by location, type, and breed. It has been our rule to include only web sites ending with .com, .org, .net, etc. (because file extensions are apt to change). Kyler Laird's Animal Rescue Resources is an exception to this rule (**www.ecn.purdue.edu/~laird/ animal_rescue**).

- *Dog Clubs—AKC Club Directory—(www.akc.org),* **Dog-On-It—** *(www.dog-on-it.com).*

- *Dog Clubs, Cat Clubs, Bird Clubs, and Critter Clubs—***Pet Station—** *(www.petstation.com).* Click on the appropriate link.

• *Pet Stores—*Locate the ones near you by using the Yellow Pages or directory assistance.

• *Local Cable TV and Radio Stations—*Locate the ones serving your area by using the Yellow Pages or directory assistance.

• *Lost and Found Newspaper Classified Ad Departments—*Use the phone directory, directory assistance, or a copy of the newspaper.

• *Lost and Found Ads Online—*These ads should be used as a supplement and are in no way a substitute for other proven effective ways of lost pet recovery. Many pets have been recovered this way and it can't hurt, as long as you are aware of the limitations of these types of ads. The Internet is still in its infancy; millions of people are not yet online, and those who are would not necessarily find your ad in the vast regions of cyberspace. Here are some web sites for placing online classifieds and lost or stolen pet notices. These do produce results and, as the Internet grows and people become more familiar with this valuable resource, they will be even more successful. It should be noted that online sites where you've uploaded a photo of your pet should be listed in the traditional newspaper classified ads that you run. That way, people reading your newspaper ad can then visit the site and see what your pet looks like.

- *Bird Hotline—(www.birdhotline.com).* Birds only/free/allows photos.

- *Pet Finder—(www.petfinder.org).* All pets/free/no photos.

- *Pets 911—(www.1888pets911.com).* All pets/free/allows photos. Pets 911, thanks to an aggressive public awareness campaign, has become very well known as a place for posting lost/found pet advertisements.

- *Pets Missing in Action—(www.pmia.com).* All pets/free/allows photos.

- *Planned Parrothood—(www.plannedparrothood.com).* Birds only/free/no photos.

• *Lost and Stolen Pets Resources—*These provide information about stolen pets, animal research, and/or assistance.

- *In Defense of Animals—(www.idausa.org)*. Pet Theft Hotline: (800) STOLEN PET, Fax: (415) 388-0388, E-mail: ida@idausa.org.
- *Last Chance for Animals—(www.stolenpets.com)*. E-mail: info@LCAnimal.org.
- *National Pet Detectives.* (See "Recovery Services" below.)
- *USDA-APHIS-Animal Care.* To obtain a list of registered animal dealers and research facilities in your area. Phone: (301) 734-4981. Also available online at **www.aphis.usda.gov/ac/publications.html**

- *Recovery Services*—These include companies and organizations (usually affiliated with some type of ID registry) that provide various pet recovery services (e.g., consulting, postcard mailing, creating flyers, contacting facilities that take in strays in and around the area where your pet was lost, etc.). These may or may not require your having pre-registered with them. It is best to sign up ahead since it will save you time.
  - *American Pet Association—(www.apapets.com)*. Phone: (800) APA-PETS, Fax: (303) 494-7316, E-mail: apa@apapets.org.
  - *National Pet Detectives—(www.nationalpetdetectives.com)*. Phone: (866) 2-RESCUE. In Pinellas County, Florida, (727) 398-2805. E-mail: info@nationalpetdetectives.com. Search and rescue is currently limited to Florida area, but they provide other services as well. Larry Maynard is very involved in the stolen pet issue and is a great resource if your pet is ever lost or stolen. National Pet Detectives also runs an e-mail support network on Yahoo Groups. This service is for members who have registered their pets with National Pet Detectives. Check it out at **www.groups.yahoo.com** and search *National Pet Detectives*. (See "Pet Detectives.")
  - *National Pet Recovery—(www.petrecovery.com)*. Phone: (800) 984-8638, E-mail: customerservice@petrecovery.com.
  - *Petfinders Pet Club of America—(www.petclub.org)*. Phone: (800) 666-5678, E-mail: petclub@capital.net.
  - *Pet Hunters—(www.pethunters.com)*. Phone: (805) 306-0810, E-mail: info@pethunters.com. In partnership with the American Humane Association, Pet Hunters employs search and rescue dogs to recover lost pets. Services are currently limited to Los Angeles and San Francisco areas. (See "Pet Detectives.")
  - *Sherlock Bones—(www.sherlockbones.com)*. Phone: (800) 942-6637, E-mail: sherlock@sherlockbones.com.
- *People Who Will Help*—Keep your Pet Partner's number here and anybody else you can think of who'd help you out. (See "Pet Partners.")

- *Disaster Resources*—If disaster were to strike, a hurricane for example, one or more of these organizations may be involved in rescue efforts.

  - *American Humane Association, Emergency Animal Relief (EAR)—(www.americanhumane.org)*. Click on the "Disaster Relief" link. Phone: (303) 792-9900, E-mail: ear@americanhumane.org.

  - *American Red Cross—(www.redcross.org)*. Contact your local chapter of the American Red Cross. E-mail: info@usa.redcross.org.

  - *Federal Emergency Management Agency (FEMA)—(www.fema.gov)*. Search the site using the keyword "pets." Phone: (202) 566-1600.

  - *Humane Society of the United States (Disaster Services)—(www.hsus.org)*. Phone: (301) 258-3103 or (301) 258-3063. E-mail: disaster@hsus.org.

  - *United Animal Nations, Emergency Animal Rescue Services (EARS)—(www.uan.org)*. Click on the "EARS" link. Phone: (916) 429-2457, E-mail: info@uan.org.

Organizing the Search

Immediately enlist as many people as you can to help in the search. Call friends, family members, neighbors, and anybody else you can think of. If you're forced to work alone or are otherwise unable to conduct the search yourself, you may want to consider hiring help. (See "Locating Help for Hire" below.)

Choose a leader and divide tasks among various team members, some of whom should begin searching immediately while others prepare flyers and put together the items listed in "Preparing for Recovery." Another team member should be making those important first few calls on the list of "Critical Contacts."

It's important that everyone is describing the same animal. You want everyone reading the same script and conveying the same accurate information about your pet when out talking to people. Make copies of the various lists: "Places to Check," "People You Should Talk To," "People You Should Call," "Places for Flyers," and log sheets for keeping track of information. Distribute them to the appropriate team members.

If you and your search team have cell phones, use them. They will greatly increase the efficiency of your efforts. Make sure each person has a list of the phone numbers of all the other team members.

Use a Map

Using a map is the best way to conduct an effective search, as it will ensure your efforts are more thorough and more organized. You can get maps at most gas stations, convenience stores, bookstores, and town halls.

Divide the map into sections. Assign a section to each member of the search team. Use different colored highlighters to mark each street each time you canvass it. Instruct everyone to use the same method: yellow for first canvass, red for second, and blue for third. Instruct team members to mark areas on the map, and record on their log sheets any of the places where they hang flyers. (This way, you'll know where the flyers are so you can replace them if they are taken down, and collect them up when your pet is found.) Using a map helps make sure that the entire area is searched systematically and thoroughly.

Maps also allow team members to keep track of each other. Team members should call in regularly to your search headquarters. This way you'll know their progress, and they can alert others to any possible sightings. A map should also be hung on the wall in your home and marked to show areas where sightings have been reported. Patterns may begin to emerge later and when they do, those areas can be heavily canvassed and blanketed with flyers and posters.

Call Your Critical Contacts

There are many contacts you will need to make. While contacting every shelter (both private and municipal), veterinarian, and rescue group within a 60-mile radius may seem an overwhelming task, by using the list of "Critical Contacts" described in "Preparing for Recovery," you can locate them easily and begin getting in touch with them right away.

Make Your Flyers and Place Your Ads

More lost pets are probably recovered through lost pet flyers and classified ads than by any other method. While an initial search can be made without them, it's important that you make and distribute flyers as soon as possible. Then call your local newspaper so you can get your classified ad in the next edition. While perhaps not quite as successful for recovering lost pets as flyers, classified ads are still quite effective. (See "Flyers and Classified Ads.")

Describing Your Pet

It's important that everybody be operating with the same information. Hopefully, you'll have photos of your pet to assist you. Sit down and write out a description of your pet to the best of your ability. If you don't have a photo and there are others present who are familiar with your pet, collaborate until you are satisfied that the description is accurate. Give copies to each person so that everyone is reading from the same script when they're out searching and talking to people, and when phone calls are being made to various facilities.

Using Log Sheets

Log sheets are indispensable for keeping track of and organizing both incoming and outgoing information, as you may need to contact people again to clarify points or to get additional information; it is easy to get confused. You will need different log sheets for different purposes. You can make these in a word processing program or download them free from our web site at **www.lostpetfoundpet.com.** You will need at least four log sheets:

- One for keeping track of flyer placement.
- One for recording information on possible sightings when out canvassing and talking to people.
- One for incoming phone calls generated by your ads and flyers.
- One for the various contacts you need to make and places you visit: shelters, veterinarians, and other agencies.

Log sheets should record every detail of any possible sightings: the person's name, address, phone number, the time, day, location, details of the animal they saw, and most importantly, which direction your pet was headed.

Use an Answering Machine

If you use your phone number on your pet's ID tags or on your flyers, you must have an answering machine. It is unlikely that someone will always be there to answer the phone. When the calls start coming in from your ads and flyers, an answering machine will prove its worth a thousand times over. Even if you are at home, trying to write down all of the information by hand can be overwhelming. An answering machine that can be set to record even the calls you answer is best. That way, the information from all the incoming calls can be recorded and transcribed onto a log sheet later.

Found Pet Classifieds

You must check the found pet classifieds every day. If you have friends in surrounding communities and suburbs, it's also a good idea to have them check their local papers as well. Be sure to check the Internet sites that list found pets, too. Investigate any ads for pets that even sound similar to yours, as people may describe your pet quite differently from the way you would. If there is even a chance that it could be your pet, make the call and check it out. If you've found a stray animal, place a found ad. Many newspapers will place them for free. (See "Found Strays.")

Searching Alone

Of course, not everyone can assemble a team of people to help them search. If you have no one to help you, there are many things that can be done from home or office. For example, you can still contact shelters, veterinarians, and rescue groups by phone, and if you have a computer or fax, you can use it to send your pet's photo or a copy of your flyer to them.

There are also recovery services available that will do many of the necessary things for you, such as mailing postcards to targeted areas in and around the place your pet was lost. Some recovery services will create flyers for you and also alert all shelters within a certain radius of where your pet went missing. (See "Critical Contacts.")

Locating Help for Hire

First, contact shelters, rescue groups, and pet clubs and see if someone would be willing to help you. If you are fortunate and find persons willing to assist purely out of kindness, you could offer to pay them. If you can't find volunteer help, there are places where you can locate people willing to help even if you have to pay.

- The local paper "Situations Wanted." Ads and flyers tacked up on bulletin boards in your local grocery store, laundromat, etc. People put ads here for a variety of odd jobs, yard work, *and* distributing flyers!
- Local colleges usually have bulletin boards, and college kids always need extra cash. Put up some flyers offering to pay for assistance. You will likely need approval from the administration, as flyers without an approval stamp will probably be removed.
- Children of friends, friends of your own children, or just kids from your neighborhood.

Recovery Services Really Can Help

Did you know that there are recovery services that will make posters for you? They can help in a lot of other ways as well. Some services will mail postcards with your pet's photo to all the residences and businesses in a certain, targeted area. Some services will fax vital information about your lost pet to all facilities that take in stray animals within a certain radius of where your pet was lost.

All these can be invaluable, especially if you are unable to do the work yourself, if you lose your pet while traveling away from home, or if your job or other commitments keep you from conducting your own extensive search effort. We've listed several recovery services in "Critical Contacts."

Find Yourself an Ally—Pet Clubs and Rescue Groups

Pet clubs and breed rescue groups can be invaluable when trying to recover a missing pet. What makes them particularly helpful is that they are part of a greater network of people who are similarly devoted to animals of a particular breed or species. There are clubs and rescue groups for every breed and type of animal.

When you lose a pet, you need as many allies as possible, and where better to turn for help and advice when your Siamese cat is lost than to a group of people who are devoted to Siamese cats? You may even be able to find club or rescue group members willing to lend assistance or to help you in your recovery efforts. They could prove critical if your pet is lost while traveling, because eventually you will be forced to return home with or without your pet. A club or rescue group member may be willing to act as a liaison for you and lend you long-distance support.

It's also important to know that veterinarians, animal hospitals, and animal shelters often work with breed rescue groups, calling on them to place the animals rather than putting them down. (This may be why you have not found your pet at the local shelter.)

Also, many rescue groups operate their own shelter facilities. Therefore, you must contact the appropriate rescue groups in your area if your pet turns up missing. These are not difficult to locate using the list of "Critical Contacts."

Use the Internet

The Internet, while not indispensable to lost pet recovery, can be of great assistance and can save you a lot of time (when compiling your list of "Critical Contacts," for example). For many people unfamiliar with navigating the Internet, it can seem very intimidating. Navigating the Net is not as difficult as it seems, and there are places where you can access the Internet where there may also be people to assist you. Here are a few suggestions:

- Friends and relatives.
- Your public library more than likely will have people available to assist you.
- Community college computer labs may or may not be available to the public. If they are just for students, they may make an exception for you under the circumstances. You could also talk to a student who could accompany you to the lab, or there are usually lab assistants to help.
- Internet cafes are places that rent computer time by the hour and usually have people to assist.
- Kinko's and other similar stores rent computer time by the hour and have staff on hand to help.

Conducting the Search

Searches should, if possible, be conducted in groups of at least two. Where you search, how quickly, and how thoroughly can make all the difference in finding your pet. Places you may think impossible for a pet to be hiding may in fact be the very place to look. A cat or ferret, for example, is much more likely to be hiding in a place you would not ordinarily think of searching. You can also combine your searching with distributing flyers and talking to people. This will save you valuable time.

Before you begin searching the neighborhood, be sure to leave the gate to your yard open just in case your pet returns on its own. Call your pet and stop to listen. If your pet has been trained to respond to a whistle, bell, clicker, squeaky toy, or even the shaking of the cat food box, bring it along and make noise as you go. If your pet has gone missing before, go to where it was found before.

Many pets are found during the early morning hours. There is less activity, so a stray tends to be more noticeable than later in the day. Early in the morning, go around your neighborhood and bring a pad and pen with you. Write down the names of any delivery trucks, as many delivery people drive the same routes every day. Talk to the drivers if you can and see if they've spotted your pet, or call and talk to whoever dispatches the trucks.

Items to Have with You When You Search

- Flyers
- Recovery Kit
- Lists: "Places to Check," "People You Should Talk To," "People You Should Call," and "Places for Flyers"
- Photos
- Contact numbers
- Cell phones
- Town map
- Pad and pen
- Log sheets
- Animal carrier

Going Door-to-Door

Be friendly and polite in your search. Display your pet's photos, and leave behind your flyers and your contact information. If the people are not home, leave flyers and information discreetly by their door. Unless they have a separate box for newspaper delivery, do not put flyers in people's mailboxes (it's illegal). Flyers can be left underneath the windshield wipers of cars. If you haven't made your flyers yet, leave a note with a description of your pet and your contact information.

Places to Check

Depending on the type of animal you have, there are many places where they might be hiding. As you're going through the neighborhood, be sure to look in the following locations:

- *Yards and Sheds*—If the people are home, ask permission to search the yard and shed. If they aren't home, at least look in the yard. Call your pet. Be sure to let all the neighbors know what you're doing so you're not mistaken for a prowler!

- *Trees and Roofs*—If the pet you are looking for can fly or climb, look up in the trees and on roofs as you walk along. Call your pet!

- *Abandoned Buildings*—Injured pets may seek out hiding places, and abandoned buildings are ideal. Check these out, too, but *never* go alone. And bring a flashlight.

- *Behind Restaurants and Stores*—Behind most restaurants, delicatessens, and grocery stores, you will find dumpsters, and where there are dumpsters, there are stray animals. If your pet has been missing for any amount of time, it will be hungry.

- *Parks and Recreation Areas*—These are good places to search. There are lots of people who walk their pets there. This may attract your pet, and certainly gives you many opportunities to talk to people about your missing pet.

- *Schools and Playgrounds*—If your pet is friendly with children, schools and playground areas are an ideal place to search. You may also get some needed help.

- *Surrounding Towns*—As time passes and you begin getting leads from your flyers and classified ads, you may need to extend your search to surrounding towns in your area. Depending on the size and type of your pet, this can extend quite a distance, as much as 60 miles or more away.

- *Some Additional Places to Search*—Wooded areas, open fields, under bridges, sewer grates, and storm drains.

People You Should Talk To

- *Joggers*—These people generally run regularly and usually follow the same routes. There is a good chance they have seen (or may see!) your pet.

- *People Walking Pets*—Fellow pet owners are a great source of information (again, they often walk the same area).

- *Children*—Talk to children. They're really good at spotting stray animals. If no adults are around, only speak to the older kids. Small children are very wisely taught to be wary of strangers. (Unfortunately, one of the biggest abduction scams is to pretend to be looking for a lost pet.) This is another reason why it is good to search in pairs.

- *Police*—If you run across officers while you're out searching, stop and ask them, too. Police cover a lot of ground, and in smaller towns police may cover the entire town several times during their shift. They'll probably be willing to keep an eye out.

- *Mail Carriers*—The folks who deliver your mail are great sources of help. They may already know and be friendly with your pet.

- *Newspaper Boys and Girls*—As with mail carriers, those who bring you your newspaper are also good people to talk to.

- *Crossing Guards*—Crossing guards are at their post every day, and they see a lot. Without distracting them from their responsibilities, ask them to watch for your lost pet. It's one more set of eyes you have working for you.

- *Landscapers*—Talk to local landscapers you see working in your neighborhood. They probably have several accounts around town and may be willing to keep an eye out for your pet.

- *Pizza and Food Deliverers*—These are good people to talk to because they normally work in the evenings when a lot of the other people you've talked to have gone home for the day.

- *Sanitation Workers*—In many small towns, people know their sanitation workers on a first name basis and even tip them at holiday time. These people cover a large area and since they pick up your garbage at your curb, they may already be familiar with your pet and willing to keep an eye out.

- *Neighborhood Watch Groups*—Many areas today have block watch groups. The best thing about them is that they watch! They see everything that is going on and may very well have seen your lost pet wandering around.

- *UPS/FedEx*—If you see one of these trucks around town, stop them and ask the drivers if they've seen your pet.

- *Meter Readers*—Ask the people who read water meters and gas meters.

- *Anyone out Walking*—It never hurts to talk to just about anyone you encounter. You'll be delightfully surprised how many people are willing to help.

People You Should Call

Some places you will need to call, others you must visit in person. Having all the information you need readily available will help you and the people you are speaking with to recover your pet.

- ***Your Newspaper***—Place a classified ad right away. Hopefully, it will be in time to make the next day's paper. Don't depend on the person on the other end of the line to help you, as they may know less about placing a successful lost pet classified ad than you do. Consider that the person at the newspaper who's taking your lost pet ad also took several yard sale advertisements and a few ads for used cars. These folks are not experts; they are there simply to take down the information you give them. Therefore, you must be the expert. (See "Flyers and Classified Ads.") Another important thing is to make sure your ad also runs in the Sunday edition, since many people subscribe only to it.

- ***Local Law Enforcement***—File a lost pet report. If some dispatcher tries to blow you off, insist that they take the report and remind them that there is always the possibility of theft. Talk to the police in person whenever possible.

- ***Animal Shelters***—Call every shelter within a 60-mile radius, alerting them that your pet is missing and giving them a description of your pet. Visit the ones in your immediate vicinity right away, and then follow up every other day. Inquire about special areas for injured or quarantined animals, and insist that you be permitted, accompanied by shelter staff, to search these areas as well. Leave copies of your flyers and all contact information so they can contact you if an animal fitting your pet's description is brought in. Fax a copy of your flyer or photos of your pet to the shelters farther away.

- ***Veterinarians and Animal Hospitals***—If your pet was injured when it escaped, it may have been taken to a local veterinarian or area animal hospital. Follow the same advice as for shelters above. Ask if they work with breed rescue groups.

- ***Breed Rescue Groups***—If a purebred is not adopted out, many shelters will contact breed rescue groups to place the animal rather than putting it down. This is also true of many veterinarians and animal hospitals. After treating injured strays, they will often call breed rescue groups and try to place the animals in homes rather than burdening the shelter. In addition, many breed rescue groups operate facilities of their own. Be sure to visit them, and fax copies of your flyers to outlying facilities. Remember, you may also find people willing to lend you some assistance.

- ***Tag, Tattoo, and Microchip Registries***—Let them know your pet has been lost, and make sure they have your up-to-date contact information. If they offer other lost pet services, take advantage of them!

- ***Anyone Else Associated with Your Pet's Tags***—Your pet is likely to be wearing more than one tag: a municipal or city license tag, a rabies tag, a veterinarian's tag, a local shelter tag, etc. Call and inform everyone associated with your pet's tags that your pet has been lost, and make sure your contact information is current.

- ***Dead Animal Retrieval***—Sadly, many pets are recovered this way. However, it is better to know the truth than to forever wonder what happened to your pet. Call your local municipal hall and get the number for Dead Animal Retrieval. Contact them and give them a thorough description of your pet. Leave your name, contact numbers, and send them a copy of your flyer. Call every day to see if they have found your pet. If they do pick up your pet, we encourage you to read some thoughts about grieving the loss of your pet. (See "Grieving.") It is important to remember that each surrounding town may have a different arrangement for this; you should call the adjacent municipalities.

- ***Local Sanitation Workers***—Call your local sanitation/recycling department, and ask if they will let their drivers know that you have a missing pet. If so, give them copies of your flyer and your contact number.

- ***Pet Stores***—If you have lost an exotic or otherwise expensive animal, someone may have stolen it. Also, someone may have simply found your pet and rather than seek out its owner, may try to sell it to a local pet store or pet supply store.

- ***Breed Clubs***—If you have a purebred animal, there may be a local breed club with people willing to offer advice or even offer some direct assistance.

- ***Local Pet Clubs***—Not all pet clubs are breed-specific. There may be a club of local animal lovers. The reference librarian at your local library might know how to locate them.

- ***Research Labs and Licensed Animal Dealers***—Strays are often picked up by "bunchers" and sold to research labs. Many city and county-operated shelters still sell unclaimed animals to registered animal dealers, through a practice known as pound seizure. Four states (Minnesota, Ohio, Oklahoma, and Utah) require that shelters turn over animals to research facilities; only fourteen states have outlawed the practice. (See "Stolen Pets.") Contact all research facilities and registered animal dealers in your area. Let them know your pet is missing, give them a thorough description of your pet, or better yet, fax them a flyer or photo along with your contact information. You can obtain a list of licensed animal dealers and registered research facilities in your area by calling the United States Department of Agriculture. (See "Critical Contacts.")

- ***Recovery Services***—If you can't make all the calls yourself, there are people who will contact all facilities in your area that take in stray animals, and will provide many other valuable services. (See "Critical Contacts.")

- ***Pet Detectives***—You may want to consider contacting a pet detective to help you in your search. (See "Critical Contacts.")

- ***Stolen Pet Resources***—If you suspect or have evidence that your pet was stolen, get in contact with one or more of the stolen pet resources we've listed. (See "Critical Contacts.")

Flyers and Classified Ads

Two of the most effective ways of recovering lost pets are through the "lost/found pet" classifieds in daily newspapers, and through the use of flyers.

Ads are helpful because they can be placed quickly, often appearing the next day. Flyers can be produced and distributed quickly, and targeted in and around the area where your pet was lost. Flyers have the added advantage of including a photograph of your lost pet, which can really be helpful. More newspapers are beginning to allow photos with lost pet ads (our local paper just began offering this option).

Many of the "lost pet" classified ads and flyers we have seen fall short of effectively communicating all the important points we know the pet owner wanted to convey. Flyers and classifieds have such a potential for success that you want to get it right the first time, because you may not get a second chance. It should also be noted that knowing what information not to include in an ad or on a flyer is almost as important as what should be included.

Most people who find a stray animal look first in the classified ads to see if the animal has been reported missing. Your lost pet classified advertisement should leave no doubt in the mind of the Good Samaritan that the stray dog he took in yesterday morning is the same one described in your ad.

At one time or another, you've no doubt seen missing pet flyers. Did they grab your attention? Were they legible and easy to read? Did they give a description that would be helpful to anyone finding someone's missing pet? Was the contact number large enough to be seen from a passing vehicle? Were there additional smaller contact numbers at the bottom of the flyers that could easily be torn off by people passing by? Was there a good color photograph of the pet? More likely than not, they looked as though they had been hastily thrown together, as though the maker was under duress. Both things were no doubt true.

How to Create "Award-Winning" Ads and Flyers

How you describe your lost pet in a classified advertisement or on a flyer (or in any other venue, for that matter) is most important. What information you put in is as important as what you leave out. You want to include only essential information surrounding your pet's disappearance, to avoid confusion. Following these guidelines will help you avoid some of the common mistakes people make, and give you what it takes to place a winning classified ad or create a successful flyer. Sample classified ads and a sample flyer can be found at the end of this section. Also, free downloadable lost pet flyers are available on our web site at **www.lostpetfoundpet.com**.

- *Avoid Descriptive Adjectives*—Telling people that your dog is "obedient" and "affectionate" is not only unnecessary, but may actually confuse rather than help. Those are probably the last adjectives that whoever found your pet would use to describe your frightened and traumatized animal. What the reader needs is concise descriptive information about your pet and specific details regarding the where, when, and how of your pet's disappearance. By eliminating unnecessary adjectives, you leave more space to include essential information. You can put more information on a flyer than in a standard classified ad, but you still want to stick to the basic facts.

- ***Give the Day and Date***—People are more likely to remember the day of the week than the date. For example, they may remember that they were out shopping on Tuesday when they came across your stray dog. They're less likely to recall that it was the 18th. At least in your initial ad, and for at least the first two weeks, include the day *and* the date.

- ***Describe Your Pet in Detail***—"LOST: Orange and white cat." That's pretty vague and not very helpful. Be specific! "LOST CAT: Orange with white paws, chest, and striped tail." Now that gives the reader a more accurate picture of the cat in question. Include any particular color patterns or distinguishing marks. Include eye color, tail length and type (e.g., long, corkscrew, or cut). Include hair length and type (e.g., short, kinky, etc.) as well as ear set (e.g., erect, cropped, tipped, etc.). Be careful when describing your pet's color, as some colors are easily confused (e.g., orange/yellow and brown/beige).

- ***Weight/Size***—"Approximately 30 pounds." You see descriptions like this on lost pet flyers and in ads all the time. Most people, however, tend to think of pets in terms of size rather than precise weights. Again, it might cost a little more, but we suggest using terms such as small, medium, large, or very large, and then giving your pet's approximate weight in pounds.

- ***Sex***—Include the sex of your dog or cat. For a lot of other animals, it isn't very useful, since gender is sometimes very difficult to determine.

- ***Age***—Another common mistake is to include the pet's age in years. It may be more confusing than helpful. The fact is that many people can't tell the age of an animal. If it's a puppy or kitten, or older animal that is showing obvious signs of aging, say so. Otherwise, just use the word "adult" or "young adult" (for adolescent animals) when describing your pet's age.

- ***Contact Information***—A phone number should be in large bold type, big enough to be seen from a passing vehicle. Also, have a row of tear-off tabs with your contact number on your flyers so people passing by can tear one off and won't be tempted to remove the entire flyer. (See "Flyer Sample.")

- ***Spay/Neuter Status***—Leave it out. Most people wouldn't be able to tell either way. Besides, the person finding your pet may be disinclined for obvious reasons to investigate the matter. Lost pets can change hands several times and are sometimes neutered after they go missing. If you say your pet was not neutered, the person finding it may conclude the stray he took in couldn't possibly be the same animal described in your ad.

- *"Last Seen Wearing"*—Because your pet might lose its collar while on the run, or because someone might have put a new collar on it, always use the words "last seen wearing" when describing what your pet had on.

- *Breed Information*—Include the name of your pet's breed, but be sure to include descriptive information about your pet as well. You can't assume that people will know anything about the breed just by the name. Granted, most people will know what a German Shepherd, a Collie, or a Dalmatian is, but only one in a thousand might know what an Australian Blue Heeler looks like.

- *Location*—This is more difficult, because lost pets have been found many miles from where they started. If you are too specific, someone farther away may not make the connection between your ad or flyer and the stray they have taken in. They may simply disregard the ad or flyer believing it to be impossible for the animal to have traveled that far. Do include the specific location, however, if your pet was lost by a shopping center, a school, or at a place where many people congregate, since it may have been found in that exact spot. Follow the specific with the general. For example: "Lost near Winkles Market/Middletown area." You might also include something like "has a tendency to wander far."

- *Be Creative*—Your flyer must capture people's attention. Obviously, you have much more room for creativity with a flyer than with a classified ad. Use bold type for portions of the text to make it stand out. If you're offering a reward, for example, that fact can be highlighted in red.

Your Pet's Photos

The importance of including a photograph of your pet on your flyer cannot be overstated. While any photo is better than no photo, ideally a flyer should include two photos: a face shot and a full body profile. (See "Flyer Sample.")

Should You Offer a Reward?

Should you offer a reward or not? People disagree about this. If you decide to offer a reward, some suggest that it be at least $300 in order to give a pet thief the incentive to return your animal. On the other hand, those who steal pets for a living have prearranged buyers and are unlikely to respond, if only out of fear of being caught. Others say it is not good to be specific, instead suggesting that you simply say "Substantial Reward."

One possible reason for not offering a reward is that it might invite a con artist. Keep in mind, however, they may not even have your pet! (See "Beware of Scams.")

Although this is really a decision that only you can make, we believe you should decide on an amount, but not put it in your ad. We suggest you just include the word "REWARD." Con artists aside, people who go out of their way to pick up a stray and then invest time and effort in trying to locate its owner are not motivated by rewards anyway. They are almost always animal lovers and pet owners themselves and are motivated by something higher than rewards.

While it is unlikely that someone seeing the word "reward" in a classified ad would then go out and search for a pet, flyers may prompt such action. Since they are more directly targeted to neighborhoods where the pet was lost, there is a good chance some neighborhood kids will see them and be motivated to search for your pet. We still suggest you not include the amount, but rather simply the word "REWARD" in bold type and capital letters and in a bright color.

Little White Lies

Some people feel you should list special needs in your ads and flyers, whether or not your pet has them. They reason that doing so stresses urgency and elicits empathy, and that someone considering keeping your pet will decide not to as animals with special needs require more time and expense. You've probably seen this type of wording on flyers: "Needs Medication," "Diabetic," or "Special Diet." It's been done so much it probably isn't all that effective anymore. It is difficult to tell who is correct on this. You be the judge.

Should You Include Your Pet's Name?

Including your pet's name in a classified ad is not helpful and it's more expensive. Flyers are different, as you are not paying for each line, and a name, especially when coupled with a photo, personalizes your flyer. This is not just one of a thousand strays; this is someone's beloved lost pet. Some people have said that a lost and frightened animal may not respond to its name, and therefore the person finding it and reading your flyer may conclude it is not the same animal. While this argument may have some merit, the positive benefits of including your pet's name on your flyer outweigh the negatives.

Should You Withhold Information?

Some have suggested holding back one or more defining characteristics of your pet in case a scam artist claiming to have your pet tries to extort money from you. Although scams do happen, fortunately they are still a rather rare occurrence. Holding back vital, descriptive, identifying information about your pet that will assist the person in making the connection between the animal described in your ad or on your flyer and the stray in their possession is unwise. There are better strategies for thwarting con artists. (See "Beware of Scams.")

How Many Flyers Does it Take to Recover a Missing Pet?

Flyers are the single most effective way of recovering a lost pet. It is reported by National Pet Recovery (NPR) that it takes approximately 200 to 1500 posters to recover a missing dog and about 100 to 400 to locate a lost cat. 73% of the pets they've recovered are the direct result of strategically placed "high visibility" posters. The more flyers you distribute, the greater the chance of recovering your lost pet.

How Wide an Area Should You Cover?

While your initial flyer placement should be concentrated in and around the immediate area where your pet was lost, you must be prepared to quickly expand your searching and flyer posting to include a much wider area. According to NPR, "More than 83% of the dogs NPR recovers are 12 to 40 miles from where they first went missing. 91% of cats we recover are within the nearest four miles from where they became missing." Fortunately, ferrets do not tend to wander very far unless carried away; therefore, you should concentrate your flyer placement in your immediate neighborhood and beyond.

This may seem overwhelming, and hopefully you have people to assist you. If not, there are places to ask for or hire help. (See "Locating Help for Hire.") When canvassing and posting flyers on foot, be sure to give one to everyone you see.

A Word of Caution

Posting signs, handbills, and similar materials is subject to municipal ordinances. Consult your city hall. Exceptions may be made even if they are not normally allowed and even permits granted. And remember, mailboxes are the property of the US Postal Service. It's illegal to put flyers in or on people's mailboxes.

Places for Flyers

BRING THE ITEMS LISTED IN YOUR RECOVERY KIT!!!

- High-volume locations in and around the area where your pet went missing. This includes gas stations, fast food restaurants, taverns, and convenience stores.

- Freestanding signs should be placed along the roadside where traffic is slow or stops completely.

- Parks, playgrounds, schoolyards, and any place where groups of children congregate; children are magnets for stray animals.

- Veterinarians, animal hospitals, and emergency clinics in the vicinity. Deliver as many as you can in person, and use a fax to get your flyers to facilities farther away.

- Get your flyers into the hands of local rescue groups.

- Any place there is a bulletin board: laundromats, community centers, coffee shops, and schools. Many towns have these in their business districts for posting local events, handbills, etc.
- Pet supply stores. The big chain stores like PETCO and PETsMART often have community bulletin boards for posting missing pet flyers. Some smaller pet stores may have these as well, or they may allow you to put a flyer in their window.
- Grocery stores. If someone finds your pet, that person will have to feed it something, and many grocery stores have bulletin boards for posting things.
- In areas where people walk their dogs (a beach or wooded area, for example), there is a good chance that if your dog is still in the area, someone out walking his or her dog may have seen it. If this is a place where you walk your own dog, it is possibly the very place you will find your dog.

Sample Classified Ads

The following is a checklist for you to consider when composing your classified advertisement. Include appropriate particulars pertaining to your pet and situation. (See "Flyers and Classified Ads.")

- AVOID DESCRIPTIVE ADJECTIVES (beautiful, smart, etc.)
- INCLUDE DAY & DATE
- DESCRIBE YOUR PET IN DETAIL
- Color patterns
- Distinguishing marks
- Hair length and texture
- Ear set
- Tail length and type
- Eye color
- WEIGHT & SIZE
- SEX
- AGE
- CONTACT INFORMATION
- BREED/SPECIES
- LOCATION
- COLLAR INFORMATION (last seen wearing)
- REWARD INFORMATION
- TATTOO INFORMATION
- OTHER PERTINENT INFORMATION

LOST

CAT–Orange with white paws, short-hair, gold eyes. Adult, female with tattoo in ear. Last seen wearing green collar. Lost near Winkle's Market in Belford area of Middletown Township on Friday 5/18. REWARD: (999) 999-9999

GERMAN SHEPHERD–Large, approx. 70lbs, adult, male, blk & tan, brown eyes, long-haired, bushy tail. One ear up, one down, small scar on nose. Last seen wearing orange collar. Lost Howell area, Sunday 5/20. (999) 999-9999. REWARD! PLEASE CALL WITH *ANY* SIGHTINGS!

PARAKEET–Green with some yellow. Lost Middletown area, Sun 5/27. REWARD. Please call (999) 999-9999. Cell: (999) 999-9999

FERRET–White with red eyes. Missing from yard in Jackson on Sat. 5/26. Last seen wearing red harness. REWARD!!! PLEASE CALL!! (999) 999-9999

REWARD!
LOST DOG

WHEN LOST: Missing since Thursday, April 26th   **NAME:** Jack

WHERE LOST: Lost in Middletown area, near Winkle's Market. Has a tendency to wander far.

AGE: **Adult**   SEX: **Male**   SIZE: **Small, approx. 18 lbs.**   BREED: **Jack Russell Terrier**

DESCRIPTION: White body with black patches on back, top of leg, and base of tail. Brown head with white at end of snout and white triangle on forehead. Brown eyes. Short straight hair. Medium length tail.

ADDITIONAL COMMENTS: He was last seen wearing a bright orange collar. He has a tattoo on his belly.

Call: 999-999-9999

| Call: 999-999-9999 Alt: 999-999-9999 | Call: 999-999-9999 Alt: 999-999-9999 | Call: 999-999-9999 Alt: 999-999-9999 | Call: 999-999-9999 Alt: 999-999-9999 | Call: 999-999-9999 Alt: 999-999-9999 | Call: 999-999-9999 Alt: 999-999-9999 | Call: 999-999-9999 Alt: 999-999-9999 | Call: 999-999-9999 Alt: 999-999-9999 | Call: 999-999-9999 Alt: 999-999-9999 | Call: 999-999-9999 Alt: 999-999-9999 |

- Recreation areas. Many towns have areas with places for people to bike, jog, run, or walk, and often have an area to rest and even restroom facilities.
- If your pet is a repeat offender, there is a good chance it will go to the same area where it was found the last time. Canvass this area very well, and blanket it with as many flyers as you can.

• Pizza parlors	• Churches	• Salons
• Dog grooming shops	• Any store or shop that will permit it	

Other Ways to Get the Word Out

Apart from bulk advertising and posting a lost pet announcement on the Internet, there are many other ways for letting people know about your missing pet. Simply apply the same techniques described above for flyers and ads. These alternative methods of advertising your lost pet can be especially helpful for the elderly, the homebound, the disabled, and others who may not be able to create and post flyers around the neighborhood. Here are some other places you can advertise a lost pet.

- *Val-Pak/Penny-Saver Mailers*—You know what these are. They're mailed out regularly, and people actually look forward to receiving them. A plus is that they can be targeted to the area where your pet was lost. The drawbacks are timeliness (mailings may only go out a few times a year, and ads may be due a month in advance) and expense (a few hundred dollars—prices vary so call for exact quotes). This is a good option if your pet has been missing for several weeks, and you refuse to give up. Remember, pets are often taken in and kept by those who find them, believing them to be abandoned or stray; your pet could literally be a few blocks from your home.
- *Direct Mail Postcards*—Mailing postcards is another way of targeting the area or neighborhood where your pet was lost and, at the current rate, they're relatively inexpensive. Postcards can be printed on your computer, and you can even insert photos of your pet. Your local library has a special phone book, the reverse directory, which lists every resident by block and house number. There are also lost pet services that will do this for you. (See "Critical Contacts.")
- *Newspaper Inserts*—This is a good way to cover a large area, and you can use the flyers you are already distributing. Like coupon mailers and direct mail postcards,

they can be targeted at a specific area. Because so few people use this approach, your insert will really get noticed! Some newspapers offer this service a few times a week. Price, however, may be a concern, as it will probably cost as much as a few hundred dollars. Contact your local newspaper for exact prices.

- *The Internet*—Be sure to check out the web sites on which you can post missing and found pet notices. Most allow you to do this by state and even by city, and many are free. Don't rely on these alone; understand that the Internet is still in its infancy. (See "Critical Contacts.")

- *Town Web Sites*—Many towns have their own web sites, and the advantage is that they're localized. They may have a bulletin board where you can alert people to your lost pet for free. You may also want to check with the city to see what space on the web site might be available for advertising.

- *Cable, TV, and Radio*—Call and see if your local cable provider and television and radio stations offer lost pet listings free as a public service. If you find you have to pay for a listing, try convincing someone at the station that it is a newsworthy story, depending on the circumstances of your pet's disappearance (e.g., if it was stolen, lost on vacation, etc.).

Some Additional Things You Can Do

Here are some additional things (some might seem extreme) which you can do if you are so inclined and if resources permit.

- Have magnetic signs made with your lost pet information on them and attach them to the sides of your car. This way, everywhere you go people will see your lost pet ad.

- Have T-shirts made with your lost pet information and even a photograph of your missing pet. You can have them made at a T-shirt shop, or if you have a computer, there are programs for making T-shirt transfers and running them off on your printer.

- Rent space on a billboard. This is expensive and perhaps extreme, but if it's within your means to do so, you might want to consider it. It certainly would attract a lot of attention!

- Mobile billboards on a trailer that you can tow around or park at different locations. There are regulations against these in some towns, so you would want to check on that first.

- Visit a pet psychic? If you are so inclined, many claim to be able to locate missing pets and persons.

Check the Animal Shelters

You will need to visit all facilities that take in stray animals in and around the area where your pet was lost, and then revisit them every other day. Contact facilities farther away (in approximately a 60-mile radius) and fax them photos of your pet along with contact information, or better yet, fax them a copy of your flyer. While faxing photos and flyers is important and should be done immediately, you can't be certain that if your pet were brought into the shelter someone would match it with your flyer or photo. Consider that your pet might appear quite different after having survived several days or weeks on the street, and giving your pet's description over the phone leaves too much room for error. You must visit as many facilities (or have someone who is familiar with your pet visit them) as you can in person; it is ultimately your responsibility to actively search for your lost pet.

Some Things You Will Need

- *Proof of Ownership*—Anything that establishes ownership, such as purchase receipts, adoption papers, breed records, photographs, etc.

- *Current Vaccination Records*—Proof of rabies vaccination. This is crucial because if your pet shows signs of having had an altercation with a wild animal, and the offending animal is unavailable for testing, your pet will be assumed to have been exposed to rabies. This could lead to your pet's being subjected to a lengthy quarantine (at your expense), or to your pet's being euthanized.

- *Log Sheets*—Use these to keep track of the contacts you make at the shelters, whom you spoke to at each facility, etc. This is important since as long as your pet remains at large you will have to follow up.

- *Flyers*—Many shelters have boards for posting lost pet flyers. Also, give several copies to the shelter workers.

- *Photographs*—Hopefully, you've included a good quality photo on your flyers. If not, then bring along photos to show and to leave with shelter workers.

- *Written Description*—Write out a description of your pet, including every detail, (unique markings, hair type and length, etc.) and give copies to the shelter workers. (See "Preparing for Recovery.")

- *License*—In most situations, you will need to prove your pet is licensed. If your pet is unlicensed, you may have to agree to obtain a license within a set period of time, and may even receive a summons.

Some Things You Should Know

- *Shelter Locations*—Animal care and control agencies operate at the local level and each town may have its own separate arrangements for the care and housing of stray animals. Each town may use a different shelter within a single county. Knowing this is critical because a pet lost in one town and picked up in another may be taken to an entirely different facility. Locating the shelters in your area is easy. (See "Critical Contacts.")

• *Special Areas*—Ask about special areas where quarantined and injured pets may be kept separate from the rest of the shelter animals. Insist that shelter workers check in these areas for your pet.

• *Pound Seizure*—The majority of states still permit the selling of surplus shelter animals to animal dealers for a variety of purposes, including for use in experimentation. Ask if the shelter practices "pound seizure." If they do, politely remind them that the Animal Welfare Act requires that they keep strays slated for this purpose for five full days. Don't antagonize the staff though; they have no control over the county's policy regarding pound seizure, and besides, you need them. After you've found your pet, write to your legislators and direct your anger at those responsible for such policies.

• *Your Pet's ID*—If your pet is tattooed or microchipped, alert the shelter workers and leave the tattoo or microchip information with them.

• *The Internet*—Ask if your local shelter has a web site. Many shelters operate web sites today and may have space for posting local lost/found pet reports.

• *Rescue Groups*—Many rescue groups operate their own shelter facilities. If your lost pet is a purebred, you will want to contact the appropriate breed rescue groups.

• *Cats*—You may think that you will recognize your cat anywhere, until you find yourself in a crowded animal shelter and realize there are a dozen cats similar to yours. It can be very difficult to tell one from another, especially with some of the common mixed breed cats. After you've peered into two dozen cages, tiger stripes can all begin to look the same. The point we are making here is that you need to take your time and search slowly and carefully.

• *Birds, Ferrets, and Other Critters*—Depending on the type of pet you have, your local animal shelter may not be permitted to house it. In many places, ferrets are considered exotics and the shelters may not be permitted to house them without a special license. They usually call on a local ferret rescue shelter. Shelters may also work with various bird rescue groups when a lost bird is brought to them. To locate breed rescue facilities see "Critical Contacts."

• *Foster Care*—Ask about foster care. Many shelters have foster care arrangements with families where animals are cared for temporarily until they can be permanently placed. If your pet was injured or sick when brought to the shelter, it may be recovering in a foster home. Your pet could remain in foster care for days, weeks, or months until the shelter deems it ready for adoption.

What You Should Expect

The most likely scenario you will encounter will be shelter workers who are dedicated animal lovers. These folks care deeply for the animals in their charge. Most will be very familiar with people searching for lost pets and will be glad to offer you assistance, encouragement, and advice. It is important, however, that you understand that shelters are very busy places. They usually do their best to get lost pets back to their owners, but cannot make guarantees.

Understand the Shelter's Limitations

Helping pet owners locate lost pets, as important as it is, is only a small part of the animal shelter's role in the community. Shelters have the awesome responsibility of dealing with animals that have been relinquished, abandoned, neglected, abused, and injured, as well as feral animals. These animals must be cared for, treated medically, put down, assessed as to whether they are candidates for adoption, neutered, etc., etc., etc. You must understand the shelter's limitations. This is why we tell you to visit them in person, and be vigilant in trying to locate your pet yourself.

Bad Shelters

We like to believe that all animal shelters are safe havens for stray animals (often people's lost pets) and that all shelter workers are benevolent people. In most cases, of course, they are. Sadly, however, this is not always the case. The fact is there are simply some terrible animal shelters with poorly-trained staff, unsanitary conditions, etc. While most people find it difficult to imagine how anyone could do shelter work without having a real love and concern for animals, for some people it may simply be a job. If you have genuine concerns about your local animal shelter, The Humane Society of the United States offers the following advice.

What to Do If You Have Concerns about Your Local Animal Shelter

"When you have concerns about the operation of your local animal shelter, The HSUS generally recommends that you contact the governing body of the organization or agency. Each shelter is an independent organization, governed by its own bylaws and board of directors (in the case of private humane organizations) or local ordinances and officials (in the case of municipal animal care and control agencies). To find out what type of organization or agency your local animal shelter is, simply contact the shelter itself or call your county or city clerk's office."

*Reprinted with permission from The Humane Society of the United States (**www.hsus.org**). Copyright 1999. All rights reserved.*

Investigating Leads

You've done all the search work and with any luck, a neighbor will call right away and say he has picked up your pet and it's fine. That's great news! If not, however, you need to be prepared to chase down dozens of bad leads, from well-intentioned people who are simply mistaken, to deliberate hoaxes perpetrated by people who apparently have nothing better to do. Worse, you may encounter someone who tries to scam you or extort money from you. While still a relatively rare occurrence, it does happen and it pays to be informed. (See "Beware of Scams.")

Although you've tried your best to give an accurate description of your pet in your ad or on your flyer, such things as color, size, breed, age, and sex pretty much go out the window when the calls start coming in. People get these things confused all the time. It is important to remember that your pet's appearance may be quite different after having survived on the street for even just a few days. In addition, it may have been injured, and therefore its physical appearance may be drastically different. The best rule to follow is to check out every lead where there is even the slightest possibility that it could be your pet. Here are a few things to consider.

A Few Things to Consider

There are three essentials for organizing the information generated by your ads and flyers: an answering machine that can be set to record (the information can be transcribed later); a log sheet or pad and pen; and a map. Because your flyers and ads will generate many calls, it is crucial that this information be well organized. (See "Organizing the Search.") Here are some additional things to consider:

- A lost pet may change hands several times during its absence, and its appearance and even physical state may have been altered. For example, your pet may have been neutered or declawed by someone who found him. Also, your pet may have been injured while it was lost and now may have a kink in its tail or a nick on its ear. The lesson here is don't ignore a report from someone claiming to have a stray fitting your pet's description, because they talk about an animal that sounds a little different from the way yours looked before it was lost.

- Another common mistake is ignoring a lead because the person reports the animal they've found has a different colored collar or no collar at all. According to National Pet Recovery, in 28% of cases in which they've recovered lost pets, the animal's collar had been changed or removed. It is important to prefix any mention of a collar with "last seen wearing" when placing an ad or making a flyer.

- When someone tells you they believe they saw an animal fitting your pet's description, ask for specifics: times, dates, street names, landmarks, etc. If they aren't sure of the street names, ask if they would be willing to return to the area and write them down. Just the other day, we spotted a stray but were unable to retrieve it. After looking in the paper, we located the possible owner, spoke with her, and then returned to the area to write down all the specifics. Someone who takes the time to call with a possible sighting is likely to be willing to do this for you. Ask for their phone number so you can call them later for additional information (don't rely on their calling you) or better yet, ask if they would be willing to lead you to the place.

• Filter out the legitimate calls from others. You're likely to get many calls from many different people with many different motivations. People may call just to harass you, to say sick things like your pet is dead, or to send you on a wild goose chase. You may also receive calls from people who are very empathetic and want to encourage you with kind words (when you get these calls you will be thankful and strengthened in your resolve). Others who have lost pets in the past may call you and even offer to assist you. Never pass up an opportunity to get some much-needed assistance. Just use your instincts. It's fairly easy to filter out the bad calls from the good, and you will soon discover that leads often lead to other leads.

You Suspect That Your Pet is Being Kept by Someone

It's possible that you may get a call from someone saying that your pet has been taken in by someone and is at such and such an address. If the caller wishes to remain anonymous, you should assure him or her that you will respect that request. People take in and keep stray animals all the time and in fact, this is where many missing pets end up. While this is wrong, it is not necessarily malicious. It's best not to assume that their motivation is negative. Here are some things you can do if you suspect your pet is being kept by someone.

• If you have reason to believe that someone has your pet, the last thing you want to do is alert them before you are positive. If they're somehow tipped off, they may try to hide your pet or send it to a friend or a relative, or fear discovery and turn the animal loose again.

• If it is within your means to do so, you might want to hire a private investigator to try to get evidence that the people you suspect do in fact have your pet.

• Try to find out the laws in your area regarding found strays. In some places, for example, it's the law that found strays be turned over to animal control or taken to a shelter. If this is the case where you live, it's important to know because you may need the police to assist you.

• If you decide to do some surveillance, do it from a safe distance. Bring along a good camera with a zoom lens, and try to snap a photo of the animal. Of course, with cats and birds, this is more difficult since they are generally kept indoors.

Cats do like to perch themselves at windows, and a bird may be kept near a window. If you can get a good clear photo, you can take it to the police who may be more inclined to assist when confronted with direct evidence. Be sure to use caution if you question neighbors, since they may alert the person who has your pet.

- Once you are certain that they are keeping your pet, and have some supporting evidence, ask the police for assistance. If you meet resistance, go right up the chain of command all the way to the prosecutor's office if you have to. Remind them that your pet is your property, and insist that the law be enforced. If you followed our earlier instructions, you've already filed a lost pet report, so the police will already be aware that you have been looking for your pet.

- Although we strongly advise against it, you may decide you want to confront the people keeping your pet yourself. If you do, do not go alone, and bring a cell phone. If they refuse to let you see the animal, phone the police, call 911, cause a scene, do whatever you need to do short of something criminal. If it's safe, plant yourself outside of their house (don't leave and give them an opportunity to whisk your pet away), and wait there until the police arrive.

- On a positive note, remember that the people who have your pet may not necessarily be mean. They may really believe they're helping an abandoned animal and may have even made an attempt to locate the owner. They may have posted flyers or even placed an ad that you simply overlooked.

Pet Detectives

Most people had probably never heard of this profession until Jim Carrey starred in the comedy movie *Ace Ventura: Pet Detective*. Although their numbers are increasing, real pet detectives are still few and far between. If you are fortunate enough to live in places like Florida, Texas, or California, you can secure the services of one of these detectives, many of whom have tracking dogs trained in the search and rescue of missing pets.

There are independent pet detectives scattered throughout the country, although there is no association or centralized directory that we are aware of. You can ask shelters, veterinarians, or rescue groups in your area, and check your local telephone directory. At the moment, this is a fairly loose and unregulated profession. That's expected to change within the next few years. National Pet Detectives, founded by Larry Maynard, has begun training other pet detectives and has even produced a lost pet video. (See figure 40.) Pet Hunters' founder Kat Albrecht recently joined forces with the American Humane Association, and they have begun training pet detectives and tracking dogs. Kat's greatest concern is for the establishment of national standards and certification, "so that when a pet owner does use this service in the future, they will be guaranteed that the dog (and the pet detective) passed

> **National Pet Detectives' Lost Pet Video**
>
> National Pet Detectives recently released their lost pet prevention and recovery video. Narrated by National Pet Detectives' founder, Larry Maynard, the video covers all the basics of preventing both pet loss and pet theft, and gives pet owners tips for recovering lost and stolen pets. To order NPD's lost pet video, contact National Pet Detectives at:
> **Phone:** (866) 2-RESCUE (273-7283); in Pinellas County, Florida (727) 398-2805
> **E-mail:** info@nationalpetdetectives.com
> **Web site: www.nationalpetdetectives.com**

FIGURE 40

a test and are legitimately trained to search for missing animals." They hope to take this program nationwide over the next five years. When we told her about our book she was excited. She did express concern, however, saying, "The worst thing that could happen would be if we had thousands of people who think this sounds like a 'great idea' run out and try to start doing this work without the proper training (of both the person and the dog). If your readers want to assist, the best thing they can do is to make a donation." (See "Resources/Pet Detectives.")

Beware of Scams

Chances are you'll be successful in locating your lost pet and won't have to deal with those who would otherwise exploit your loss. Even if someone else does find your pet, the odds are that person has good intentions. Nevertheless, there are criminals whose stock trade is lost pets—pet thieves and scam artists who have a whole arsenal of schemes at their disposal, that are very successful with emotionally distraught pet owners. Here are some common tricks and how to avoid becoming a victim:

Pet Scammers Make Their TV Debut

Those close to the issue of lost and stolen pets have been warning people for a long time about con artists who prey on vulnerable pet owners distraught over having lost a beloved pet. The issue was recently catapulted into the national spotlight, when on Friday, July 20, 2001, the news magazine program DATELINE NBC aired a segment titled *Dog Gone Shame*.

The program recounts a California couple's desperate attempt to recover their lost dog Sasha through a series of collect telephone calls from a man who identified himself only as Mike. Mike didn't claim to have the dog, but he knew who did, and he had a plan to help get her back. The plan was, of course, contingent on the couple wiring one third of the $1000 reward, via Western Union, with no ID required to pick up the money at the other end: a sure sign that his claims were fraudulent.

Fortunately, this couple followed their better instincts and contacted the police, who advised them to record the phone calls. They wanted so much to believe this man really knew who had their beloved Sasha that, hoping against hope, they put themselves through an emotionally grueling volley of telephone calls.

Mike described Sasha in every detail, right down to her unusual eyes, one blue and one green. This information, of course, he had easily gleaned from a newspaper ad the couple had placed some time before. With each call, however, it became clearer that this man had no knowledge of their dog's whereabouts; he was nothing more than an opportunist.

The Lost Pet Scam

Thieves use lost pet ads to get in touch with anxious pet owners. More often than not, they choose ads that offer cash rewards and they usually ask that money be turned over before the animal is returned. A refusal can bring a threat of physical harm to the pet, which usually induces the owner to pay.

• Demands for money or threats to harm your pet if money is not sent in advance should immediately send up a red flag.

• Don't be intimidated or fearful for your pet. People who pull this scam are simply opportunists who have come across your ad or flyer and most likely don't even have your pet. (See figure 41.)

• Most of these con artists will request that you wire the money to them. The reason is that money wired to one location can be picked up at another, so you can't have the police waiting for them. Another reason is that unless you specifically request it, they are not required to show identification. If you insist on their showing ID they will likely give up. The best rule is never to send money to someone claiming to have your pet, until the animal is returned safely or brought to an animal shelter (see "The Trucker/Traveler Scam" below). Insist on a meeting, but never go alone and always meet in a public area. If they really have your pet, they will agree.

- A blocked caller identification number may not necessarily be an indication of a scam. If it is, there will be some other supporting evidence such as probing questions and requests for money in advance of returning your pet to you.

- Trust your instincts; if your gut tells you something is wrong, something probably is. If you suspect you are being targeted for a scam, call the police.

Con Man's Prey: Pet Owners
INDICTMENT SAYS HE PRETENDS TO FIND LOST ANIMALS, POCKETS REWARDS

By Lisa Fernandez

"A Hayward man has been indicted in two states in an unprecedented nationwide pet scam for allegedly cheating forlorn animal owners who expected him to unite them with their missing dogs and cats.

"William Arnold Muniz, 39, was charged with a total of 18 felony counts of wire fraud and illegally obtaining money by federal grand juries in Nevada and the U.S. District Court in San Francisco. He allegedly scoured lost-pet ads across the country, called the owners to say he had found their animals, and pocketed a total of $10,000 from at least 16 owners who wired him cash, but never got their pets.

"Indictments filed this week in the U.S. District Court in San Francisco, and last week in the U.S. District Court of Nevada, allege that from October to February, Muniz scanned newspapers, flyers, and the Internet for lost-pet ads. Speaking in a fake French Canadian accent, he called the owners, claiming he'd found their pets, but would need a few hundred dollars for their safe return or to reimburse him for veterinary expenses."

FIGURE 41

The Found Pet Scam

In this ruse, a professional pet thief, a lowlife involved in dog fighting, or some other creep calls a well-intentioned person who found a stray animal and placed a found pet ad in the newspaper. In the ad, this person has inadvertently supplied the crook with a description of the animal. The con artist pretends to be the grateful owner, picks up the animal, and then turns around and sells it to an animal dealer where it will likely meet a horrible fate as a research specimen in a lab or as bait for an illegal dog fight. (See "Stolen Pets.") There are more proper ways for handling found strays. (See "Found Strays.")

- Hold back one or more identifying marks or distinguishing characteristics when placing a found stray ad.

- Be aware of callers who only seem to solicit information. Don't volunteer anything. If it is the pet's owners, they will be able to describe the animal without any help from you.

- Be sure to ask the claimant to the found stray for pet records, photographs, papers, etc., before turning the animal over.

The Team Scheme

In this one, an advance person calls the number on a flyer or in an ad, talks to the owner sympathetically, and draws out information about the animal. After learning what he needs to know, the shill will usually say it's not his animal after all. A little later, his partner will call with an exact description of the animal and demand money. (See the tips for "The Found Pet Scam" above.)

The Trucker/Traveler Scam

The con artist claims to be someone who, while traveling through your area, found a stray animal that fits your pet's description. The crook will say something like the pet needed emergency veterinary care (which he paid for, of course, and for which he wants to be reimbursed). He may even ask for additional money to send the pet back with another driver who will, according to him, be coming through the owner's area soon. (According to the Humane Society of the United States, this scheme has become so widespread that some police departments have issued press releases warning pet owners.)

- Although it's not an impossible scenario, the trucker/traveler gambit is more than likely illegitimate.

- Think about it. This person claiming to have your pet was benevolent enough to pick up a poor wounded stray animal and then travel all the way home with it. He then takes it for emergency medical treatment, pays for it out of his own pocket, and then takes the time to read through the classified ads from a newspaper published in a city some distance from where he lives. Then, he suddenly turns into a money-grubbing fiend and begins demanding money? Obviously, this makes no sense.

- Suggestion: Ask for the name of the veterinarian where the animal was treated and call to verify.

- If it is simply a matter of transporting the animal, you could agree to go and retrieve the animal yourself. If it is a scam, however, the trip will be wasted and time that could have been spent looking for your pet will be lost. A better solution is to locate a shelter in the area where this person lives, that agrees to act as a liaison. Explain the situation to the shelter director. If he or she agrees to help, direct the person claiming to have your pet to bring it to the shelter. Tell him you will compensate him for any money dispensed on your pet's behalf, and pay the reward you have offered once it is confirmed, beyond doubt, that the animal is indeed your pet. This can be done by faxing photos (although with many breeds it is difficult to determine through photos), describing markings that are "unique" to your pet, (e.g., a scar, a nicked ear, or an unmistakable color pattern) or ideally by permanent ID, such as a tattoo or microchip. If it cannot be determined with 100% certainty that the animal in question is your beloved pet, then only pay the money after your pet is safely home.

The Charity Scam

In this rip-off, someone goes through the classified ads and calls people who have recently lost a pet. This person doesn't claim to have your pet. Instead, what they do is exploit the pet owner's emotionally vulnerable state. They may not even let on that they know you've lost a pet. They claim to represent a charity that's related to pets in distress (e.g., lost, stolen, or abused). They will then ask for a donation and try to obtain a credit card number, or offer to send a courier to pick up the donation (this is a common way they avoid the more serious offense of mail fraud).

- Don't donate to any pet charity requesting money that is unwilling to first send you literature. It's a sure sign that it is fraudulent.
- If the timing of the call coincides with the recent loss of your pet, be especially wary.

The "To a Good Home" Ad Scam

The con man or woman in this one will answer ads placed by people looking for good homes for pets they can no longer keep. He will tell the pet owner that he runs a placement service and, for a fee, will make certain the pet is placed in a loving home. After he's gotten the money and the animal, he will then sell it to some other equally vile person for profit, or perhaps simply dump it by the side of the road.

- If you must relinquish your pet, don't place a "to a good home" ad until all your other options have been explored. First, try placing the animal with a family member or a friend. Or if it's a purebred, try placing it with a breed rescue group.
- If you do place your pet through a "to a good home" ad, thoroughly check out the respondents. In their *Guidelines For Finding A Responsible Home For A Pet*, the Humane Society of the United States offers this advice: "Finding a new home for

a pet can be difficult. A 'good' home means a home where the animal will live for the rest of his or her life, where he or she will receive attention, veterinary care, proper nutrition, and be treated as part of the family." They urge you to screen potential homes carefully and warn you not to be fooled.

- Ask lots of questions. Any legitimate animal-loving person will have no problems with questions concerning your pet's care.

- Ask for identification, especially one with a photograph (e.g., a driver's license).

- Ask if they would mind if you visited their home.

- Ask if they have other pets and, if so, who their veterinarian is.

For more information, visit The Humane Society of the United States' *Pet Information Center* at **www.hsus.org**., and read their *Guidelines For Finding A Responsible Home For A Pet*.

Special Recovery Situations

When it comes to losing a pet, there are so many variables that it is nearly impossible to develop a universal recovery plan, one that covers every situation and circumstance. Under normal circumstances, there are specific steps pet owners can follow to maximize their chances of a speedy recovery. There are special situations, however (losing a pet during a disaster, having a pet stolen), where one needs to respond a little differently. Our recovery plan, coupled with a little common sense and a brief reading of this special section, will cover almost any situation. The following list of special situations will be kept brief. Always follow the recovery plan as closely as possible, and read through this section to address the particulars that are unique to your situation.

Recovery: Travel

If you lose your pet while traveling or on vacation, follow the recovery plan as closely as possible, tailoring it to your situation:

- Enlist someone to give you long-distance support. Eventually, you will have to return home, leaving your pet with no one searching for it. Here are some people who may be willing to help:

  - Members of pet clubs, rescue group members, members of local animal organizations, shelter workers (shelters often employ volunteers; who better to ask. Offer to pay them, and also offer a reward as an incentive for finding your pet.) Use the "Critical Contacts" list to locate them.

- There are places where you can hire help. "Situations Wanted" ads in the local newspapers, for example. (See "Locating Help for Hire.")

- Know exactly where you were when your pet was lost. Write down street names, highway markers, any landmarks.

- Go to the borough hall or to a bookstore and get copies of town maps.

- If you were on the road, do not continue on to your destination; instead, check into a hotel in the area.

- Contact a recovery service. There are many things they can do for you, such as contacting every facility that takes in stray animals in the area where your pet was lost.

- Get your flyers out immediately. Include contact numbers where you are staying in the area. Also include a contact number for someone back home: a friend, family member, or your Pet Partner. If you have been fortunate enough to locate someone in the area, you were traveling, and they are willing to help, you can include their number as well. A cell phone with nationwide service is ideal.

- Contact the news media: radio stations, local TV stations. This is a good source for getting the word out if you lose your pet away from home. Try to convince them that a pet lost hundreds of miles from home is newsworthy; play on the emotion of it. Your pet is lost, has not been recovered, and you will be forced to leave it behind. This is good stuff, especially for local newspapers.

- Place a classified ad in the paper.

Recovery: Air Travel

If your pet was lost by an airline, follow the recovery plan as closely as possible, tailoring it to your situation.

- *Make a lot of noise!*

- *Contact airline officials immediately.*

- *Find out the circumstances.* Was your pet lost in the cargo hold, in the terminal, etc.?

- *Insist that the plane be grounded in order to search for your pet.*

- *Contact an attorney.* This has proven to be successful. A judge can order the plane to be grounded and searched thoroughly.

- *Contact the news media.* If there is one thing that airlines hate, it is bad PR.

- *File an Air Travel Incident Report.* These can be downloaded from the Internet at The Humane Society of the United States' *Pet Information Center* at **www.hsus.org**. Search keyword "travel" and choose *"File a Complaint Against an Airline."*

Recovery: Pet Sitters, Boarding Kennels, and Caretakers

If your pet is lost while in the care of a sitter, boarding kennel, or other caretaker, follow or have them follow the recovery plan as closely as possible, tailoring it to the situation.

How to proceed will best be determined by what you can discover about the event, and if you are able to help in the recovery effort. Find out as many details as possible from whomever was caring for your pet. Try to determine the exact nature of and circumstances surrounding your pet's disappearance. Ask a lot of questions. Ask:

- Who was in charge of the care of your pet at the time it went missing?
- Did someone actually witness the event, and if so, who?
- If no one actually witnessed the event, then who discovered that your pet was missing?
- What was the location?
- How much time has elapsed?
- Who have they actually contacted so far?
- Is there a possibility that your pet was stolen?
- What, if anything, has been done so far to recover your pet?

Once these things have been determined, it will give you a better idea of exactly how to proceed. Here are some options:

- Return home, if at all possible, to help in the recovery effort.
- Use your Pet Partner or some other designated person to begin the search for your lost pet.
- Contact a recovery service immediately so they can get the word out about your lost pet. Some recovery services will mail information about your lost pet to all shelter facilities in and around the area where your pet was lost. If you are a thousand miles away from home, this type of service can make a real difference.
- Copy and fax the pages from the recovery plan (e.g. "People You Should Call," "Places to Check," etc.) to whomever was caring for your pet.

Recovery: Accidents

Being involved in an accident is a unique situation in terms of pet loss. You may be completely unconscious, or injured and unable to go after your pet. Or your pet may be at home, and depending on the type of pet, this could have tragic consequences. How you proceed will be determined by your situation; hopefully you've made arrangements in advance.

Accidents clearly illustrate the importance of preparing ahead. Please read "Accidents" in the "Prevention" section, and take the necessary precautions. Seriously consider a service such as Pet Guardian Angels of America's Pet Alert. It can really make a difference in an accident situation. If you are injured or incapacitated, you will not be able to search for your pet yourself. You will have to rely on others. The important thing when relying on others is to give them the tools they need to conduct an effective search for your lost pet: this book for example. Here are a few people who can assist you.

- Friends or family.
- Your Pet Partner.
- A recovery service.
- Paid assistance. (See "Locating Help for Hire.")

If you were not seriously injured, it may be that your pet escaped in the confusion. However, you can't just leave the scene of the accident to chase after your pet, so in this situation:

- Alert police and Emergency Medical Technicians and see if someone could assist you. Give them a thorough description of your pet and the direction it ran off in.
- Stress the urgency of the situation, and ask if there is any way to expedite the process.
- Ask police if, once insurance and other information is exchanged, you could have your car pulled to the side, or even towed so you can go after your pet.

If you are injured in an accident, and your pets are at home:

- Contact people such as friends, family, or a neighbor, to care for your pets. Do this as soon as you are able; depending on the type of pet you have, it may not be able to survive on its own for very long. This is one reason to seriously consider using static cling window decals and an emergency notification wallet card to let emergency workers know that you have pets, and let them know who to contact if you are seriously injured.

Recovery: Moving

If you lose your pet while in the process of moving, follow the recovery plan as closely as possible, tailoring it to your situation.

Understand that the moving company may require that someone be at the final destination, with final payment, before they will unload your things. Some of your options would be to:

- Have a friend or family member meet them at the new address.

- Arrange for someone else to meet the movers at your new address. If you are relocating for work, ask your company to arrange this for you.

- Ask if your belongings can be temporarily put into storage. Many moving companies have storage facilities.

- Halt or delay the move if you have not actually hit the road yet.

- Rely on your Pet Partner to assist you.

- Contact a recovery service.

- If your pet was lost in transit, see the above section on losing a pet while traveling.

Recovery: Stolen Pets

If you believe your pet was stolen, follow the recovery plan as closely as possible, tailoring it to your situation.

The first thing you should do is call your local police and file a report. Then contact other professionals with the expertise to help. Here are some people you should contact.

- In Defense of Animals. Phone: (800) STOLEN-PET (786-5367).

- National Pet Detectives. Phone: (866) 2-RESCUE (273-7283); in Pinellas County, Florida at (727) 398-2805. Also visit National Pet Detectives, E-group at **www.groups.yahoo.com** and search National Pet Detectives. This group is for those who have registered their pets with National Pet Detectives. NPD founder Larry Maynard is very knowledgeable in the area of lost and stolen pets. You can e-mail NPD for information and/or advice at info@nationalpetdetectives.com.

- The USDA-APHIS-Animal Care. Phone: (301) 734-4981. Stolen pets are often sold to research facilities through registered animal dealers. Alert animal dealers and research facilities in your area; fax them photos, flyers, and your contact information. You can obtain a list of the animal dealers and research facilities in your area by contacting the USDA. Also available online at **www.aphis.usda.gov/ac/publications.html**

- Check the "For Sale" advertisements in the paper, especially if your pet was a purebred or an expensive bird. And have friends and family check the papers in outlying communities as well.

- Contact pet stores, bird jungles, local breeders, or breed clubs, especially if your stolen pet was an expensive breed or exotic animal. Call everywhere a person might try to sell an expensive animal.

- Talk to your neighbors, and ask if any suspicious persons or vehicles were seen in your neighborhood. If you have a neighborhood watch program, contact them.

Recovery: Holidays and Parties

If your pet is lost during a holiday or party, follow the recovery plan as closely as possible, tailoring it to your situation.

- Know that your local shelters may be closed on major holidays. Each shelter sets its own schedule, so call immediately to find out. You do not want to waste time visiting shelters that are closed.

- If you are having a party or have company for the holidays, this could be a blessing in disguise, since there will be additional people available to help.

- If you have been drinking, stop immediately. You need to be thinking clearly. Also, someone will need to drive around the area searching for your pet. Do not drive if you've been drinking.

Recovery: Disasters

If your pet is lost during a disaster, follow the recovery plan as closely as possible, tailoring it to your situation.

- Rely on local officials who should be able to keep you abreast of what is happening.
- Use your list of "Critical Contacts."
- Find out what disaster relief efforts are being coordinated in your area. The following organizations may be of assistance and may already be involved in the rescue and relief efforts.

  - *The American Humane Association, Emergency Animal Relief (EAR)— (www.americanhumane.org)*. Click on the "Disaster Relief" link. Phone: (303) 792-9900, E-mail: ear@americanhumane.org.

  - *The American Red Cross—(www.redcross.org)*. Contact your local chapter of the American Red Cross. E-mail: info@usa.redcross.org.

  - *The Federal Emergency Management Agency (FEMA)—(www.fema.gov)*. Search the site using the keyword "pets." Phone: (202) 566-1600. Call to get the number of your regional FEMA office.

  - *The Humane Society of the United States (Disaster Services)—(www.hsus.org)*. Phone: (301) 258-3103 or (301) 258-3063. E-mail: disaster@hsus.org

  - *United Animal Nations, Emergency Animal Rescue Services (EARS)— (www.uan.org)*. Click on the "EARS" link. Phone: (916) 429-2457, E-mail: info@uan.org.

- *Cooperate with animal rescue workers.*
- *Visit temporary or emergency shelters.* In the aftermath of a major disaster,

emergency or temporary animal shelter facilities are often set up to care for animals displaced by the disaster, many of which are people's lost pets. You must visit these facilities, and bring along photographs of your pet and your pet records.

- *Examine photo albums carefully.* The temporary shelter facilities will probably have photo albums with pictures of pets that were recovered. It is important to realize that your pet may look quite different in these photographs, so examine them closely. Here is a perfect example of where a tattoo or microchip would eliminate any confusion. Shelters may also set up a web site with pet photos.

- *Follow the local news broadcasts.* When a disaster strikes, some people are so traumatized that they cannot even watch the news coverage. As difficult as this may be, for your pet's sake, you must follow the local news broadcasts. After the fires in Oakland, California, the local news media broadcast photographs of pets that had been rescued; many pets were reunited with their owners this way.

- Leave strong-scented articles of clothing around your property if you discover your pet is missing upon your return, or if your pet went missing prior to your having to evacuate. Also leave your pet's bedding, kitty litter pan, carrier or cage, a can of open sardines, or anything that may lead your pet home.

- Follow the recovery plan as closely as possible, once you are permitted to return to your home.

Recovery: Birds

How you proceed when trying to recover a lost bird can be quite different from looking for a dog or cat. Obviously, if your bird did indeed fly off and is still in your sight, the important thing is not making phone calls, or passing out flyers, or placing advertisements. Keep your eye on your bird!

When it first flies away, it will probably fly only a short distance and then perch itself in a nearby tree or on a rooftop. Remember, your bird is not used to open flight and is probably more frightened than you are. Keep calling your bird and whistling to it. The sound of your voice is the only thing familiar to it at this point and, hopefully, will keep it from flying farther away.

Be very careful of well-intentioned but misguided advice. We once lost our beloved cockatiel, Tra, on a trip to the veterinarian, for her wing clipping ironically enough. We could see her sitting on a tree branch, but were unable to coax her down. It was near sunset, and we didn't know what to do. We contacted an animal control officer, and he told us that she wouldn't fly off at night. He advised us to go home and return early in the morning before sunrise to get our bird. We were hesitant, but we did as he suggested. He was wrong. We never saw our bird again.

To Coo or Pursue—That is the Question

We posed this question to Jackie Mount of Second Chance Wildlife, Middletown New Jersey, a bird rescuer who has been involved in wild bird rehabilitation for many years. Her advice to me was that it is better to first try to coo rather than pursue your bird. "Pursuing a frightened bird," she says, "may have the effect of chasing the bird further away and eventually losing sight of it. Remember your bird is frightened and may be hesitant to come so this may take some time; you need to be patient."

When to Coo

- Since you don't want to lose sight of your bird (or your bird to lose sight of you), stick close to your bird. Quickly enlist the help of others to gather the following recovery items: your bird's travel cage, its mate, a long light-handled net, gloves, binoculars, a flashlight, and a ladder. There are also some other important recovery items you will need. (See "Preparing for Recovery.")

- Place its cage in an open area where your bird can see it, and then gently coo and call your bird. You want to assure your bird in a familiar and comforting tone. If you lose sight of your bird altogether, leave its cage outside, with the door open, and put fresh food and water inside. The cage is familiar and may offer a sense of security. Keep an eye out for other birds, as they will also be attracted by the food. If they begin to gather, chase them off.

- If your bird has a mate, place it in a separate cage next to its travel cage or in a smaller cage inside of a larger one so it won't fly off or be attacked by wild birds. This alone may be enough to entice your bird down.

- If crowds of people begin to gather, ask them to please keep their distance. Too many people may increase your bird's reluctance to come down or frighten it away.

- If you've made tape recordings of your bird and/or its mate prior to the escape, place the recorder inside the cage and play the tape. If you haven't done this, it's not too late. Have someone call local pet stores and ask if they have a bird of the same species, and if they will record or allow you to record the bird's calls. Also, consider distributing copies of the recording to friends and neighbors in the area where your bird was lost, and asking them to play it.

- If you are a bird owner, chances are you know others who own birds who will probably be willing to lend you assistance, and even lend you a bird of the same breed as yours as a decoy.

- If you lose sight of your bird for a short time, don't give up too easily and leave the area. Your bird may circle back. Keep calling your bird and waiting. It's hard to say exactly how long to wait. If you do have to leave, be sure to return to the same area later.

- Knock on doors in the area, and alert people to the fact that you've lost your bird. Ask them to keep an eye and ear out for it, and to put out food to attract your bird. Also, be sure to leave your contact information with them.

When to Pursue

- If your efforts to coo your bird down fail, another option is to attempt to climb up and get the bird yourself. This should be done with the utmost caution, however; not simply because you may cause the bird to fly farther away, but because you could fall and be injured.

- Use a net with a long, lightweight handle to capture your bird. These are available in some catalogs (we've included a couple of places in our resources where you can purchase these).

- The time of day plays a role in how best to proceed. If it's close to sundown, you can wait because your bird may be less likely to fly off and you may have an easier time approaching it. Try to get close enough to daze the bird with the light from a powerful flashlight, and then grab it.

- Using a hose to knock the bird down is an option, and water will also limit its ability to fly. The risk of injuring your bird, however, is quite high. Besides, if you fail, you don't want your bird to be wet at night.

- If your bird is perched on electric or telephone wires or on a transformer, DO NOT attempt to climb up or use a ladder. Call the fire department or local police for assistance.

Additional Tips for Recovering Lost Birds

If your attempts to coo or pursue your bird have failed and your bird has flown off or otherwise is lost and you have no idea where it is, go immediately to our recovery plan and begin organizing your search and get those flyers out there. Meanwhile, here are some additional recovery methods particular to birds.

- Call pet stores, bird jungles (a finder may try to sell it), and veterinarians (especially if they specialize in avian care) in your area and alert them. If someone tries to keep your bird, they will eventually need to take it for veterinary care. If your bird is banded, be sure to give them the band number.

• Contact bird clubs, rescue groups, and bird rehabilitation facilities in your area. Alert them, and try to enlist allies for your search efforts. Bird lovers often have feeders in their yards and many lost birds have been found at backyard feeders in the very neighborhoods where they went missing. Put up a feeder yourself. Also, someone finding your bird may, after a failed attempt at locating you, the owner, turn it over to a rescue group or a bird rehabilitator.

Tips for Finding and Coaxing Down an African Grey Parrot

(This applies to most birds.)

"Always look for an African Grey *before* sunup and *after* sundown because they are the most vocal and most active then.

"The third day is when they get hungry enough to come in for food. They will go to just about anyone at that time if they are tame.

"Always have a recording of your African Grey when he is playing and having the most fun. Play this recording intermittently as you look for him.

"Throw food on rooftops. Place a small cage on the roof of your house or wherever your African Grey has been seen.

"Tell people to put him in a pillowcase if they find him. Sometimes African Greys are caught by inexperienced holders, and they don't know what to do with them. If the person gets bitten, he might drop your bird and off it goes again.

"Water hoses do work if you can spray him shortly after his escape. Hit him with as much water as you can all at once. He is [probably] heavy from not having exercise, and the water throws him off enough to ground him for a bit. However, don't use this approach just before dark unless you are sure you can get him.

"Contact organizations up to 50 miles away. Sometimes people find stray pet birds while traveling and take them home with them. Fifty miles? African Greys can get that far just flying.

"Give all the children in the neighborhood a buck, and tell them there is more if they can locate your bird. (Kids will tell on people who are hiding birds also.)

"If someone spots your African Grey, have him watch the bird until you can get there or you can arrange for help.

"If you try to climb the tree, it frequently will scare your bird farther up in the branches. Instead, use a long branch, and try to coax him onto the branch. An alternative is to raise his cage to where he is.

"Have friends and family miles away in other cities watch the lost and found ads."

- Ask your local shelter if they house stray birds. Shelters often send found birds who are brought to them to bird rescues, since they are often better equipped for caring for birds.

- If your bird has the ability to talk, it's important to include that fact (and what words it can say) when placing an ad or making flyers.

- Check the classified ads in the local newspapers for "Birds For Sale," and contact anyone trying to sell a bird fitting your bird's description. Be aware that someone trying to sell your bird through the classifieds may try to disguise the bird by giving a less than accurate description. Don't ignore ads where there is the slightest chance it could be your bird.

- Online advertisements— **www.birdhotline.com** and **www.plannedparrothood.com** both have free space for posting lost or stolen bird reports, and both report successful recovery stories. Be sure to read through the ads for found birds as well.

Recovery: Ferrets

Once you've determined that your ferret really is lost and not napping in a pile of clothes or trapped somewhere in your home, it's time to extend your search. Follow our recovery plan, tailoring it to your situation. To help you, there are some things unique to recovering missing ferrets that you need to know.

Ferret Recovery Tips

- Put your ferret's cage or carrier outside in the yard. Put its bedding and its favorite food along with some water inside the cage. This will usually entice your wayward ferret home. Ferrets have a healthy appetite and

Fortunately, Ferrets Don't Tend to Wander Far

Fortunately, ferrets are unlikely to stray too far from home. They are usually found in the general vicinity of where they went missing, unless they are picked up by someone and carried away. It is important to know, however, that even if your pet wanders just a few yards away, "[ferrets] do not have the ability to find their way home as a cat or dog would," according to Angela Espinet, of *For Ferrets Only* (**www.craftycreatures.com**). She also says there is a real need to act quickly because "adverse weather conditions, lack of food and water could prove to be deadly. The sooner the ferret is found, the better; the ferret is neither nocturnal or diurnal therefore day or night, the search should continue, being aware that at any time the ferret could have found a comfortable spot to take a nap!"

need to eat frequently. This also has the added benefit of discouraging your ferret from traveling to nearby homes in search of food, where it could encounter a dog or a cat.

• Set a humane trap. If you have to resort to using a trap, make sure it's a humane trap (e.g., Havahart). Often, you can borrow one from your local humane society, animal control facility, or local cat or ferret rescue organization. Humane traps are cages that capture the animal inside without harming it. Put some of your ferret's favorite food inside to lure it into the trap, and set it out in a likely area. Check it several times each day.

• Use your training device. If your ferret is trained to respond to a bell, a whistle, a clicker, or some other sound, use it while out searching.

• Focus your initial search on the immediate neighborhood; ferrets are unlikely to travel far. Go door-to-door and talk to everyone you see. Remember, ferrets are very friendly and will be more than happy to go right up to just about anybody they encounter.

• Talk to children in the neighborhood. Children are good sources of information since they are often outside playing and are likely to have seen your ferret or heard that someone else has seen your animal.

• Contact local animal shelters and veterinarians in your area.

• Contact ferret rescue groups, since many times local animal shelters call on ferret rescues to place ferrets that are brought to them. Animal control will likely take a found ferret to a ferret rescue shelter. Your local ferret rescue may also have some other suggestions, and you may even enlist an ally to help in your search. The American Ferret Association maintains a directory of ferret shelters on their web site at **www.ferret.org.**

Recovery: Other Critters

This chapter, more than any other, demonstrates just how useful the Internet can be when trying to recover a lost pet. When it came to recovering lost critters, we found it to be an invaluable resource. For the following bits of advice, we turned to various critter experts and enthusiasts. Each one offered something a little different, and although each reply is critter-specific, many of the suggestions apply to other animals as well. For example, the mouse, rat, and hamster information may also apply to gerbils and other rodents.

Mice

We received this answer from Beth after a posting on the "Critter Medley" message board on the PetStation.com web site:

"I have fancy pet mice and spiny mice and occasionally breed them. What I do when a fancy mouse escapes is bait a live trap with peanut butter, place it in the room in which the mouse escaped (in a mouse-friendly location, like under a piece of furniture), go to bed, and check the trap first thing in the morning. I have caught uninvited guests (wild mice) in this fashion, also. The brand name of my live trap is Havahart. They are available in several different sizes, according to the size of the animal you need to catch. My mouse-breeder friend uses a straight-sided metal wastebasket to catch her strays. She empties the wastebasket, puts a mouse treat in the bottom, places the wastebasket in the room where the mouse was last seen… if a mouse jumps in to obtain the treat, it can't get back out (due to the slippery straight sides). Good luck!"

Hamsters

We received this e-mail from Lorraine Hill, author of the "Complete Hamster" site (**www.petwebsite.com/hamsters.htm**); she lives in the United Kingdom. Miss Hill has been involved with keeping and breeding hamsters since 1983 and has been involved in establishing various hamster clubs throughout her country.

"Hamsters are nocturnal and so even when escaped are most active at night. They will usually find somewhere dark and quiet to hide and sleep, particularly during the day. Good places to find a hamster are usually behind or under furniture.

"They rarely leave much evidence to make it easy for you to locate them. But you may notice things have been chewed. They may chew up bits of paper, furniture, etc., to use for nesting material.

"They often don't travel far, so may still be in the room where the cage is located. Often shutting this room off and setting a humane trap will find the hamster.

"You can set a humane trap by placing a bucket in the room or waste paper basket—something that once the hamster is inside, it cannot pull itself out from. Build some steps up to the top of the bucket or basket on the outside (books prove useful for building steps). Place some soft bedding in the bucket, along with some food and a piece of apple (this gives off a good enticing smell!) A few seeds on the books will entice the hamster up the steps. Once it reaches the top, it will smell the apple and drop in the bucket to the soft bedding placed inside. Voilà! You have recovered your hamster who will now sit and wait for you to come and find it!

"The trap obviously works best if left overnight, as the hamster is most likely to be caught at this time when it is awake and foraging for food. If the hamster is suspected to have escaped some time ago, a trap can be set up in each room. Sometimes it may take a few nights, but this method does seem to catch the majority of hamsters within a week."

Rats

Kristin Johnson from The Wererat's Lair (**www.wererat.net**), a great place to get questions answered on every aspect of rat care, referred us to this terrific online article by Sarah Shuman Skilling. Miss Shuman Skilling has written numerous articles for the Rat and Mouse Club of America. In addition, she has written for the Rat and Mouse Fanciers for Excellence, a club that she co-founded. Many of her fine articles on rat care can be viewed on her web site, **www.greeneyedesigns.com**. She gave us permission to reprint her article on lost and found rats here:

Lost and Found: When Your Rattie Goes Rambling

"*Things to Do Right Away*—Once the rattie is beyond your immediate reach, the first thing you should do is eliminate hazards. Put the dog or the cat or what-have-you in another room. (Although I have to say sometimes a friendly dog is good for pointing out the rat's hiding place. But if you have any doubts about whether your dog might harm the missing rattie, put him in another room.)

"Also, close all doors, windows, or other methods of leaving the room, assuming you know which room the rattie is currently in. Buckets of water, toilets, or any other standing water should be drained or covered. Make sure no toxic materials, including poisonous plants, are within reach of the rattie. These are things that should be done in any area where a rat is allowed to play, but when your rat gets loose in an area that is not ratproof, these considerations must be attended to.

"Remove any source of noise… If there is total silence, then you can hear the rattie moving, in many cases… You are listening for little rustling sounds as the rattie moves around. This will hopefully help you pinpoint the rat's location. If the rat has been out for a while and fallen asleep, obviously this won't work.

"*If You Know What Room the Rat is in But Can't See or Hear Her*—If there is a sofa or recliner in the room, DO NOT allow anyone to sit on it, because if the rat is inside it may end up being crushed. In fact, try to keep everyone out of the room until the rat is found. If she has fallen asleep, this may take quite a while. Once the room is cleared and exits are closed and hazards are eliminated, make a 'home' area for the rat to return to. If you have a small aquarium or carrier handy, this is simple to make. Take some of the bedding from the rat's own cage and put it in the container. If the rat has nesting material, put some of that in, too, in a little box that the rat could curl up in. Put something tasty inside, something that has a strong smell—a little peanut butter thinly spread on toast can work. (Be careful. Too much peanut butter can choke your little friend.) Also put in a water bottle or other water source. The point is to make this 'home' area attractive and safe to the rat so she will go in, eat, drink, and possibly fall asleep there. What if you are using an aquarium and your rat is too little to easily get in? Take books and stack them to form a 'stairway' that the rat can climb up and jump into the cage.

"If Once You Locate the Rat It Won't Let You Pick It Up—There are a number of things to try. If the rat is under something, like a piece of furniture or a cabinet, or behind something, like a dresser, first try to call the rat and see if it will come. A lot of times they are too scared for that. You can also try bribing the rat with a treat, but that often fails for similar reasons. Another thing you can try is having someone make a loud noise from the other end of where the rat is so that it may come to you for safety... If the rat will come and sniff you but won't come far enough out for you to pick her up, one thing that works really well is to take a tube (paper towel tube, plastic pipe, or in a pinch even a paper bag) and hold the opening near the rat's face. Many times they will be reassured by that dark, enclosed space (it can be made even more attractive by inserting a treat if you have one handy) and once the rat fully enters the tube or bag you can pick the whole thing up. Be careful, as the rat may feel panicky and try to jump out of the tube or bag to the floor.

"Remember the natural activity cycle of rats. If they escape during the day, they will probably find a place to hide and sleep. They will become active and begin searching for food and water in the late evening. It is often helpful to go into the area where the rat was last seen (they seldom stray too far from their cages) and sit silently, with dimmed light in the late evening. Listen very carefully.

"When the Rat is Found and Recaptured—Remember that this has been an extremely stressful and unsettling experience for the rat, especially if she was at large for a long time. She may act very wild at first. The best thing to do is usually to put her in her cage and leave her there for at least an hour, better two or three. This allows her to calm down and feel safe again... As the rat matures and gets used to you, she will not hesitate to come to you if she gets loose. In fact, it is very wise to train your rattie to come when you call her by holding treats just out of reach and rewarding her when she steps towards your hand, then slowly increasing the distance the rat must come to get the treat... [Rat] youngsters can be helped to learn this behavior by allowing them to observe older rats coming when called and being rewarded for it."

Snakes and Lizards

Recovering these reptiles can be difficult. It is best not to lose them in the first place and some contend, with good reason, that it is improper to keep them as pets at all. If you have one that gets lost, here are a few tips from an exchange we had with Damien N. Oxier, Director and licensed Wildlife Rehabilitator at Arrowhead Reptile Rescue located in Cincinnati, Ohio:

Question: Do you have any information for preventing the loss of snakes and lizards, and more importantly, how to recover one lost in your home or in your yard?

Answer: Prevention is difficult. A secure cage is obviously the most important factor.

Question: Do they seek out certain places, warm or wet places?

Answer: They usually like to find a dark quiet place to curl up. They may be near a heat source if they find one. Most semi-aquatic reptiles would seek a moist environment.

Question: How do you recapture one? Can you set a safe trap? How would you entice them out from wherever they may be hiding?

Answer: Set a trap—good luck—none that I know of. Entice out—doubtful. Usually they don't want to come out for anything unless they are literally starving or freezing to death, which can take a while. Catching them usually involves a great deal of time and searching, as well as equipment like rabies poles, snake tongs, or snake hooks to protect us and the reptile.

Question: What are the particular hazards faced by snakes or lizards and other reptiles that get lost in the house?

Answer: Depends on the species and if there are small children or pets around. Most reptiles are carnivores. Many species get quite large, have sharp claws, or are designed to kill large prey items (such as the household pet). Some are poisonous, but they should not be kept as pets in a house.

Additional Critter Recovery Tips

- If possible seal off the room completely.
- Confine other pets immediately.
- Sprinkle powder on the ground to trace your critter's steps.
- Use the Internet to contact other critter enthusiasts; people involved in rescue work for whatever particular critter you've lost, pet clubs, and various critters web sites, etc. They are a great source of information, as this chapter demonstrates. Use a search engine and enter your critter type. We have included several in our "Resources" section as well. (See "Resources/Ferrets and Other Critters.")

Question: Would a local rescue group be a good place to call for assistance? Is there some directory of reptile rescue groups and/or clubs?

Answer: A rescue group would be the place to call. At least around here if you call the zoo, aquarium, most vets, park naturalists, police, fire, etc., etc., about a reptile they give you our name and number. If you have online access, try going to **www.anapsid.org** for a really great list of reptile rescue groups across the country.

Section III

ADDITIONAL TOPICS

You've Found Your Pet! *Now What?*

"Hello?"

"Hi. My name is John Williams. I live over on Chestnut Street. I have a dog here. He looks like a Lab mix, black. He's got a white patch on his chest, and his tail kind of bends to the left. My son brought him home yesterday. Anyway, the dog wasn't wearing any tags, and so I almost took him over to the shelter. But I figured first let me pick up a newspaper and go through the lost/found ads. When I went to the store to get the paper, I saw this flyer in the window with a photo and a description that pretty much matched the dog my kid found. Anyway, I tore off the phone number and gave a call."

"Yes! Yes, and thank you so much. That sounds like Prince all right. He's been gone nearly three days. We've all been worried sick. My son's been especially upset. I mean, that dog is his life. Give me your address, and I'll be right over to pick him up. And thank you again. Thank you!"

Your lost pet has been found, your search effort successful. That detailed description and photo on your flyer paid off. You have much to be thankful for. So now what? Once you've recovered your lost pet, there are some important things you need to do.

- Assess its overall condition. Check it closely for wounds. A good bath is probably in order, too.

Birds are particularly vulnerable to the elements, and if accosted by a cat (which is not always easy to tell) will need immediate antibiotic therapy. It is recommended that recovered birds be taken for a veterinary visit, regardless of how long they were lost.

- Offer it food and water in small quantities at first, depending on how long it's been gone.

- If your pet has been missing for a couple of days or more, or if there are any signs that it has had an altercation with another animal or an injury of any kind, an immediate visit to your veterinarian is a must. You can't afford to take any chances.

- Call everyone who may still be looking for your pet (friends, volunteers, shelters, veterinarians, rescue groups, etc.) to alert and thank them.

- Pay any reward that has been offered.
- Go around and gather up the flyers that you've posted.
- Promptly purchase and replace any missing tags.

Don't Let it Happen Again

You need to figure out how your pet escaped and take steps to prevent it from happening again. We implore you to read carefully through the "Prevention" section of the book, to implement the various strategies we've detailed there, and to familiarize yourself with every aspect of prevention and preparedness. Here are a few examples of common ways pets escape and some simple solutions:

- Did your dog escape by tunneling under the fence or is it a jumper or a climber? Perhaps the fence is not adequate for the size of your dog. It's also important to remember that, fence or no fence, it is not a good idea to leave your dog in the yard unsupervised for long periods of time. A standing kennel is one solution; there are solutions to tunneling behavior, as well. Electronic fencing may be an option for you. Did it escape through a gate inadvertently left open? Posting "PLEASE CLOSE GATE" signs is one solution, or you could simply lock the gate. They also make spring-loaded gates that close themselves. (See "Roaming and Escaping.")

- Did your son or daughter leave the door open again? Educating youngsters about pet safety is an on-going process. Every so often, talk to your kids about the rules that will help keep their pet happy and safe.

- Was your cat lurking by the door, waiting for the opportune moment when your attention was focused elsewhere so he could dart out as soon as someone came knocking? Post signs as a constant reminder to yourself and others to be careful when opening the door. Some cats are perfectly content as house cats, while others are very difficult to keep indoors. Some cats constantly yearn to be outside and will stop at nothing to get there. If this describes your kitty, consider building a cat enclosure.

- Did your bird simply fly out of an open door or window? The best solution for preventing bird loss is keeping its wings clipped on a regular schedule since this virtually eliminates the possibility of escape. Be vigilant in keeping windows screened and putting your bird in its cage when the doorbell rings. (See "Prevention: Birds.")

Dealing with Persistent Escape Artists

Most methods for preventing pet loss rely on some form of containment, which is often all many people know about preventing escape. While containment can be very effective, it has its limits and should not be seen as a long-term solution. Long-term solutions only come about when the underlying problems are addressed.

If you have a persistent escape artist, then you are probably already aware of the limitations of pet containment. You're reading this section because you've just recovered your pet. You're fortunate. You've gotten your pet back and been given another chance. Unfortunately, one of these days your dog may not return, or your cat may have used up its ninth life. It is time to explore other avenues for preventing escape.

Many escape artists return on their own, often at suppertime. While we are grateful when the prodigal returns, this is by no means a reliable method for recovering a pet who has run off. No matter how many times your pet has returned home on its own, it is your responsibility to actively search for it each time and without delay.

When your dog returns, it is important that you not let your anger get the best of you. Punishment will probably have the opposite of the desired effect. For one thing, your dog may begin to associate his return home with punishment, and subsequently stay away longer the next time or simply not return at all. For another, it may be that the excitement of being out romping around seems to your dog worth whatever the consequences; the crime being worth the punishment so to speak. Are you spending enough quality time with your dog? Is he getting enough exercise? It is up to you to provide the things at home that your dog is seeking outside.

If your escape artist is not sterilized, spaying or neutering may be enough to solve the problem. (See "Roaming and Escaping.")

Training your pet is one of the most effective ways of preventing pet loss. Even something as simple as teaching your pet tricks can have a positive impact on escaping behavior. (See "Training.")

Does your cat return hours later with a mole or mouse and anxiously await your approval? The need to hunt is very strong in some cats. There are, however, things that you can do to gratify and/or redirect this instinctual behavior. Playing games, especially those that involve hunting or stalking an object (something as simple as a feather, or a string with several knots on the end) can be enough to meet this need in your cat. Does your cat constantly meow to go out, frustrating you to the point of allowing it to roam freely? While many cats are happy leading sedentary lives, others are extremely curious about the outside world. For these, often a window perch will help to satisfy them. There are many things you can do to gratify your cat's natural curiosity and hunting instinct, and thus prevent escape attempts. (See "Roaming and Escaping.")

Found Strays

Doing the Right Thing

When some people see a stray running loose in the neighborhood, they remain unconcerned and take no action. Since you are reading this book, it is unlikely you could be that apathetic. Of course, some very well-meaning people don't do anything about stray animals they see because they're afraid to approach them. On the other hand, they think that if they call animal control, the animal will be taken to the shelter and probably be destroyed.

While it is understandable and even prudent in many instances not to attempt to capture a stray dog yourself, it is not necessarily the case that it will be destroyed at the local animal shelter. In fact, the animal has a better chance of being reunited with its owner if it is taken to the shelter, than it does running around the neighborhood streets.

We are not necessarily recommending that you try to capture any stray animals you encounter, but we are urging you to "do the right thing" and take some kind of action. Call your local police or animal control agency and report the loose animal; the owner may have already filed a lost pet report with them. Besides, they have the expertise and equipment to capture it safely, and they will bring it to the local animal shelter which is where most people first turn when looking for a lost pet. If you are concerned about the animal's remaining unclaimed and eventually being euthanized, ask about "first chance adoption."

The Humane Society of the United States publishes a list of very helpful guidelines at their *Pet Information Center* (**www.hsus.org**) titled "What To Do When You Find a Stray Dog or Cat." (See figure 42.)

Taking in a Stray

People end up with stray animals in any number of ways. They may capture the animal themselves, their children may bring a dog home with them, or a cat may simply show up at their back door. Often, the animal has no visible means of identification and, therefore, there is no way of contacting its owner. Although it's sadly true that many strays are pets who have simply been abandoned by their owners, it should always be assumed that the animal, regardless of appearance or lack of identification tags, does belong to someone who cares deeply. So what do you do?

The Humane Society of the United States Says Be Ready to Rescue

"If you know in your heart that you're a rescuer, why not equip yourself to do the best possible job? Here are some things to have in your car at all times.
- Cell phone.
- Phone numbers of local animal control, animal shelters, and a 24-hour emergency veterinary clinic.
- Cat carrier or cardboard box.
- Collars and strong leashes for dogs.
- Blanket.
- Water bowl and water.
- Strong-smelling foods (e.g., canned tuna or dried liver).
- Animal first-aid kit."

To read this entire pamphlet, *What To Do When You Find a Stray Dog or Cat*, visit The HSUS's *Pet Information Center* at **www.hsus.org**.

FIGURE 42

Most people who are concerned enough to take a stray animal into their home are willing to make some effort to locate the owner, even if they do nothing more than call animal control and have the animal taken to the local shelter. There is nothing wrong with this. In fact, it is the minimum that should be done, and depending on where you live, the law may require that you do so.

Other people, however, want to do more than that, but simply don't know what to do. There are several other things you can do to locate the owner of a missing pet. Posting found pet flyers, placing a found pet classified ad (these are usually free) and canvassing the neighborhood door-to-door are a few examples. We firmly believe that once you take in a stray, you must go the extra mile. Turn the situation around. If your pet were lost and picked up by someone, wouldn't you want them to intervene on your pet's behalf? There is hardly a greater feeling in the world than helping to reunite a lost pet with its worried owner.

A Few Precautions

If you do take a stray into your home and you own other pets, there are certain precautions you need to take. First, do not let the stray come in contact with your other animals until it is checked out and cleared by a veterinarian, and you've followed the gradual approach for introducing pets to each other. (For help with this see the article *Getting to Know You: When New Pet Meets Old Pet*, by Ann Smalley, on The Humane Society of the United States' "Pets for Life" web site at **www.petsforlife.org**.) You certainly don't want your pets picking up contagious and dangerous diseases; don't allow your pets and the stray to share food or water dishes. It is best to confine the stray to the garage, basement, carrier, or some other separate area while you get busy trying to get the animal back to its home.

Several Ways of Locating the Owner

- *Check Its Tags*—Of course, if it has an identification tag with a phone number, that could make your job a lot simpler. Also, license and rabies tags can usually be traced through your local city hall.

- *Check for Tattoos*—Once you feel comfortable that the animal is not a danger, check it for tattoos. Tattoos are usually placed in the ear, on the belly, or on an inner thigh. The two main tattoo registries—Tattoo-A-Pet and the National Dog Registry—both use prefixes that identify them ("T" for Tattoo-A-Pet, followed by a two-letter state code such as NJ; and "NDR" for the National Dog Registry). Even if the animal was tattooed by another company, both Tattoo-A-Pet and the National Dog Registry will go to amazing lengths to locate the owner. After some 30 years of dealing with tattoos, they are very familiar with the various markings; they can and do cross-reference with other registries. The phone number for Tattoo-A-Pet is (800) TATTOOS (828-8667) and for the National Dog Registry it is (800) NDR-DOGS (637-3647). (See "Tattoos.")

- *Have It Scanned for a Microchip Implant*—If you feel the animal is safe to handle, you can take him to your veterinarian or local shelter where, as a free service, they will scan the animal for a microchip implant and make the necessary calls. You can locate a veterinarian in your area who does microchip implants by calling AVID (FriendChip) at (800) 336-AVID (2843) or by visiting the Schering-Plough (Home Again microchip) web site at **http://usa.spah.com**.

- *Canvass the Area*—Knock on doors and talk to people in the neighborhood where you found the animal.

- *Post Found Pet Flyers*—Post them all around the area where you found the animal and beyond. This can and should be done even if you have taken the animal to a shelter, which you can make known on your flyer. Follow the guidelines for creating lost pet ads and flyers. (See "Flyers and Classified Ads.") It is better not to include the sex of the animal in your flyer or classified ad unless you are 100% certain, as it can be difficult to correctly determine an animal's sex. Neutered males, for example, can easily be mistaken for females. This is a common mistake; a mistake we've made ourselves. We once noticed a cat wandering up and down our street. She was obviously lost and not a roamer from the neighborhood. We took her in, fed her (she was starving), made up some flyers, placed half a dozen of them around the immediate neighborhood, then took her to our local shelter. They took down the information and off we went. When we arrived home, the shelter called to let us know that she was, in fact, a he. Fortunately we had only placed a few flyers, which we quickly gathered up and replaced. The best advice we can give is to take the animal to your local shelter first and ask them to determine its sex, then place your found pet flyers and ads.

- *Place a Found Pet Classified Ad*—Most local newspapers will run found pet ads for free, although they usually limit you to three or four lines. Therefore, include only the essentials. Place ads in your local paper and in other area newspapers. Beware, however, of crooks who read such ads looking for animals they can sell to people involved in the illicit animal trade. Withhold at least one distinguishing mark when placing a found pet ad. Be wary of callers who seem only to solicit information. Don't volunteer anything; if it really is their pet, they will not need your help to describe the animal in detail. Never turn a found stray over to anyone unless they support their claim of ownership with some supporting documentation, such as photos or adoption papers. (See "Beware of Scams.")

- *Check the Ads*—Look in the paper every day for a lost pet ad describing an animal that matches the stray you took in, and have friends or relatives check the lost pet classifieds in the newspapers in the areas around your town.

- *Call the Police*—To file a found pet report and to check if anyone has made a lost pet report on an animal fitting the description of the one you've found.

- *Call Animal Shelters and Area Veterinarians*—Alert them about the stray. Ask them about breed rescue groups, as these groups may have already been alerted to a missing pet of that breed. Besides, breed rescue groups may also offer to accept and help place the animal if the owners aren't located.

- *Call Lost Pet Services*—The Pet Club of America is a good example of such services that compile lost pet reports. (See "Critical Contacts.")

- *Call the Media*—See if your local radio and cable TV stations make lost/found pet announcements.

- *Post a Lost/Found Ad Online*—Post a found pet ad online at some of the missing pet sites, many of which will accept photographs, too. Also, read through the lost pet ads (they are usually listed by state). Pets911, **www.1888pets911.com** is a great, easy-to-use site, and, thanks to an aggressive public awareness campaign, has become very well known as a site to locate missing pets. For more online classified sites see "Critical Contacts."

Keeping a Stray

Many people feel completely justified taking in and keeping a stray. They often point to its tattered or scruffy appearance, or to the fact that it has no identification tags, as evidence of abandonment or neglect. This is not necessarily the case. Identification tags can be lost and a mangy appearance may only be the result of its surviving on the streets, perhaps for many days or even weeks. People can't be faulted for falling in love with an animal they've rescued, but remember there may be someone else out there whose heart is broken over the same animal.

It is important that you begin with the assumption that the animal you've taken in is someone's pet, and that they are searching for it. It's a wonderful thing to be willing to open your home and adopt a stray pet. It is wrong, however, to keep the animal without first making a concerted effort to locate the owner.

Found Birds

The founders of **www.birdhotline.com** pose the following question on their web site: "Why is it that when a dog or cat is found, the immediate thought is to find the animal's home, yet when a bird is found, the immediate thought is to buy a cage?" This is just plain wrong. Lost birds are loved and missed by their owners every bit as much as lost cats and dogs. If you find a lost bird, the only proper action is to make every effort to locate its owner. When you find a lost bird, you will do many of the same things you would if you'd found a stray cat or dog. Here are some other things you should know:

- Since the bird may have flown quite some distance, extend the area of search significantly.

- Locate classified sites online that are bird-specific; **www.birdhotline.com** and **www.plannedparrothood.com** both provide space for lost/found bird ads.

- Have the bird scanned for a microchip. Your local shelter may have a scanner, or they should be able to direct you to someone who does. Locating a local veterinarian who does microchip implants is easy by calling AVID (Friendchip) at (800) 336-AVID (2843) or by visiting the Schering-Plough (Home Again microchip) web site at **http://usa.spah.com.**

- Look for a leg band. Write down any numbers recorded on the band and give the numbers to whomever you call.

• When calling people, be sure to call bird jungles, bird rescue groups, and clubs in your area. Also, call veterinarians who specialize in avian care.

A Brief Note about Stray Ferrets

Ferrets are very friendly and will likely come right up to the first person they see. Unless the animal was picked up by someone and carried away, its owner should be found in close proximity to where the ferret was found. Follow the above instructions for locating the owner of a stray dog or cat, concentrating your efforts in the immediate area where you found the animal. Also, ferret rescue groups are a good source of information. If the owner isn't located and you're not interested in keeping the ferret, these groups will likely pick up the animal and place it. The American Ferret Association has a directory of ferret shelters on their web site at **www.ferret.org**.

Knowing When to Give Up

How long should you keep searching for your missing pet? William E. Campbell, in his *Owner's Guide to Better Behavior in Cats and Dogs*, says that you should "keep searching for at least six months before resigning yourself to the fact that your dog or cat is, indeed, gone from your life." The key words here are "at least." Suppose your pet has been missing for six months, you've exhausted all your options, done everything you know to do. Now what?

This difficult question has troubled us greatly because we know from personal experience the anxiety we felt when we lost a pet. We knew instinctively that we had to put our loss behind us at some point. Yet during the course of researching and writing this book, we read incredible stories of pets being found months and even years after they went missing.

For many pet owners, it is not a matter of loving or not loving their pets. For them, time, resources, family concerns, and any of a variety of other factors may dictate how long and how aggressively they can search. The fact is that this is not an ideal world, and not everyone has the freedom to continue an active search indefinitely. This is why prevention and preparedness are so important.

We believe that if one is physically able, the effort to recover a lost pet, in the beginning at least, should take on the sense of a mission. If, as the months pass, however, the search begins to negatively affect other areas of your life, you must at that point try to put it in perspective. There must come a time when you begin to accept at least the possibility that your pet may never return. This does not mean you must abandon all hope, as miracles do happen.

Answering the question of when to give up is so important for people who have lost a beloved pet that we wanted to get it right. We didn't want to tell people to prematurely abandon the search, nor did we want to give people an unrealistic hope that would keep the wound open indefinitely. So we wrote to people involved in searching for and recovering lost pets and sought their advice. We have come to the conclusion that, although six months is acceptable as a general rule, it's simply impossible to tell someone else when to give up an active search. We agree with Larry Maynard of National Pet Detectives, who said, "You will know in your heart when all possible avenues have been exhausted."

A Heartfelt Letter

We recently received a letter from Lisa Messmer, a woman whose Dalmatian was stolen four years ago. We decided to include it below because it is insightful, heartfelt, and comes from personal experience:

"No one can say when the 'right time' to give up a search is for anyone else, other than themselves. Some people have no hope and give up nearly right away, some give up after a few weeks or months, and some do not give up until the life expectancy for their dog has passed.

"Mourning a missing pet is a personal thing. How long one mourns, how long one searches, is up to the individual. No one should judge another, whether that person decides to accept their loss or decides to never give up, as long as that pet is searched for in some manner.

"It's a matter of the heart. There are those of us who can't or won't give up, and we are sure that our friends and family cannot understand this…it seems that it is more 'normal' (or expected) for missing pet owners to accept the loss and give up looking. We also think that it is just as acceptable to NOT give up hope, no matter how long that hope holds out.

"No matter when a person gives up, it does not mean that we don't still love our missing pets, nor does it mean that we cannot love other pets if we still go on searching. I have five Dalmatians here now who I probably would not have if my Dulcie had not disappeared. Much good has come from her loss and from my efforts to help others, as I have gotten very involved in 'pet theft' issues as well as Dalmatian Rescue. Her loss has helped to alert others as to how easily our pets can be taken from us, and I feel she is helping others to be more diligent in preventing any losses. I try to look at the 'good' as the silver lining in the dark cloud of her loss.

"And still, even with the rumor of her death, we keep a small thread of hope alive. We can't help but get very choked up over her loss, and it has been nearly four years since we last saw her. We are sure many think we're nuts to do so, but we'd deny that allegation."

Best regards
Lisa Messmer

Grieving

Some Thoughts on Grieving for a Lost Pet

Our main intent in writing this book was to help people learn the importance of preventing and preparing for pet loss. We wanted to do something that would have a positive impact on the alarming numbers of pets that go missing each year and are never recovered. We were excited because we knew that if we could get this book into the hands of pet owners, their pets would be safer. We knew, of course, that no matter how well prepared we all are, pets are sometimes lost forever.

The knowledge that your pet has died is in some ways less traumatic than losing a pet that is never recovered. If you know your pet has died, there is a sense of finality. But as long as a lost pet remains missing, the absence of closure means the pain of your loss can go on indefinitely. This uncertainty complicates an already difficult situation and yet at some point, the grieving must begin.

The question then becomes, can grieving begin without completely surrendering hope? For two reasons, we believe the answer is yes. One, the grieving process is about loss, loss of any kind. Your pet is missing, and so you can justifiably begin grieving your loss whenever you feel the need. Two, as pets have been recovered long after they went missing, you can let the grieving begin while still keeping hope alive.

Elisabeth Kubler-Ross identified the five stages of grief in her book *On Death and Dying*. We include a summary of these as they relate to pet loss, in the hope that they can help guide you through your grief by allowing you to understand the validity of your many and varied emotions:

1. ***Denial***—Denial will be your first reaction upon learning that your pet is missing. This quite normal reaction is simply a natural defense mechanism which allows you to slowly assimilate an emotionally overwhelming experience. Denial acts as sort of a temporary buffer against the immediate shock. You may insist that your pet is simply hiding or has been taken in by someone who is searching for you.

2. ***Anger***—As reality begins to set in, denial gives way to anger. You may be angry at your pet for running off, or at the person who let the animal out, or at yourself for not being more careful. Such anger is often misdirected, sometimes spilling over onto innocent parties, total strangers, and even inanimate objects. This is a healthy sign that we are moving out of the denial stage and beginning to accept the facts. We may feel like we are being tossed back and forth between fits of anger and bouts of sadness until we are finally tossed onto the shore of the next stage, bargaining.

3. ***Bargaining***—Bargaining is a normal reaction to the feelings of vulnerability and helplessness we have in a situation over which we have no control. "Dear God, if

you help me find my pet I promise to be more careful. I will walk the dog on a leash and will never let it run loose again." Attempting to negotiate with our higher power is an attempt to reach beyond ourselves and gain control over the painful reality that our pet is gone, and had we only done something different, this would not have happened. This feeling of responsibility for the loss, whether accurate or not, leads us to the fourth stage, depression.

4. *Depression*—Regret has clouded our vision, and now worry and sadness dominate the emotional landscape. While depression may make us feel like we are in a bottomless pit, it is also evidence that we have begun to mourn. Often a sympathetic ear, a hug, a shoulder to cry on, or just a few kind words are enough to reach down and lift us from the depths of despair. When we begin to face the possibility at last that our pet is indeed gone, and may never be found, the light of acceptance begins to break on the horizon.

5. *Acceptance*—Acceptance is a gift, not a given, and unfortunately, not everyone finds their way to accepting the loss. It takes time to get here. In the beginning, time is your nemesis because most lost pets that are recovered are found quickly. Once some time has passed and you begin to accept the reality that your lost pet may never be recovered, time assumes another role, that of friend and healer.

Resources for Those Who are Grieving

From books to counseling hotlines to the Internet, there are many resources available to pet owners for help in dealing with the loss of a pet:

- *Books*—There are over twenty books on the topic of pet loss and grieving, and each year it seems there are several new ones. While these books often focus on pet loss of a permanent nature (e.g., the death of a pet), the dynamics of grieving are such that much of the information will be helpful to those who are grieving a missing pet as well. Some pet loss grieving books are written specifically for children, for whom the loss of a family pet can be a particularly devastating experience. It is not uncommon for young children to feel they are responsible in some way. A suggested reading list for both adults and children, as well as many other helpful grieving resources, can be found by visiting The Humane Society of the United States' *Pet Information Center* at **www.hsus.org**. (See figure 43.)

- *Hotlines*—Hotlines can help you through the grieving process, especially in the early stages. Experienced phone counselors are trained to deal specifically with issues surrounding grief and pet loss. (For example, the University of Florida's College of Veterinary Medicine operates a hotline that grieving pet owners are invited to call and leave a message with anytime. A volunteer trained in grief counseling—very often a veterinary student—will get in touch with you. You can reach the hotline at (352) 392-4700, ext. 4080 between 7:00 p.m. and 9:00 p.m., EST. For a complete listing of pet loss grief support hotlines see "Resources/Grieving."

- *Support Groups*—Many animal shelters facilitate or provide space for pet loss support groups. Make some phone calls to shelters, veterinarians, and therapists and find out what is available in your local area.

- *Web Sites*—Specifically designed for grieving pet owners, these sites contain a variety of valuable information and links to other sites, chat rooms, message boards, and memorial sites.

- **Lightning Strike— www.lightning-strike.com** has many helpful grieving resources. Be sure to check out "Lightning Links." Also check out the Association for Pet Loss and Bereavement's web site. A truly comprehensive site with lots of resources for grieving pet owners. (See figure 44.)

- *Chat Rooms*—One of the wonderful things about chat rooms in regard to grieving a pet loss is that people—literally from around the world—can come together and offer one another much-needed support, all while allowing everyone to remain anonymous. Chat rooms are great for people who have a hard time talking face-to-face to others about their feelings.

Help for Grieving Pet Owners from The Humane Society of the United States

The Humane society of the United States *Kindred Spirits Memorial Program* was created to help pet owners come to terms with the loss of a beloved pet. If you or someone you know has lost a pet, please visit the Kindred Spirits web site. There you will find many helpful resources and thoughtfully written articles on the subject of pet loss and grieving. Has someone you know recently lost a pet? Make a donation in their pet's memory and The HSUS will send a sympathy card to that person's family acknowledging your thoughtful donation. Sign up for *Kindred Spirit News*, a quarterly newsletter that includes true stories, educational articles, valuable resources, and helpful hints. Enter your beloved pet into the Diary of Kindred Spirits, a special way to honor the friend and companion who shared your life, while supporting the hundreds of animal protection programs of The HSUS.

Visit Kindred Spirits today at **www.kspirits.org**
Grieving resources available at the site include:
- *Coping with Pet Loss.*
- Pet Loss Support Hotlines.
- Resources & Internet Links.
- Suggested Reading List (for both adults and children).

Coping with Pet Loss is also available in print form by calling The HSUS and requesting the article by title. (See "Resources/Humane Organizations.")

FIGURE 43

• *Message Boards*—These can be used to post a question, which can then be answered by others for you to read. You can post the story of the loss of your pet and express your sense of loss, so that others can offer their own advice and kind words.

• *Cyber Memorials*—When you visit one of these sites and read the heartfelt stories and the tremendous impact the pets memorialized there had on their owners, you can't help but feel the kinship. Reading the stories of people who have had a similar experience is a tremendous help to anyone struggling with the grief of having lost a pet. You can then begin to create your

---

The Association for Pet Loss and Bereavement (APLB)

The APLB is one of the best grieving resources we have come across. The site was founded by author and professional bereavement counselor Dr. Wallace Sife, and we highly recommend it to anyone who is dealing with the loss of a beloved pet. Dr. Sife recently expanded his very popular 1993 book, *The Loss of a Pet*, to include, among other things, a section on grieving as it relates to lost and missing pets. The APLB recently hosted the First International Conference on Pet Loss and Bereavement in New York City and have hosted an annual picnic in Washington, DC, for the last two years. Their web site is truly comprehensive and includes a newsletter, a memorial page, chat rooms, as well as listings of grief hotlines, support groups, and counselors who are trained in pet loss and bereavement. Visit their site at **www.aplb.org**.

FIGURE 44

---

own memorial, post photos, poems, tell the story of how much joy your pet brought to your life, and how grateful you are for the time you had together.

We have only touched on some of the basic issues associated with grieving. There are many other creative ways to grieve the loss of your pet. We encourage you to make use of the various resources at your disposal to help you make it through this difficult experience. For additional grieving help, see "Resources/Grieving."

Afterword

It is our sincerest wish that this book serve its intended purpose—safeguarding your pets from becoming lost. Or, should your pet ever go missing, assisting you in recovering your lost pet quickly.

Lost, missing, and stolen pet information is continually changing—from new statutes and regulations to new pet registries and recovery services, as well as innovative pet products designed to aid in lost pet prevention or recovery. Even new methods of pet identification are in development to track your lost pet as you would your lost car!

For this reason, we anticipate the need to keep updating this book in order to bring you the latest and most accurate information. We want each new edition of this book to be the best it can be, and we invite you to share with us any ideas or suggestions you may have for its improvement. We would welcome any information you may have that would aid pet owners in lost pet prevention and recovery.

We would also like to request that you please feel free to share your own lost/found pet stories with us. We want to hear about your successes as well as your failures, and what worked and what did not work in your own pet recovery efforts. We hope that through the sharing of your experiences with us, we can make the next edition of this book even more helpful in reuniting lost pets with their owners—or in preventing them from becoming lost in the first place.

Sincerely,
The Authors

Wanted

Lost/found pet stories for future editions of this book. Please provide the circumstances that led to your pet's disappearance, the steps you took to find your missing pet, and how your pet was eventually found. If possible, enclose a clear photo of your pet, one that you will not need returned to you. Thank you.

All responses can be sent to the authors at the following address:
El Jebel Press
P.O. Box 288
Atlantic Highlands, NJ 07716
Or share your story at:
www.lostpetfoundpet.com

Attention Professionals:

Animal control officers, shelter directors, shelter employees and volunteers, kennel managers, humane organization staff, animal welfare advocates, veterinarians, animal trainers, and anyone whose job involves regular contact with lost pets: We would welcome any information you may have that would aid pet owners in lost pet prevention and recovery.

Index to Resources

Our web site was created to assist our readers by making it easy to access the Internet sites found throughout our book and listed in this resource section. Just log on to **www.lostpetfoundpet.com**, and click on the "For Our Readers" link.

Birds

The Association of Avian Veterinarians
(Locate avian veterinarians at AAV web site)
P.O. Box 811720
Boca Raton, FL 33481-1720
E-mail: aavctrlofc@aol.com
Web site: **www.aav.org**

Python Products (Purchase bird nets)
7000 W. Marcia Road
Milwaukee, WI 53223
Phone: (414) 355-7000
Fax: (414) 355-1144
Web site: **www.pythonproducts.com**

Birds: Books and Other Resources
(All books are available in bookstores and online)

A Step by Step Book about Training Your Parakeet
Darlene Campbell, Elaine Radford, J. Darlene Campbell / Paperback / TFH Publications, Inc. / March 1990

The African Grey Parrot Handbook
Mattie Sue Athan, Dianalee Deter / Paperback / Barron's Educational Series, Inc. / April 2000

The Cockatiel Handbook: Everything About Purchase, Housing, Care, Nutrition, Behavior, Breeding, and Diseases, with a Special Chapter on Raising Cockatiels
Matthew M. Vriends, Michele Earle-Bridges (Illustrator) / Paperback / Barron's Educational Series, Inc. / August 1999

The Parakeet Handbook: Everything About the Purchase, Diet, Diseases, and Behavior of Parakeets, with a Special Chapter on Raising Parakeets
Immanuel Bermelin, I. Bermelin, Annette Wolter / Paperback / Barron's Educational Series, Inc. / February 2000

Hornbecks (Great source of bird supplies. Cages, travel cages, nets, play gyms, bird harnesses, etc. Everything necessary for a safe and happy bird.)
Phone: Toll-free (888) 224-3247
Web site: **www.creativebird.com**

Birds: Internet Resources

The American Cockatiel Society
www.acstiels.com

Avian Fashions: Flight Quarters (Order bird harnesses)
Web site: **www.flightquarters.com**

BirdHotline (Post or view lost/found bird ads)
E-mail: birdhotline@birdhotline.com
Web site: **www.birdhotline.com**

Bird Talk (Locate bird clubs by state)
Web site: **www.birdtalk.com**

Fred Bird Company (Order bird harnesses)
Web site: **www.fredbird.net**

Parrot Pages
www.parrotpages.com

Parrot Science
www.parrotscience.com

PETsMART (Order bird harnesses under the brand name Feather Tether Bird Harness)
Web site: **www.petsmart.com**

Pet Station (Locate bird clubs and associations. Click on the "Bird Station" link)
Web site: **www.petstation.com**

Planned Parrothood (Post or view lost/found bird ads)
E-mail: parrot@plannedparrothood.com
Web site: **www.plannedparrothood.com**

Disasters

American Humane Association
63 Inverness Drive East
Englewood, CO 80112-5117
Phone: (303) 792-9900
E-mail: (Emergency Animal Relief/EAR)
ear@americanhumane.org
Web site: **www.americanhumane.org**

American Red Cross (Contact your local Red Cross Chapter)
Web site: **www.redcross.org**

Federal Emergency Management Agency (FEMA)
500 C Street, SW
Washington, DC 20472
Phone: (202) 566-1600
Web site: **www.fema.gov** (Search under "Pets")

**Ferret Friends Disaster Response
International**
c/o Ferret Friends of Indian River County
8775 20th Street, Lot 614
Vero Beach, FL 32966
Phone: (561) 567-0994
Fax: (561) 562-5696
E-mail: agedog1@aol.com
Web site: **www.geocities.com/ffdri**

The Humane Society of the United States
2100 L Street, NW
Washington, DC 20037
Attn. Disaster Services
Phone: (Disaster Services) (301) 258-3063 or
(301) 258-3103
Web site: **www.hsus.org**

**The Independent Living Resource Center
San Francisco**
649 Mission Street
San Francisco, CA 94105
E-mail: herb@ilrcsf.org
Web site: **www.ilrcsf.org**

United Animal Nations
5892 A South Land Park Drive
P.O. Box 188890
Sacramento, CA 95818
Phone: (916) 429-2457
Fax: (916) 429-2456
E-mail: info@uan.org
Web site: **www.uan.org** (Click on the "EARS"
link)

Disasters: Book Resources

Emergency Animal Rescue Stories: True Stories About People Dedicated to Saving Animals from Disasters
Terri Crisp / Hardcover / Prima
Communications, Inc. / October 2000

First Aid Companion for Dogs and Cats
Amy D. Shojai / Paperback / Rodale Press /
February 2001

Operation Pet Rescue
Gregory N. Zompolis / Hardcover / J.N.
Townsend Publishing / August 1994

Out of Harm's Way: The Extraordinary True Story of One Woman's Lifelong Devotion to Animal Rescue
Terri Crisp, Samantha Glen / Paperback /
Simon & Schuster Trade / April 1997

Pet First Aid: Cats and Dogs
Bobbie Mammato, American Red Cross,
The Humane Society of the United States /
Paperback / Mosby Consumer-Health & Safety
/ April 1997

Disasters: Internet Resources

The Emergency Email Network (receive
e-mail alerts for disasters and emergencies)
www.emergencyemailnetwork.com

DNA

American Kennel Club (AKC)
Attn: DNA Services
5580 Centerview Drive
Raleigh, NC 27606-3390
Phone: (919) 816-3508 (DNA Services)
Fax: (919) 816-3627
E-mail: dna@akc.org

Avian Biotech International
4500 Shannon Lakes Plaza Unit 1, Suite 138
Tallahassee, FL 32308-2285
Phone: Toll-free (800) 514-9672
Or (850) 386-1145
Fax: (850) 386-1146

E-mail: contact@mail.avianbiotech.com
Web site: **http://avianbiotech.com**

Celera AgGen

For birds: Attn:. Avian Services
For dogs: Attn:. Canine Services
1756 Picasso Avenue
Davis, CA 95616
Phone: Gene Match for Birds, Toll-free (800)
995-BIRD (2473)
Phone: Canine, Toll-free (800) 362-DOGG
(3644)

Therion Corporation

Rensselaer Technology Park / 185 Jordan
Road
Troy, NY 12180-7617
Phone: (518) 286-0016
Fax: (518) 286-0018
E-mail: therion@theriondna.com

United Kennel Club (UKC)

DNA Department
100 E. Kilgore Road
Kalamazoo, MI 49002-5584
Phone: Toll-free (888) 548-7362
Or (616) 343-9020
Fax: (616) 343-7037
Web site: **www.ukcdogs.com**

Ferrets and Other Critters

American Ferret Association

PMB 255
626-C Admiral Drive
Annapolis, MD 21401

Phone: Toll-free (888) FERRET-1 (337-7381)
Fax: (516) 908-5215
E-mail: afa@ferret.org
Web site: **www.ferret.org**

The Ferret Company

P.O. Box 7161
Redwood City, CA 94063-7161
Phone/Fax: (650) 851-5775
E-mail: publisher@ferretcompany.com
Web site: **www.ferretcompany.com**

Ferret Friends Disaster Response International

c/o Ferret Friends of Indian River County
8775 20th Street, Lot 614
Vero Beach, FL 32966
Phone: (561) 567-0994
Fax: (561) 562-5696
E-mail: agedog1@aol.com
Web site: **www.geocities.com/ffdri**

Ferretsfirst.com (Extensive list of plants that are poisonous to ferrets)

Patricia Curtis
P.O. Box 2368
Weatherford, TX 76086
E-mail: director@ferretsfirst.com
Web site: **www.ferretsfirst.com**

For Ferrets Only

P.O. Box 1760
Dunnellon, FL 34430-1760
Phone: Toll-free (888) 340-7671
Or (352) 465-7541
Fax: (352) 465-7541
E-mail: shelterwoman@yahoo.com
Web site: **www.craftycreatures.com**

Ferrets and Other Critters: Internet Resources

All pets
Pet Station
www.petstation.com

Ferrets Central
Web site: **www.ferretcentral.org**

Gerbils
The Gerbil Information Page
Web site: **www.gerbil-info.nl.com**

The National Gerbil Society
Web site: **www.gerbils.co.uk**

Hamsters
All About Hamsters
Web site: **www.allabouthamsters.com**

The Complete Hamster Site
www.petwebsite.com/hamsters.htm

Rats
The Rat and Mouse Club of America
13075 Springdale Street, PMB 302
Westminster, CA 92683
Web site: **www.rmca.org**

The Wererat's Lair
Web site: **www.wererat.net**

Ferrets and Other Critters: Book and Video Resources

ASPCA Pet Care Guides for Kids
Mark Evans / Dorling Kindersley Publishing /
1992-93

The Ferret Handbook
Gerry Buscis, Barbara Somerville / Paperback
/ Barron's Educational Series, Inc. / January
2001

Ferrets!: For Today's Pet Owner from the Publishers of Ferrets USA Magazine
Karen Dale Dustman, Renee Stockdale
(Photographer) / Paperback / BowTie Press /
April 1998

Pocket Pet Series Videos (No phone orders,
only available through the mail or online)
S.E.I.
P.O. Box 6663
Los Osos, CA 93402
E-mail: info@pocket-pet-series.com
Web site: **www.pocket-pet-series.com**

Rat & Mouse Gazette
Rat and Mouse Club of America (See above.)

Training Your Pet Ferret
Gerry Buscis / Paperback / Barron's Educational Series, Inc. / October 1997

Grieving

**The Association for Pet Loss and
Bereavement**
(A terrific resource for anyone who has lost a
beloved pet, founded by Dr. Wallace Sife,
author of *The Loss of a Pet* [see below]. Their
web site has grief support chat rooms, a list of
grief support groups by state, and much more.)
P.O. Box 106
Brooklyn, NY 11230
Phone: (718) 382-0690
E-mail: aplb@aplb.org
Web site: **www.aplb.org**

Grieving: Internet Resources

American Veterinary Medical Association (AVMA)
(Click on the "Care for Animals" link)
Web site: **www.avma.org**

The Association for Pet Loss and Bereavement
(See above)

The Humane Society of the United States' *Pet Information Center*
Web site: **www.hsus.org**

In Memory of Pets
Web site: **www.in-memory-of-pets.com**

LightningStrike
Web site: **www.lightning-strike.com**

PetLoss.com
Web site: **www.petloss.com**

Rainbows Bridge
Web site: **www.rainbowsbridge.com**

Grieving: Book Resources

Goodbye, Friend: Healing Wisdom for Anyone Who Has Ever Lost a Pet
Gary Kowalski / Paperback / Stillpoint Publishing / August 1997

Pet Loss: A Thoughtful Guide for Adults and Children
Herbert A. Nieburg, Arlene Fischer / Paperback / HarperCollins Publishers, Inc. / March 1996

The Loss of a Pet: New Revised and Expanded Edition
Wallace Sife / Paperback / Howell Books / June 1998

Pet Loss Audio Book: Journey Through Pet Loss Revised Edition
Deborah Antinori, MA, RDT, LPC, NBCCH / Two cassette albums, 3 hrs. 8 mins. 28-page booklet. (Order online at Amazon or by phone through Book ClearingHouse, Phone: Toll-free (800) 431-1579

When Children Grieve: For Adults to Help Children Deal with Death, Divorce, Pet Loss, Moving, and Other Losses
John W. James, Russell Friedman / Hardcover / HarperCollins Publishers, Inc. / June 2001

When Only the Love Remains: The Pain of Pet Loss
Emily Margaret Stuparyk / Hardcover / Emil G. Keller / February 2000

Pet Loss Grief Support Hotlines

Chicago Veterinary Medical Association (630) 603-3994

Colorado State University (970) 491-1242

Iowa State University, Toll-free: (888) 478-7574

Michigan State University (517) 432-2696

Tufts University School of Veterinary Medicine (508) 839-7966

University of California (530) 752-4200

University of Florida, Toll-free: (800) 798-6196

University of Pennsylvania (215) 898-4525

Virginia–Maryland Regional College of Veterinary Medicine (540) 231-8038

Washington State University (509) 335-5704

For additional grief support hotlines visit The Humane Society of the United States' *Pet Information Center* at **www.hsus.org.**

Humane Organizations

American Humane Association

63 Inverness Drive East
Englewood, CO 80112-5117
Phone: Toll-free (800) 227-4645
Or (303) 792-9900
Fax: (303) 792-5333
E-mail: animal@americanhumane.org
(Animal Protection Services)
Web site: **www.americanhumane.org**

American Society for the Prevention of Cruelty to Animals (ASPCA)

424 East 92nd Street
New York, NY 10128
Attn: Humane Education Department (for Material orders)
Phone: (212) 876-7700 ex. 4400 (for Material orders)
E-mail: information@aspca.org
E-mail: education@aspca.org (to request a catalog)
Web site: **www.aspca.org**
Web site: **www.animaland.org** (AnimaLand just for kids)

Dumb Friends League

Attn: Behavior Department
2080 S. Quebec Street
Denver, CO 80231
Phone: (303) 696-4941
Web site: **www.ddfl.org**

The Humane Society of the United States

2100 L Street, NW
Washington, DC 20037
Phone: (202) 452-1100
Web site: **www.hsus.org**
Web site: **www.kindnews.org** (Just for Kids)

ID Tags

Cat Finder (Unique tag product for locating a pet hiding in the home. Purchase online through HouseCat Premier Services Inc.)
Web site: **www.housecat.com**

GoTags.com
421 Date Place
Mattawa, WA 99349
Fax: (509) 932-5131
E-mail: pets@gotags.com
Web site: **www.gotags.com**

Ideclare Talking Pet Tag (Purchase from Interplanetary Pet Products, Inc.)
Phone: Toll-free (888) 477-4732
Web site: **www.interplanetarypets.com**

Small Pet Necklace Tag (Purchase through TagXpress)
Phone: (904) 819-0210
Web site: **www.tagxpress.com**

Traveltag
Salamander Design
14576 64th Avenue
Surrey, BC, V3S, 1X4 Canada
Phone: Toll-free (877) 246-4744
Or (604) 572-9905
E-mail: sheena@blaze.ca
Web site: **http://salamander.bc.ca**

Pet Clubs and Breed Rescue Groups

Pet clubs and breed rescue groups can be located in many pet magazines. The greatest source of information, however, is online. Here are a few web sites for locating them.

Dog Clubs

American Kennel Club Directory (Locate both breed clubs and breed rescue groups)
www.akc.org

Dog-On-It (Locate both breed clubs and breed rescue groups)
www.dog-on-it.com

Dog, Cat, Bird, and Critter Clubs

Pet Station (An extensive listing for all pet clubs, especially bird clubs and associations)
www.petstation.com

Breed Rescue Groups

Kyler Laird's Animal Rescue Resources (Incredible site, thousands of rescue groups, listed by state and country)
www.ecn.purdue.edu/~laird/ animal_rescue

Pet Guardian Angels of America (An extensive listing)
www.pgaa.com

Pet Containment

Electronic Fencing

Innotek Inc.
1 Innoway
Garrett, IN 46738
Phone: Toll-free (800) 826-5527
Fax: (219) 357-3160
E-mail: sales@pet-products.com
Web site: **www.pet-products.com**

Invisible Fence (IF)
493 Danbury Road
Wilton, CT 06897
Phone: Toll-free (800) 578-DOGS
Web site: **www.invisiblefence.com** (Search for local distributor)

Radio Fence Distributors, Inc. (Radio Fence and Spray Control [Citronella] Radio Fence)
1133 Bal Harbor Boulevard, Suite 1153
Punta Gorda, FL 33950
Phone: Toll-free (800) 941-4200
Or (941) 505-8220
Fax: (941) 505-8229
E-mail: info@radiofence.com
Web site: **www.radiofence.com**

Sonic Fence
ICO ClickShopping
7042 NW 46th Street
Miami, FL 33166
Phone: Toll-free (800) 327-1033
Or (305) 592-6069
Fax: (305) 599-0936
E-mail: info@petbehave.com
Web site: **www.petbehave.com**

Cat Fencing and Enclosures

Just4cats.com (Safe Cat Outdoor
Enclosures manual)
c/o The Montgomery family
2127 Old Bainbridge Road
Tallahassee, FL 32303
E-mail: jm4vision@aol.com
Web site: **www.just4cats.com**

Cat Fence-In
P.O. Box 795 Dept. E.
Sparks, NV 89432
Phone: Toll-free (888) 738-9099
E-mail: fenceinfo@catfencein.com
Web site: **www.catfencein.com**

Pet Detectives

Bloodhound Investigations (Texas)
Phone: (817) 239-0066
E-mail: hndgchad@swbell.net

National Pet Detectives (Florida Area)
Phone: (866) 2-RESCUE (273-7283) in
Pinellas County, Florida (727) 398-2805
E-mail: info@nationalpetdetectives.com
Web site: **www.nationalpetdetectives.com**

Pet Hunters (San Francisco and
Los Angeles)
P.O. Box 940638
Simi Valley, CA 93094-0638
Phone: (805) 306-0810
Fax: (805) 306-1183
E-mail: info@pethunters.com
Web site: **www.pethunters.com**

Rabies

American Veterinary Medical Association
1931 North Meacham Road, Suite 100
Schaumburg, IL 60173-4360
Phone: (847) 925-8070
Fax: (847) 925-1329
E-mail: avmainfo@avma.org
Web site: **www.avma.org** (Search under
"Rabies.")

**The National Institute of Allergy and
Infectious Diseases**
Office of Communications and Public Liaison
Building 31, Room 7A-50
31 Center Drive MSC 2520
Bethesda, MD 20892-2520
Phone: (301) 496-5717
Web site: **www.niaid.nih.gov** (Search under
"Rabies.")

PETCO
Low-cost vaccinations are available at most
PETCO stores. Contact your nearest PETCO
store for details.
Web site: **www.petco.com**

PETsMART
Many PETsMART stores offer low-cost vacci-
nations. For details contact your local
PETsMART.
Web site: **www.petsmart.com**

**U.S. Centers for Disease Control
and Prevention**
Mail Stop A-26
1600 Clifton Road, NE
Atlanta, GA 30333
Phone: Toll-free (888) 232-3228
Web site: **www.cdc.gov** (Search under
"Rabies.")

Record Keeping

Record Keeping: Software

Health-Minder Software
P.O. Box 1041
Larchmont, NY 10538
Phone: (914) 576-1831
E-mail: info@health-minder.com
Web site: **www.health-minder.com**

Registries and Recovery Services

ID Tag Registries

1-800-HELP-4-PETS
8721 Santa Monica Blvd., PMB 710
Los Angeles, CA 90069
Phone: Toll-free (310) 652-9837
Fax: (310) 652-2022
E-mail: mail@help4pets.com
Web site: **www.help4pets.com**

American Pet Association (Guardian
Collar/Tag)
P.O. Box 7172
Boulder, CO 80306-7172
Phone: Toll-free (800) APA-PETS (272-7387)
Fax: (303) 494-7316
E-mail: apa@apapets.org
Web site: **www.apapets.org**

Doctors Foster and Smith (Lost Pet
Service Kit)
P.O. Box 100
2253 Air Park Road
Rhinelander, WI 54501
Phone: Toll-free (800) 826-7206
E-mail: customerservice@drsfostersmith.com
Web site: **www.drsfostersmith.com** (Search
under "Lost Pet Service Kit.")

Keepet
P.O. Box 18135
Cleveland, OH 44118-0135
Phone: Toll-free (888) 4-KEEPET (453-3738)
E-mail: info@keepet.com
Web site: **www.keepet.com**

National Pet Detectives
Phone: (866) 2-RESCUE (273-7283); in
Pinellas County, Florida (727) 398-2805
E-mail: info@nationalpetdetectives.com
Web site: **www.nationalpetdetectives.com**

National Pet Network
P.O. Box 258
Cloverdale, MI 49035
Phone: (616) 623-7250
Fax: (866) 851-7540
E-mail: sales@nationalpetnetwork.com
Web site: **www.nationalpetnetwork.com**

National Pet Recovery (Club 55)
Attn: Customer Service
704 Greengate Circle
St. Johns, MI 48879
Phone: Toll-free (800) 984-8638
Or (517) 224-3210
Fax: (517) 224-8509
E-mail: customerservice@petrecovery.com
Web site: **www.petrecovery.com**

Pet Club of America (Pet Finders)
661 High Street
Thurman, NY 12810
Phone: Toll-free (800) 666-5678
E-mail: petclub@capital.net
Web site: **www.petclub.org**

Tattoo Registries

National Dog Registry (NDR)
P.O. Box 116
Woodstock, NY 12498
Phone: Toll-free (800) NDR-DOGS
(637-3647)
E-mail: info@natldogregistry.com
Web site: **www.natldogregistry.com**

Tattoo-A-Pet
6571 SW 20th Court
Ft. Lauderdale, FL 33317
Phone: Toll-free (800) TATTOOS (828-8667)
Or (954) 581-5834
Fax: (954) 581-0056
E-mail: info@tattoo-a-pet.com
Web site: **www.tattoo-a-pet.com**

Microchip Registries

AKC Companion Animal Recovery
(Home Again Microchip)
5580 Centerview Drive Suite 250
Raleigh, NC 27606
Phone: Toll-free (800) 252-7894
Fax: (919) 233-1290
E-mail: found@akc.org
Web site: **www.akccar.org**
Schering-Plough web site:
http://usa.spah.com (Locate a Home Again
Vet)

AVID (FriendChip)
3179 Hamner Avenue
Norco, CA 92860
Phone: (United States) Toll-free (800)
336-AVID (2843)
Or (International) (909) 371-7505
Fax: (909) 737-8967
E-mail: avid@avidid.com
Web site: **www.avidid.com**

Roaming and Escaping

Spay and Neuter Resources

SPAY/USA
2261 Broadbridge Avenue
Stratford, CT 06614
Phone: Toll-free (800) 248-SPAY (7729)
Fax: (203) 375-6627
E-mail: alwaysspay@aol.com
Web site: **www.spayusa.org**

Feral Cat Resources

Feral Cat Coalition
9528 Miramar Road
PMB 160
San Diego, CA 92126
E-mail: rsavage@feralcat.com
Web site: **www.feralcat.com**

Safe Haven for Cats
270 Redwood Shores Parkway PMB #139
Redwood City, CA 94065-1173
Phone: (650) 802-9686
Web site: **www.safehavenforcats.com**

Roaming and Escaping: Books

Cat Home Alone: Fifty Ways to Keep Your Cat Happy and Safe While You're Away
Regen Dennis, Regen Davis / Paperback /
Andrews & McMeel / October 1997

Pet Sitters, Boarding Kennels, and Caretakers

American Boarding Kennels Association

1702 East Pikes Peak Avenue
Colorado Springs, CO 80909
Phone: (719) 667-1600
Fax: (719) 667-0116
E-mail: info@abka.com
Web site: **www.abka.com**

National Association of Professional Pet Sitters (NAPPS)

#6 State Road, Suite 113
Mechanicsburg, PA 17050
Phone: (717) 691-5565
Fax: (717) 691-3381
E-mail: nappsmail@aol.com
Web site: **www.petsitters.org**

Pet Mates Professional Pet Care Service Pet Mates, Inc.

322 East 55th Street, Suite D
New York, NY 10022
Phone: (212) 414-5158
Fax: (212) 688-0661
E-mail: info@petmates.com
Web site: **www.petmates.com**

Pet Sitters International (PSI)

418 East King Street
King, NC 27021-9163
Phone: (336) 983-9222
Fax: (336) 983-3755
E-mail: info@petsit.com
Web site: **www.petsit.com**

Pet Sitters, Boarding Kennels, and Caretakers: Internet Resources

The Doggie Directory
www.doggiedirectory.com

The Humane Society of the United States
(Information on choosing a boarding kennel or professional pet sitter at The HSUS's *Pet Information Center*
www.hsus.org

Yahoo Yellow Pages
www.yahoo.com

Stolen Pets

In Defense of Animals (IDA)

131 Camino Alto, Suite E.
Mill Valley, CA 94941
Phone: (415) 388-9641
Pet Theft Hotline: Toll-free (800) STOLEN-PET (786-5367)
Fax: (415) 388-0388
E-mail: ida@idausa.org
Web site: **www.idausa.org**

Last Chance for Animals

8033 Sunset Boulevard, Suite 35
Los Angeles, CA 90046
Phone: (310) 271-6096
E-mail: info@lcanimal.org
Web site: **www.stolenpets.com**

National Crime Prevention Council

1000 Connecticut Avenue, NW/13th Floor
Washington, DC 20036
Phone: (202) 466-6272
Fax: (202) 296-1356
Web site: **www.ncpc.org**

National Pet Detectives (Florida Area)
Phone: (866) 2-RESCUE (273-7283); in
Pinellas County, Florida (727) 398-2805
E-mail: info@nationalpetdetectives.com
Web site: **www.nationalpetdetectives.com**

USDA-APHIS-Animal Care (For a list
of registered animal dealers and research
facilities)
4700 River Road, Unit 84
Riverdale, MD 20737-1234
Phone: (301) 734-4981
Web site: **www.aphis.usda.gov/ac/
publications.html**

Stolen Pets: Book Resources

Stolen for Profit
Judith Reitman, Michael W. Fox (Introduction) /
Paperback / Kensington Publishing
Corporation / March 1994

Training

Association of Pet Dog Trainers
66 Morris Avenue, Suite 2A
Springfield, NJ 07081
Phone: Toll-free (800) PET-DOGS (738-3647)
E-mail: information@apdt.com
Web site: **www.apdt.com** (Search to locate
a trainer near you.)

Cats International (Request their free
25-page manual: see below.)
193 Granville Road
Cedarburg, WI 53012
Phone: (Behavior Hotline) (262) 375-8852
Web site: **www.catsinternational.org**

Dumb Friends League
2080 S. Quebec Street
Denver, CO 80231
Phone: (303) 696-4941
Web site: **www.ddfl.org**

Perfect Paws (Great training articles available
at Perfect Paws web site.)
Phone: (415) 647-8000
Fax: (650) 745-2647
E-mail: mail@perfectpaws.com
Web site: **www.perfectpaws.com**

PETCO
Pet training classes are available at your local
PETCO. For details contact a store near you.
Web site: **www.petco.com**

PETsMART
PETsMART Smart Pets courses are available
at your local PETsMART. Contact a store near
you for details.
Web site: **www.petsmart.com**

Sunshine Books, Inc. (Clicker training
books and aids)
49 River Street, Suite #3
Waltham, MA 02453-8345
Phone: Toll-free (800) 47-CLICK (472-5425)
or (781) 398-0754
Fax: (781) 398-0761
E-mail: sales@clickertraining.com
Web site: **www.clickertraining.com**

Training Books

American Humane Association's Guide to Humane Dog Training

Order direct from AHA by calling (866) AHA-1877

A Step by Step Book about Training Your Parakeet

Darlene Campbell, Elaine Radford, J. Darlene Campbell / Paperback / TFH Publications, Inc. / March 1990

Training Your Pet Ferret

Gerry Buscis / Paperback / Barron's Educational Series, Inc. / October 1997

Catch Your Dog Doing Something Right: How to Train Any Dog in Five Minutes a Day

Krista Cantrell / Paperback / Penguin USA / December 1997

Cats on the Counter: Therapy and Training For Your Cat

Larry Lachman, Frank Mickadeit / Hardcover / St. Martin's Press, Inc. / October 2000

Clicking with Your Dog: Step-by-Step in Pictures

Peggy Tillman, Foreword by Karen Pryor / Paperback / Sunshine Books, Inc. / March 2001

Dogs on the Couch: Behavior Therapy for Training and Caring for your Dog

Larry Lachman, Frank Mickadeit / Hardcover / Overlook Press / April 1999

Dog Tricks

Arthur J. Haggerty, Carol Lea Benjamin / Hardcover / Black Dog & Leventhal / May 1996

Dog Tricks for Dummies

Sarah Hodgson, Nikki Moustaki (Editor) / Paperback / Hungry Minds, Inc. / September 2000

Don't Shoot the Dog

Karen Pryor / Paperback / Bantam Books, Inc. / August 1999

From the Cat's Point of View

Gwen Bohnenkamp / Paperback / Perfect Paws, Inc. / April 1991

How to Live Happily Ever After With Your Cat

(Free 25-page manual from Cats International) (See Cats International above.)

How to Teach Your Old Dog New Tricks

Ted Baer / Paperback / Barron's Educational Series, Inc. / February 1991

Training Videos and Kits

Amazing Trick Training Videos

Yours To Keep Productions, LLC
8086 S. Yale, Suite 199
Tulsa, OK 74136
E-mail: y2k@amazingtricks.com
Web site: **www.amazingtricks.com**

Association of Pet Dog Trainers (Maintains a list of recommended videos and books on training)
Web site: **www.apdt.com**

Dogwise.com
Maintains a complete list of dog training books, videos, and more. This site has everything you will ever need, and items can be purchased right from the site.
Web site: **www.dogwise.com**

Getting Started Clicker Training for Dogs Kit and Clicker Magic Video By Karen Pryor (Order through Sunshine Books: See "Resources/ Training."

Traveling with Pets

Pet Guardian Angels of America (Pet Alert)
(Prepare ahead for accidents)
8283 Main Street
Bokeelia, FL 33922
Phone: Toll-free (888) 560-6129
E-mail: pgaa4me@aol.com
Web site: **www.pgaa.com**

The United States Department of Agriculture – Animal and Plant Health Inspection Service Voice Response Service (Find out what the regulations are for crossing borders with pets.)
Phone: Toll-free (800) 545-USDA (8732)

Traveling with Pets: Internet Resources

DogFriendly.com, Inc.
1390 Broadway, #B282
Placerville, CA 95667
Phone: (530) 672-5316
Fax: (413) 228-6037
E-mail: info@dogfriendly-inc.com
Web site: **www.dogfriendly.com**

Petswelcome.com
9 Conklin Street
New Hamburg, NY 12590
Web site: **www.petswelcome.com**

Takeyourpet.com
Net Publishing LLC
2545 South Lafayette Street
Denver, CO 80210
Phone: (303) 744-6320
Fax: (303) 722-7449
E-mail: general@takeyourpet.com
Web site: **www.takeyourpet.com**

Traveldog.com
P.O. Box 19724
Sacramento, CA 95819
Phone: (916) 455-3476
E-mail: td@traveldog.com
Web site: **www.traveldog.com**

Traveling With Pets: Book Resources

Fodor's Road Guides USA: Where to Stay with Your Pet
Manufactured by Fodor / Paperback / Crown Publishing Group / June 2001

Pets Welcome: A Guide to Hotels, Inns and Resorts That Welcome You and Your Pet
Kathleen Devanna Fish, Robert Fish / Paperback / The Millennium Publishing Group / June 1998

Traveling with Your Pet 2000: The AAA Pet Book
Cynthia Psarakis / Paperback / AAA / April 2000

Vacationing with Your Pet: Eileen's Directory of Pet-Friendly Lodging in the United States and Canada
Eileen Barish, Greg Myers / Paperback / Pet-Friendly Publications, Inc. / June 1999

Transporting Your Pet

The Humane Society of the United States' Pet Information Center (Download an Air Travel Incident Report form)
Web site: **www.hsus.org** (Click on Pet Care Link.)

United States Department of Agriculture – APHIS – Animal Care
(To register a complaint against an airline)
Deputy Administrator
USDA-APHIS-Animal Care
4700 River Road, Unit 84
Riverdale, MD 20737-1234
Phone: (301) 734-4981

Transportation Services

Air Animal Inc. (Relocation only)
Mildred A. Woolf, President
Air Animal, Inc.
4120 West Cypress Street
Tampa, FL 33607
Phone: Toll-free (800) 635-3448
Fax: (813) 874-6722
E-mail: petsfly@aol.com
Web site: **www.airanimal.com**

Happy Tails (Arrangements made for both relocation and vacationers)
4325 N. Camino Colibri
Tucson, AZ 85718
Phone: (520) 615-9800
Fax: (877) 585-7327
E-mail: info@happytailstravel.com
Web site: **www.happytailstravel.com**

Independent Pet and Animal Transportation Association, Inc. (IPATA)
(Locate a professional pet shipper near you)
Route 1, Box 747, Highway 2869
Big Sandy, TX 75755
Phone: (903) 769-2267
Fax: (903) 769-2867
E-mail: info@ipata.com
Web site: **www.ipata.com**

Jet-A-Pet (Relocation only)
6 Big Pine Road
Westport, CT 06880
Phone: Toll-free (888) JET-A-PET (538-2738)
Fax: (203) 454-3080
E-mail: mugsy1@jet-a-pet.com
Web site: **www.jet-a-pet.com**

Professional Pet Transports Inc. (Ground transport only. A great service for those traveling long distances who do not feel comfortable shipping their pets by air.)
HCR 56 Box 424
John Day, OR 97845
Phone: (866) ARE-PETS (273-7387)
E-mail: questions@pro-pet-transports.com
Web site: **www.pro-pet-transports.com**

Additional Resources
Books

The Humane Society of the United States' Complete Guide to Dog Care

Marion S. Lane, The Humane Society of the United States Staff / Hardcover and Paperback / Little, Brown & Company / May 1998

Coming in the summer of 2002
The Humane Society of the United States' Complete Guide to Cat Care

Wendy Christensen, The Humane Society of the United States Staff / Paperback / St. Martin's Press

Catalogs and Magazines

Pet magazines and pet catalogs are a terrific source of many of the products and services mentioned in this book. There are many great pet magazines and catalogs and it would be impossible to list them all. Here are a select few of our favorites:

Pet Catalogs

All Pets
Phone: Toll-free (800) 346-0749
Web site: **www.allpets.com**
Good variety of products for all pets. Exceptional web site—highly recommended.

The Dog's Outfitter
Phone: Toll-free (800) FOR-DOGS (367-3647)
Web site: **www.dogsoutfitter.com**
Another great catalog. Geared towards the professional groomer, but pet owners welcome. Cat products included. Nice web site. Added bonus: ships most items in 12 hours!

Dogwise
Phone: Toll-free (800) 776-2665
Web site: **www.dogwise.com**
Large variety of dog (and some cat) books and videos. Be the best "guardian" you can be. Educate yourself in all aspects of your pet's care. Pet products are available from their web site.

Doctors Foster & Smith
Phone: Toll-free (800) 826-7206
Web site: **www.drsfostersmith.com**
5 stars! Maybe 10! Exceptional catalog. We can't say enough good things about this catalog. A must for every pet owner.

Hornbecks
Phone: Toll-free (888) 224-3247
Web site: **www.creativebird.com**
Great source for bird supplies. Cages, travel cages, nets, play gyms, bird harnesses, etc. Everything necessary for a safe and happy bird.

That Pet Place
Phone: Toll-free (800) 842-8738
Web site: **www.thatpetplace.com**
Another great catalog for a variety of pets. Terrific web site—worth a visit.

Pet Magazines

A large variety of pet magazines are available at most of the Super Pet Stores and the Super Bookstores.

Or go to your favorite search engine and type in "Animal Magazines."

Fancy Publications
Phone: Toll-free (800) 456-6049
Web site: **www.animalnetwork.com**
has a great selection.

Magazine City
Web site: **www.magazinecity.net** has
a nice selection also.

Internet Resources

All Pets
www.allpets.com

PETCO
www.petco.com

PETsMART
www.petsmart.com

Miscellaneous

Ferretsfirst.com (Extensive list of plants that
are poisonous to ferrets)
Patricia Curtis
P.O. Box 2368
Weatherford, TX 76086
E-mail: director@ferretsfirst.com
Web site: **www.ferretsfirst.com**

**National American Society for the
Prevention of Cruelty to Animals
Animal Poison Control Center**
1717 S. Philo Road, Suite #36
Urbana, IL 61802
Phone: (888) 4ANI-HELP (426-4435) (This is a
pay service)
Web site: **www.napcc.aspca.org**

Videos

Clicker Magic Video
By Karen Pryor
Sunshine Books, Inc.
49 River Street, Suite #3
Waltham, MA 02453-8345
Phone: Toll-free (800) 47-CLICK (472-5425)
or (781) 398-0754
Fax: (781) 398-0761
E-mail: sales@clickertraining.com
Web site: **www.clickertraining.com**

Pocket Pet Series Videos (No phone orders,
only available through the mail or online)
S.E.I.
P.O. Box 6663
Los Osos, CA 93402
E-mail: info@pocket-pet-series.com
Web site: **www.pocket-pet-series.com**

**Prevention and Recovery of Missing, Lost,
and Stolen Pets Video**
By Larry Maynard (National Pet Detectives)
Phone: (866) 2-RESCUE (273-7283); in
Pinellas County, Florida (727) 398-2805
E-mail: info@nationalpetdetectives.com
Web site: **www.nationalpetdetectives.com**

Visit our web site at www.lostpetfoundpet.com

TELEPHONE ORDERS: Call 888-PETS-222 toll-free. Have your credit card ready.
INTERNET ORDERS: www.lostpetfoundpet.com
CUSTOMER SERVICE: (732) 872-2414
POSTAL ORDERS: El Jebel Press, P.O. Box 288, Atlantic Highlands, NJ 07716. Please enclose check or money order in the amount of $23.95 per book. Add $5.00 for shipping and handling per book. All orders shipped priority mail. (For more shipping options call us or visit our web site: **www.lostpetfoundpet.com**). Make check payable to El Jebel Press.
SALES TAX: Please add 6% for all books shipped to New Jersey addresses.

Please use order forms below and leave the above order information for other pet owners who may need a copy of this important book. Thank you!

Please send me_____ copies of ***The Complete Guide to Lost Pet Prevention & Recovery.***

Name: _____

Address: _____

City: _____ State: _____ Zip:_____

Please enclose check or money order in the amount of $23.95 per book. (Add $5.00 for shipping and handling per book. All orders shipped priority mail.) Make check payable to El Jebel Press. Or call us toll-free to order: 888-PETS-222.

Sales Tax: Please add 6% for all books shipped to New Jersey addresses.

Mail this order form to: El Jebel Press, P.O. Box 288, Atlantic Highlands, NJ 07716
Order online at: **www.lostpetfoundpet.com**

Please send me_____ copies of ***The Complete Guide to Lost Pet Prevention & Recovery.***

Name: _____

Address: _____

City: _____ State: _____ Zip:_____

Please enclose check or money order in the amount of $23.95 per book. (Add $5.00 for shipping and handling per book. All orders shipped priority mail.) Make check payable to El Jebel Press. Or call us toll-free to order: 888-PETS-222.

Sales Tax: Please add 6% for all books shipped to New Jersey addresses.

Mail this order form to: El Jebel Press, P.O. Box 288, Atlantic Highlands, NJ 07716
Order online at: **www.lostpetfoundpet.com**